Checkmate

Competency Based Questions (CBQs)

Economics

CBSE Class 12

Author
Sonam Arora
(M.A. Economics, M.Com, B.Ed.)

arihant
SUCCESS AND NOTHING LESS

Checkmate

arihant
SUCCESS AND NOTHING LESS

ARIHANT PRAKASHAN (SCHOOI DIVISION SERIES), MEERUT

Administrative & Production Offices

Regd. Office
'Ramchhaya' 4577/15, Agarwal Road, Darya Ganj, New Delhi -110002
Tele: 011- 47630600, 43518550

Head Office
Kalindi, TP Nagar, Meerut (UP) - 250002
Tel: 0121-7156203, 7156204

Sales & Support Offices
Agra, Ahmedabad, Bengaluru, Bareilly, Chennai, Delhi, Guwahati, Hyderabad, Jaipur, Jhansi, Kolkata, Lucknow, Nagpur & Pune.

PRICE ₹245.00

PO No : TXT-XX-XXXXXXX-X-XX

Published by Arihant Publications (India) Ltd.

For further information about the books published by Arihant, log on to www.arihantbooks.com or e-mail at info@arihantbooks.com

Follow us on

Checkmate CBQs Series

MASTER YOUR COMPETENCY!

01 **All types of Competency-Based Questions (CBQs)**, including Multiple Choice Questions (MCQs), Assertion-Reason, Correct/Incorrect Statements, Case-Based/Source-Based, and Subjective/Open-Ended Questions, providing a well-rounded preparation.

02 Meticulously selected **competency-based questions from past exams** to ensure thorough preparation and familiarity with question formats.

03 **Detailed Solutions** for effective self-study and a deeper understanding of each topic, enabling you to learn at your own pace.

04 **Self Scoring feature** to track your performance and progress on your own, helping you identify strengths and areas for improvement.

05 **Indication of suggested time** with each set of questions to help you learn time management skills to maximize your efficiency and confidence during exams.

केन्द्रीय माध्यमिक शिक्षा बोर्ड

(शिक्षा मंत्रालय, भारत सरकार के अधीन एक स्वायत संगठन)

Central Boards of Secondary Education

(An Autonomous Organisation Under the Ministry of Education, Govt. of India)

CBSE/ACADEMIC/JS (SH)/2024/ 3rd April, 2024 Circulars No. Acad 30/2024

The changes for classes IX-XII year-end Board Examinations (2024-25)

(Classes IX-X)

Particulars	**Academic Session 2023-24**	**Academic Session 2024-25** (No change from previous academic session)
Composition of question paper for year-end examination/ Board Examination (Theory)	• Competency Focused Questions in the form of MCQs/ Case Based Questions, Source-based Integrated Questions or any other type = 50% • Select response type questions (MCQ) = 20% • Constructed response questions (Short Answer/Long Answer Type Questions, as per existing pattern) = 30%	• Competency Focused Questions in the form of MCQs/Case Based Questions, Source-based Integrated Questions or any other type = 50% • Select response type questions (MCQ) = 20% • Constructed response questions (Short Answer/Long Answer Type Questions, as per existing pattern) = 30%

(Classes XI-XII)

Particulars	**Academic Session 2023-24**	**Academic Session 2024-25**
Composition of question paper for year-end examination/ Board Examination (Theory)	• Competency Focused Questions in the form of MCQs/ Case Based Questions, Source-based Integrated Questions or any other type = 40% • Select response type questions (MCQ) = 20% • Constructed response questions (Short Answer Questions/Long Answer type Questions, as per existing pattern) = 40%	• Competency Focused Questions in the form of MCQs/ Case Based Questions, Source-based Integrated Questions or any other type = 50% • Select response type questions (MCQ) = 20% • Constructed response questions (Short Answer Questions/Long Answer type Questions, as per existing pattern) = 30%

Curriculum document released by the Board for the Academic Session 2024-25 and the Sample Question Papers may also be referred to for details of the QP design of individual subjects. Learning frameworks for various subjects for classes IX-XII are available at the link https://cbseacademic.nic.in for reference.

Contents

PART A Introductory Macroeconomics

PART B Indian Economic Development

Syllabus

Theory : 80 Marks | Project : 20 Marks

Units		Marks	Periods
Part A	Introductory Macroeconomics		
1	National Income and Related Aggregates	10	30
2	Money and Banking	6	15
3	Determination of Income and Employment	12	30
4	Government Budget and the Economy	6	17
5	Balance of Payments	6	18
		40	**110**
Part B	Indian Economic Development		
6	Development Experience (1947-90) and Economic Refroms Since 1991	12	28
7	Current Challenges facing Indian Economy	20	50
8	Development Experience of Inida - A Comparison with Neighbours	08	12
		40	**90**
Part C	Project Work	20	20

Part A Introductory Macroeconomics

Unit 1 National Income and Related Aggregates — 30 Periods

What is Macroeconomics ?

Basic Concepts: Consumption Goods, Capital Goods, Final Goods, Intermediate Goods; Stocks and Flows; Gross Investment and Depreciation.

Circular Flow of Income (two sector model), Methods of Calculating National Income - Value Added or Product Method, Expenditure Method, Income Method.

Aggregates Related to National Income: Gross National Product (GNP), Net National Product (NNP), Gross and Net Domestic Product (GDP and NDP) - at Market Price, at Factor Cost; Real and Nominal GDP. GDP Deflator, GDP and Welfare

UNIT 2 Money and Banking — 15 Periods

Money - Meaning and Functions, Supply of Money - Currency Held by the Public and Net Demand Deposits Held by Commercial Banks.

Money Creation by the Commercial Banking System.

Central Bank and Its Functions (example of the Reserve Bank of India): Bank of issue, Govt. Bank, Banker's Bank, Control of Credit through Bank Rate, CRR, SLR, Repo Rate and Reverse Repo Rate, Open Market Operations, Margin Requirement.

UNIT 3 Determination of Income and Employment — 30 Periods

Aggregate Demand and its Components.

Propensity to Consume and Propensity to Save (average and marginal).

Short-run Equilibrium Output; Investment Multiplier and its Mechanism.

Meaning of Full Employment and Involuntary Unemployment.

Problems of Excess Demand and Deficient Demand; Measures to Correct Them - Changes in Government Spending, Taxes and Money Supply.

UNIT 4 Government Budget and the Economy 17 Periods

Government Budget - Meaning, Objectives and Components.

Classification of Receipts - Revenue Receipts and Capital Receipts; Classification of Expenditure – Revenue Expenditure and Capital Expenditure.

Balanced, Surplus and Deficit Budget - Measures of Government Deficit

UNIT 5 Balance of Payments 18 Periods

Balance of Payments Account - Meaning and Components; Balance of Payments-Surplus and Deficit.

Foreign Exchange Rate - Meaning of Fixed and Flexible Rates and Managed Floating.

Determination of Exchange Rate in a Free Market, Merits and Demerits of Flexible and Fixed Exchange Rate. Managed Floating Exchange Rate System.

Part B Indian Economic Development

UNIT 6 Development Experience (1947-90) and Economic Reforms Since 1991 28 Periods

A brief introduction of the State of Indian Economy on the Eve of Independence.

Indian Economic System and Common Goals of Five Year Plans.

Main Features, Problems and Policies of Agriculture (Institutional Aspects and New Agricultural Strategy), Industry (IPR 1956 ; SSI-role & importance) and Foreign Trade.

Economic Reforms since 1991

Features and appraisals of Liberalisation, Globalisation and Privatisation (LPG Policy);

Concepts of Demonetisation and GST

Unit 7 Current Challenges facing Indian Economy 60 Periods

Human Capital Formation: How people become resource; Role of Human Capital in Economic Development; Growth of Education Sector in India.

Rural Development: Key Issues-Credit and Marketing - Role of Cooperatives; Agricultural Diversification; Alternative Farming - Organic Farming.

Employment: Growth and Changes in workforce participation rate in formal and informal sectors; Problems and Policies.

Sustainable Economic Development: Meaning, Effects of Economic Development on Resources and Environment, Including Global Warming.

Unit 8 Development Experience of India 12 Periods

A Comparison with Neighbours.

India and Pakistan.

India and China.

Issues: Economic Growth, Population, Sectoral Development and other Human Developmental Indicators.

Part C Projects in Economics 20 Periods

Prescribed Books:

1. Statistics for Economics, NCERT
2. Indian Economic Development, NCERT
3. Introductory Microeconomics, NCERT
4. Macroeconomics, NCERT
5. Supplementary Reading Material in Economics, CBSE

Note : The above publications are also available in Hindi Medium.

Question Paper Design

Economics *(Code No. 030)*

SN	Typology of Questions	Marks	Percentage
1.	**Remembering and Understanding:** Exhibit memory of previously learned material by recalling facts, terms, basic concepts, and answers. Demonstrate understanding of facts and ideas by organizing, comparing, translating, interpreting, giving descriptions, and stating main ideas	44	55%
2.	**Applying:** Solve problems to new situations by applying acquired knowledge, facts, techniques and rules in a different way	18	22.5%
3.	**Analysing, Evaluating and Creating:** Examine and break information into parts by identifying motives or causes. Make inferences and find evidence to support generalizations. Present and defend opinions by making judgments about information, validity of ideas, or quality of work based on a set of criteria. Compile information together in a different way by combining elements in a new pattern or proposing alternative solutions.	18	22.5%
	Total	**80**	**100%**

PART A

Introductory Macroeconomics

CHAPTER - 1

National Income and Related Aggregates

Types & Nos. of Questions

Multiple Choice Questions	–	35
Assertion-Reason Questions	–	10
Correct/Incorrect Statements	–	10
Case Based Questions	–	2 Cases, *each with four Questions*
Subjective Questions	–	22

Trend Analysis

On the basis of analysis of last 2 years' papers, it is found that on an average 3 Multiple Choice Questions and 2 Short Answer Type Questions (Statement Based and Numerical) are asked from this chapter. No case based question is asked but may be asked in coming exams.

Focus Topics of the Chapter

- Basic Concepts in Macroeconomics
- Circular Flow of Income
- Aggregates related to National Income
- Methods of Measuring National Income

Multiple Choice Questions

No. of Questions : **35** Suggested Time : **55 Minutes**

Direction Each of the question given below is Multiple Choice Question (MCQ) i.e. there are Four Options/ Choices for answer, out of which ONLY ONE is correct. You have to select the correct option.
A response box is given with each option, mark (✓) in the box of the correct option. For each correct answer you will get 1 mark, while there is no penalty for incorrect answer or missed out questions.

1. Which of the following best defines intermediate goods?

(A) Goods purchased by consumers for personal use ☐
(B) Goods used as raw materials or inputs in the production of other goods ☐
(C) Goods used for investment purposes ☐
(D) Goods exported to foreign markets ☐

2. In an economy, households provide labour and other services to firms and receive wages, rent and dividends in return. This exchange of services for payments is a key aspect of the economic system.

This flow of money across different sectors is termed as ....

(A) capital flow ☐ (B) money flow ☐
(C) income distribution ☐
(D) fiscal transfer ☐

3. Which of the following statements is true regarding final and intermediate goods?

(A) Intermediate goods are included in the calculation of Gross Domestic Product (GDP), while final goods are excluded ☐
(B) Final goods are included in the calculation of Gross Domestic Product (GDP), while intermediate goods are excluded ☐
(C) Both final and intermediate goods are included in the calculation of Gross Domestic Product (GDP) ☐
(D) Neither final nor intermediate goods are included in the calculation of Gross Domestic Product (GDP) ☐

4. Identify the item that best illustrates a capital good, serving as a long-term investment to enhance productivity and facilitate economic development in a manufacturing context.

(A) Industrial machinery acquired by a manufacturing company for production processes ☐
(B) Software purchased by a graphic design studio for creative projects ☐
(C) Steel used in the manufacturing of automobiles ☐
(D) Decorative fixtures installed by a retail store to enhance aesthetic appeal ☐

5. Which of the following is/are considered as stock?

(i) Wealth
(ii) Number of machines in a plant
(iii) Exports (iv) Profits

Codes

(A) (i) and (iii) ☐
(B) (i) and (iv) ☐
(C) (ii) and (iv) ☐
(D) (i) and (ii) ☐

6. What does fixed business investment refer to?

(A) Addition to machinery, factory buildings and equipment ☐
(B) Purchase of stocks and bonds ☐
(C) Spending on advertising and marketing ☐
(D) Investment in residential housing facilities ☐

7. What does residential investment entail?

(A) Addition to the stock of raw materials ☐

(B) Purchase of land for future development ☐

(C) Increase in the value of inventories ☐

(D) Addition of housing facilities ☐

8. Which of the following best describes unplanned accumulation of inventories?

(A) Unexpected rise in sales leading to increased stock levels ☐

(B) Anticipated increase in production to meet demand ☐

(C) Planned decrease in inventory levels to optimise costs ☐

(D) Unexpected fall in sales resulting in excess unsold goods ☐

9. When calculating national income using the income method, what is the primary source of interest income?

(A) Interest earned by households on savings accounts ☐

(B) Interest earned by firms on investments in financial markets ☐

(C) Interest paid by households on mortgages and loans ☐

(D) Interest paid by the government on public debt ☐

10. During the early 20th century, a global economic crisis known as the great depression shook economies around the world. Sparked by the stock market crash of 1929, industries faced significant decline in production and businesses struggled to stay afloat amidst plummeting demand.

Governments implemented various policies in attempts to alleviate the crisis, but recovery was slow and arduous.

During the great depression, what characterised the economic situation globally?

(A) Rapid economic growth and prosperity ☐

(B) Widespread unemployment and poverty ☐

(C) Stable market conditions and high consumer confidence ☐

(D) Booming industrial production and increased consumer spending ☐

11. On the basis of the figure given below, identify the type of flow indicated by B and D. *[CBSE 2023]*

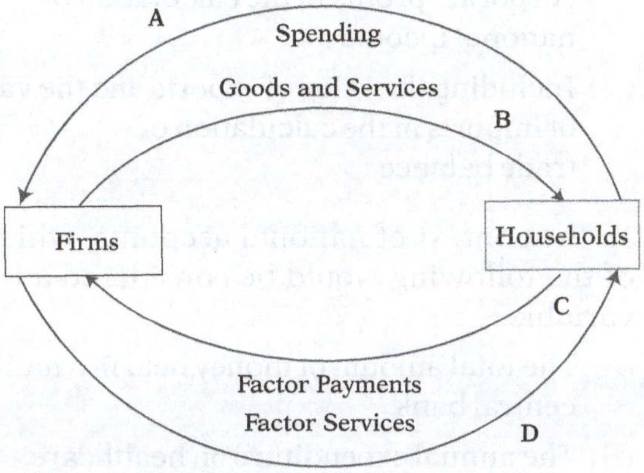

(A) Real flow ☐

(B) Money flow ☐

(C) Nominal flow ☐

(D) National flow ☐

12. Read the following figure carefully and choose the correct pair from the alternatives given below.

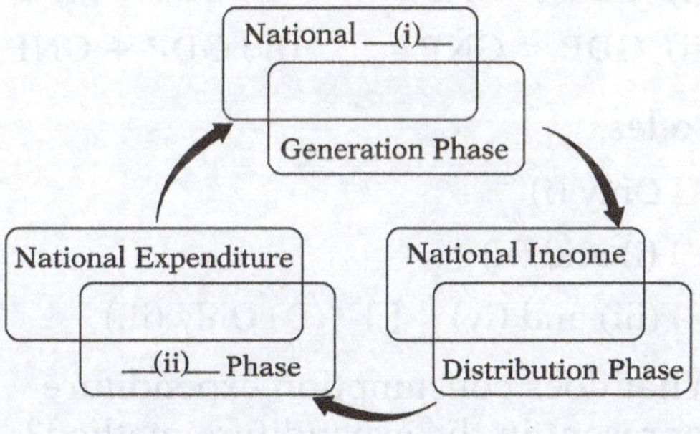

(A) Output, Production ☐

(B) Value added, Production ☐

(C) Output, Disposition ☐

(D) Wealth, Development ☐

13. Which of the following illustrates an instance of double counting within economic analysis?

(A) Including both investment spending and government purchases in Gross Domestic Product (GDP) ☐
(B) Counting the value of intermediate goods and the value of final goods in the GDP calculation ☐
(C) Incorporating both household income and corporate profits in the calculation of national income ☐
(D) Including the value of exports and the value of imports in the calculation of trade balance ☐

14. In the context of national accounts, which of the following would be considered a flow variable?
(A) The total amount of money held in a nation's central bank ☐
(B) The annual expenditure on healthcare services within a country ☐
(C) The total number of automobiles produced by a country's automotive industry ☐
(D) The value of residential properties owned by households in a country ☐

15. For a closed economy (with no foreign trade), which of the following is correct?
(i) GDP = GNP (ii) GDP > GNP
(iii) GDP < GNP (iv) GDP + GNP = 0

Codes
(A) Only (i) ☐
(B) (i) and (ii) ☐
(C) (iii) and (iv) ☐ (D) Only (iii) ☐

16. What does consumption expenditure represent in the expenditure method?
(A) Expenditure by households on goods and services for current consumption ☐
(B) Expenditure by firms on new machinery and equipment ☐
(C) Expenditure by the government on infrastructure projects ☐
(D) Expenditure by households on savings and investments ☐

17. Which component of the expenditure method includes spending by firms on capital goods?
(A) Consumption expenditure ☐
(B) Investment expenditure ☐
(C) Government expenditure ☐
(D) Net exports ☐

18. What does government expenditure represent in the expenditure method?
(A) Spending by households on goods and services ☐
(B) Spending by firms on new factories and equipment ☐
(C) Spending by the government on goods and services, as well as transfer payments ☐
(D) Spending by foreigners on domestically produced goods and services ☐

19. When calculating national income using the income method, which of the following is not included in the category of operating surplus?
(A) Corporate profits ☐
(B) Proprietor's income ☐
(C) Rental income ☐
(D) Wages and salaries ☐

20. If the Gross Domestic Product at Factor Cost (GDP_{FC}) of a country is ₹ 500 billion and the Net Factor Income from Abroad (NFIA) is ₹ 50 billion, what is the Gross National Product at Factor Cost (GNP_{FC})?
(A) ₹ 450 billion ☐ (B) ₹ 550 billion ☐
(C) ₹ 500 billion ☐ (D) ₹ 50 billion ☐

21. How are basic prices related to factor cost and market prices?
(A) Basic prices include net production taxes and product subsidies ☐
(B) Basic prices include net production taxes but not net product taxes ☐
(C) Basic prices exclude production taxes but include product subsidies ☐
(D) Basic prices exclude both production taxes and product subsidies ☐

22. Gross Domestic Product (GDP) is calculated by summing up which of the following components?
(A) Consumption expenditure, investment expenditure, government expenditure and net exports ☐
(B) Compensation of employees, operating surplus, mixed income and taxes minus subsidies ☐
(C) Gross value added at basic prices and net product taxes ☐
(D) Compensation of employees, operating surplus and net product taxes ☐

23. Which of the following represents the total income earned by residents of a country, both domestically and abroad, minus income earned by foreigners within the country?
(A) Gross Domestic Product (GDP) ☐
(B) Gross National Product (GNP) ☐
(C) Net Domestic Product (NDP) ☐
(D) Net National Product (NNP) ☐

24. How is real GDP calculated?
(A) By summing up the total market value of all final goods and services produced within a country in a specific period, not adjusted for inflation ☐
(B) By adjusting nominal GDP for changes in the price level using a base year ☐
(C) By adding net foreign factor income to Gross Domestic Product (GDP) ☐
(D) By subtracting depreciation from Gross Domestic Product (GDP) ☐

25. Which of the following statements is correct regarding nominal GDP?
(A) It reflects changes in both the quantity of goods and services produced and changes in their prices over time ☐
(B) It only reflects changes in the quantity of goods and services produced over time ☐
(C) It only reflects changes in the prices of goods and services over time ☐
(D) It does not reflect changes in either the quantity of goods and services produced or changes in their prices over time ☐

26. Which of the following represents an increase in nominal GDP but a decrease in real GDP?
(A) An increase in both the quantity of goods and services produced and an increase in their prices ☐
(B) A decrease in both the quantity of goods and services produced and a decrease in their prices ☐
(C) An increase in the quantity of goods and services produced but a decrease in their prices ☐
(D) A decrease in the quantity of goods and services produced but an increase in their prices ☐

27. In a hypothetical economy, a firm produces clothing. It purchases raw materials worth ₹ 20,000. If the firm sells its clothing for ₹ 50,000, what is the value added by the firm?
(A) ₹ 50,000 ☐ (B) ₹ 20,000 ☐
(C) ₹ 30,000 ☐ (D) ₹10,000 ☐

28. In an economy, a firm produces goods worth ₹ 100 per year. It uses intermediate goods valued at ₹ 20 and incurs depreciation (consumption of fixed capital) worth ₹ 10. What is the Gross Value Added (GVA) and Net Value Added (NVA) by the firm per year?
(A) GVA = ₹ 100, NVA = ₹ 80 ☐
(B) GVA = ₹ 90, NVA = ₹ 70 ☐
(C) GVA = ₹ 80, NVA = ₹ 70 ☐
(D) GVA = ₹ 100, NVA = ₹ 90 ☐

29. If in an economy the value of net factor income from abroad is ₹ 200 crore and the value of factor income to abroad is ₹ 40 crore. Identify the value of factor income from abroad.
(A) ₹ 200 crore ☐ (B) ₹ 160 crore ☐
(C) ₹ 240 crore ☐ (D) ₹ 180 crore ☐

30. Complete the table. [CBSE 2023]

Producer	Value of Output	Intermediate Consumption	Value Added
Farmer	2,000	—	2,000
Baker	...(i)...	2,000	2,000
Retail Seller	4,400	...(iii)...	400
Total	...(ii)...	6,000	...(iv)...

(A) 4,000, 10,400, 4,000, 4,000 ☐
(B) 4,000, 10,400, 4,000, 4,400 ☐
(C) 2,000, 6,000, 6,000, 4,400 ☐
(D) 4,000, 10,400, 6,000, 4,000 ☐

31. Which of the following equations represents the expenditure method to calculate national income?

(A) National Income = Consumption Expenditure + Investment Expenditure + Government Expenditure + Net exports ☐
(B) National Income = Consumption Expenditure + Investment Expenditure − Government Expenditure + Net Exports ☐
(C) National Income = Consumption Expenditure − Investment Expenditure + Government Expenditure + Net Exports ☐
(D) National income = Consumption Expenditure + Investment Expenditure + Government Expenditure − Net Exports ☐

32. Match the following

Column I	Column II
A. Real flow	(i) Balance of payment
B. Money flow	(ii) Physical flow
C. Microeconomics	(iii) Nominal flow
D. Macroeconomics	(iv) Price theory

Codes

	A	B	C	D	
(A)	(ii)	(iii)	(i)	(iv)	☐
(B)	(ii)	(iii)	(iv)	(i)	☐
(C)	(ii)	(iv)	(iii)	(i)	☐
(D)	(ii)	(i)	(iv)	(iii)	☐

33. From the statements given in Column I and Column II, choose the correct pair [CBSE 2023]

Column I	Column II
A. Vegetables grown in the personal garden	(i) Non-marketing activity
B. A car used as a taxi	(ii) Consumer good
C. An air conditioner used by household	(iii) Capital good
D. Scholarship given to students by government	(iv) Factor income

Codes

(A) A-(i) ☐ (B) B-(ii) ☐
(C) C-(iii) ☐ (D) D-(iv) ☐

34. Match the following

Column I	Column II
A. NFIA is negative	(ii) Intermediate consumption is zero
B. NIT is positive	(ii) FITA > FIFA
C. Value added = Value of output	(iii) NIT = 0
D. MP = FC	(iv) IT > Subsidies

Codes

	A	B	C	D	
(A)	(ii)	(i)	(iv)	(iii)	☐
(B)	(ii)	(iv)	(iii)	(i)	☐
(C)	(ii)	(iii)	(i)	(iv)	☐
(D)	(ii)	(iv)	(i)	(iii)	☐

35. Match the following

Column I	Column II
A. NDP at MP	(ii) NDP at MP + NFIA − NIT
B. NNP at MP	(ii) GDP at FC + NFIA
C. GNP at FC	(iii) GDP at MP − Dep. + NFIA
D. NNP at FC	(iv) GNP at MP − Dep. − NFIA

Codes

	A	B	C	D	
(A)	(iv)	(iii)	(ii)	(i)	☐
(B)	(iv)	(iii)	(i)	(ii)	☐
(C)	(iv)	(ii)	(iii)	(i)	☐
(D)	(iv)	(i)	(ii)	(iii)	☐

Assertion-Reason Questions

No. of Questions : **10** Suggested Time : **15 Minutes**

Direction Each of the question given below consist of the two statements; one labelled as **Assertion** (A) and other as **Reason** (R). List of common options applicable for each question is given below

(A) Both Assertion (A) and Reason (R) are true and Reason (R) is the correct explanation of Assertion (A)

(B) Both Assertion (A) and Reason (R) are true, but Reason (R) is not the correct explanation of Assertion (A)

(C) Assertion (A) is true, but Reason (R) is false

(D) Assertion (A) is false, but Reason (R) is true

You have to select the codes as *A, B, C* or *D* as your answer to the question by marking (✓) in the response box given against each option.

1. **Assertion** (A) Final goods contribute directly to GDP, while intermediate goods do not.

   Reason (R) Intermediate goods are used in the production process and are not counted separately in GDP calculations.

   (A) ☐ (B) ☐ (C) ☐ (D) ☐

2. **Assertion** (A) Gross investment represents the total amount of capital invested in an economy, while net investment excludes depreciation.

   Reason (R) Depreciation reflects the appreciation of capital assets over time, increasing the value of gross investment.

   (A) ☐ (B) ☐ (C) ☐ (D) ☐

3. **Assertion** (A) Stock variables represent quantities measured at a specific point in time, while flow variables represent quantities measured over a period of time.

   Reason (R) Stock variables, such as the level of inventory, are dynamic and subject to change, while flow variables, such as income or expenditure, are static and remain constant.

   (A) ☐ (B) ☐ (C) ☐ (D) ☐

4. **Assertion** (A) The circular flow of income model illustrates the continuous flow of goods, services and payments between households and firms in an economy.

   Reason (R) Through this model, households provide factors of production, such as labour and capital, to firms in exchange for income, while firms produce goods and services, which are then sold to households for consumption.

   (A) ☐ (B) ☐ (C) ☐ (D) ☐

5. **Assertion** (A) The value added method calculates GDP by measuring the difference between the value of output and the cost of intermediate goods used in production.

   Reason (R) This method focuses on the final value of goods and services produced in an economy, without considering the contributions of various sectors to the overall output.

   (A) ☐ (B) ☐ (C) ☐ (D) ☐

6. **Assertion** (A) GNP_{MP} represents the total economic output produced by a nation's normal residents, measured at market prices, including both domestic production and net factor income from abroad.

Reason (R) GNP_{MP} is calculated by adding GDP_{MP} (measured at market prices) to Net Indirect Taxes (NIT), reflecting the total income earned.

(A) ☐ (B) ☐ (C) ☐ (D) ☐

7. **Assertion (A)** Real gross domestic product is a better indicator of economic growth of a nation as compared to nominal gross domestic product.

Reason (R) Real gross domestic product measures the value of goods and services at current year prices. *[CBSE 2024]*

(A) ☐ (B) ☐ (C) ☐ (D) ☐

8. **Assertion (A)** Externalities, such as pollution and traffic congestion, can have significant impacts on social welfare by affecting health, well-being and the environment.

Reason (R) Despite their importance for societal welfare, externalities are often not accounted for in GDP calculations, leading to an incomplete assessment of economic well-being.

(A) ☐ (B) ☐ (C) ☐ (D) ☐

9. **Assertion (A)** The concept of domestic territory in macroeconomics refers to the geographical area within a country's borders, excluding land, water and airspace.

Reason (R) Domestic territory is essential for calculating national income and other macroeconomic indicators, as it defines the scope of economic activity under a nation's jurisdiction.

(A) ☐ (B) ☐
(C) ☐ (D) ☐

10. **Assertion (A)** Double counting occurs when the same economic transactions or activities are counted more than once in the calculation of GDP.

Reason (R) Double counting can distort the measurement of GDP by inflating the value of economic output, leading to inaccuracies in assessing the true level of economic activity.

(A) ☐ (B) ☐ (C) ☐ (D) ☐

Correct/Incorrect Statements

No. of Questions : **10** Suggested Time : **15 Minutes**

Direction Each of the question given below consist of the two statements. List of common options applicable for each question is given below

(A) Statement I is correct and Statement II is incorrect

(B) Statement I is incorrect and Statement II is correct

(C) Both statements are correct

(D) Both statements are incorrect

You have to select the codes as *A, B, C* or *D* as your answer to the question by marking (✓) in the response box given against each option.

1. **Statement I** An item that is meant for final use and will not pass through any more stages of production or transformations is called a final good.

Statement II Final goods will not undergo any further transformation at the hands of any producer. It may, however, undergo transformation by the action of the ultimate purchaser.

(A) ☐ (B) ☐ (C) ☐ (D) ☐

2. **Statement I** Capital goods are durable goods used by industries to produce consumer goods or other goods for further production.

Statement II The purchase of new machinery by an automobile manufacturer to increase production capacity is not an example of investment in capital goods.

(A) ☐ (B) ☐ (C) ☐ (D) ☐

3. **Statement I** Stock refers to the quantity of goods or assets accumulated at a specific point in time, while flow represents the rate of change in the quantity of goods or assets over a period.

Statement II A company's inventory level is an example of stock, while the rate of production is an example of flow.

(A) ☐ (B) ☐
(C) ☐ (D) ☐

4. **Statement I** Depreciation refers to the decrease in the value of an asset over time due to wear and tear, obsolescence or other factors.

Statement II Depreciation is considered as a non-accounting concept.

(A) ☐ (B) ☐
(C) ☐ (D) ☐

5. **Statement I** The aggregate consumption by the households of the economy is equal to the aggregate expenditure on goods and services produced by the firms in the economy.

Statement II In income generation phase, the income received by factors of production, is spent on the goods and services produced by firms.

(A) ☐ (B) ☐ (C) ☐ (D) ☐

6. **Statement I** In economics, the stock of unsold finished goods or semi-finished goods, or raw materials which a firm carries from one year to the next is called inventory.

Statement II In case of an unexpected fall in sales, the firm will have unsold stock of goods which it had not anticipated. Hence, there will be planned accumulation of inventories.

(A) ☐ (B) ☐ (C) ☐ (D) ☐

7. **Statement I** Examples of transfer incomes included in the income method are wages, salaries, rent, interest and profits.

Statement II The income method calculates national income by summing up all factor incomes earned by individuals and businesses within an economy over a specific period.

(A) ☐ (B) ☐ (C) ☐ (D) ☐

8. **Statement I** Real GDP adjusts for inflation or deflation by expressing the value of goods and services produced in constant prices of a base year.

Statement II Nominal GDP does not adjust for changes in the price level and reflects the value of goods and services produced at current market prices.

(A) ☐ (B) ☐ (C) ☐ (D) ☐

9. **Statement I** Gross Domestic Product (GDP) is the sum total of the gross market values of all the final goods and services added by all the sectors in the economy during a final year.

Statement II Gross Value Added at Market Price (GVA_{MP}) is equal to the excess of value of output over intermediate consumption.

[CBSE 2023]

(A) ☐ (B) ☐ (C) ☐ (D) ☐

10. **Statement I** Externalities refer to the benefits or harms caused by firms or individuals to others for which they are compensated or penalised.

Statement II GDP account for externalities, such as pollution, which can have negative effects on well-being, leading to an overestimation of actual welfare.

(A) ☐
(B) ☐
(C) ☐
(D) ☐

Case Based Questions

No. of Questions : **2** Suggested Time : **10 Minutes**

Direction This section contains 2 cases each having 4 questions of 1 mark each. You have to write the answer of each question based on the context of the related case.

Case 1 In a town, there are several industries contributing to the local economy. Among them are farmers cultivating various crops and a textile factory that processes cotton into fabric. The farmers sell their cotton to the textile factory, which in turn produces cloth used by local garment manufacturers.

Additionally, there is a carpentry workshop that specialises in crafting wooden furniture. The carpenters purchase timber from local sawmills, which source their wood from nearby forests. The furniture produced by the carpentry workshop is sold to residents and businesses in the town.

Also, there is a recycling plant in the town that collects scrap metal from households and businesses.

The plant processes the scrap metal into raw material used by construction companies for building new infrastructure in the town.

Questions

(i) ...... industries represents the production of intermediate goods in this case.

(ii) ...... is the final good produced in this case.

(iii) How does the purchase of timber by the carpentry workshop affect the GDP of the town?

(A) It increases the GDP directly ☐
(B) It increases the GDP indirectly ☐
(C) It does not affect the GDP ☐
(D) It decreases the GDP ☐

(iv) What role does the recycling plant play in the production process described?

(A) It produces final goods ☐
(B) It produces intermediate goods ☐
(C) It contributes to the recycling industry ☐
(D) It is not involved in the production process ☐

Case 2 The Budget Estimate of total spending for 2021-22 is ₹ 34.83 lakh crore. The Revised Estimate (RE) for total central spending in 2020-21 is ₹ 34.5 lakh crore. The Gross Domestic Product (GDP) deflator — if one takes 14.4% nominal GDP growth projection for 2021-22 given in the budget and 11% real GDP forecast given in the latest Economic Survey comes to 3.4%.

This means that central spending should have increased to at least ₹ 35.7 lakh crore to keep it unchanged in real terms. The fact that it has not happened implies that the 2021-22 budget entails a negative fiscal stimulus to the economy.

To be sure, one could argue that 2020-21 was an abnormal year — and therefore, the government is justified in rolling back its welfare spending push, as the economy gets unlocked and vaccination gains momentum. [CBSE QB]

Questions

(i) With the rise in real national income, the economic welfare of the people .... (rises/falls).

(ii) If GDP Deflator = 125, Nominal GDP = ₹ 15,000 crore then Real GDP is equal to ....

(iii) **Assertion** (A) Real GDP is always equal to Nominal GDP.

Reason (R) Real GDP is a better measure to make periodic comparison in the physical output of goods and services over different years.

Alternatives

(A) Assertion (A) is true and Reason (R) is false ☐

(B) Assertion (A) is false and Reason (R) is true ☐

(iv) State the significance of GDP Deflator.

Subjective Questions

Free Response Questions, Open-ended Questions etc.

No. of Questions : **22** Suggested Time : **110 Minutes**

1. Consider a scenario where a domestic resident purchases a new car produced by a foreign-owned automobile company operating within the country. Is the revenue from the sale of the car included in national income? Why or why not?

2. In a country with a large population of migrant workers sending remittances back home, how are these remittances treated in national income accounting?

3. Explain why transfer payments, such as social security benefits and welfare payments, are excluded from national income calculations.

4. How are non-market activities, such as household production and volunteer work, treated in national income accounting? Give reasons for their inclusion or exclusion from national income calculations.

5. The following headline is indicated in the newspaper

"India's GDP growth pegged at 7.3% for FY24, government's first advance estimate shows."

Do you think that welfare in the economy will also increase by the same rate? Justify.

6. The good which is used by a producer in the production process is a producer good, then how can you categorise the good into intermediate and capital good?

7. "Disposition phase of circular flow of income involves flow of factor income, which comprises of rent, wages, interest and profits from firms to housholds."

Defend or refute the statement, giving valid reasons in support of your answer. [CBSE 2024]

8. What aspect of income does the following image represents?

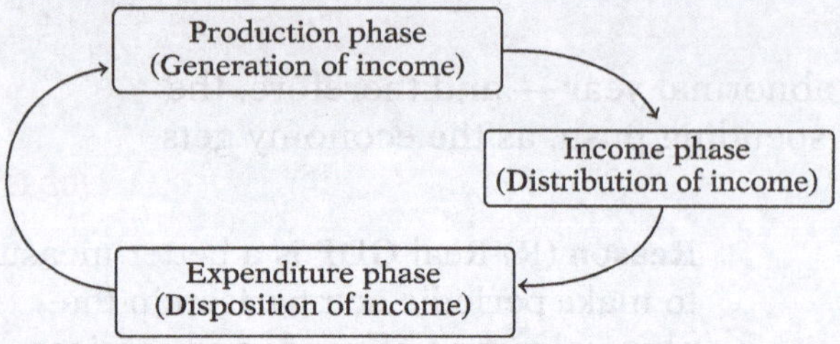

9. "Delhi-Mumbai Industrial Corridor (DMIC) has been envisaged as one of the largest infrastructure projects being implemented in India, along with Smart Cities Mission, Bharatmala and Sagarmala – both in financial as well as geographical terms."
Elaborate the impact of these projects on GDP and welfare.

10. Sarah recently moved into a new apartment and decided to buy some household items to furnish her living space. She purchased a variety of items, including a sofa set, a dining table and a refrigerator. These items were essential for her daily living and were classified as durable goods because they were expected to last for several years.
Additionally, Sarah bought some new dinnerware, such as plates, glasses and cutlery. While these items were not as long-lasting as the furniture, they could be used multiple times before needing replacement.
To complete her shopping, Sarah also bought groceries, including milk, vegetables and bread. These items were consumed relatively quickly and needed to be replenished frequently.
(i) What category do the groceries purchased by Sarah fall into?
(ii) What type of goods are the dinnerware items purchased by Sarah?

Numerical Questions

11. Calculate GDP_{FC}, if
(i) NDP_{MP} = ₹ 16,000 crore
(ii) Consumption of fixed capital = ₹ 2,000 crore
(iii) Net factor income from abroad = ₹ 200 crore
(iv) Income tax = ₹ 120 crore
(v) Corporate tax = ₹ 20 crore
(vi) GST = ₹ 100 crore
(vii) Subsides = ₹ 30 crore

12. Calculate national income, if
(i) GDP_{MP} = ₹ 43,500 crore
(ii) Current replacement cost = ₹ 1,200 crore
(iii) Net factor income to abroad = ₹ 600 crore
(iv) GST = ₹ 200 crore
(v) Indirect taxes = ₹ 500 crore
(vi) Subsidies = ₹ 700 crore
(vii) Factor income from abroad = ₹ 100 crore

13. Calculate domestic income, if
(i) GNP_{MP} = ₹ 18,800 crore
(ii) Current replacement cost = ₹ 1,200 crore
(iii) Net factor income from abroad = ₹ 300 crore
(iv) Excise duty = ₹ 50 crore
(v) Income tax = ₹ 30 crore
(vi) GST = ₹ 40 crore
(vii) Subsidies = ₹ 20 crore
(viii) Factor income to abroad = ₹ 100 crore
(ix) Profit = ₹ 300 crore

14. Suppose in a financial year, the Gross Domestic Product (GDP) at market price of a country was ₹ 1,100 crore, the net indirect taxes was ₹ 150 crore and national income was ₹ 850 crore.
Calculate the value of depreciation, on the basis of above information. *[CBSE 2023]*

15. Calculate NFIA, if
(i) GDP_{MP} = ₹ 21,000 crore
(ii) NNP_{FC} = ₹ 19,800 crore
(iii) Consumption of fixed capital = ₹ 400 crore
(iv) Indirect tax = ₹ 400 crore
(v) Subsidies = ₹ 200 crore

16. Calculate NNP_{MP}, if
(i) Change in stock = ₹ 50 crore
(ii) Purchase of raw material = ₹ 20 crore
(iii) Factor income from abroad = ₹ 60 crore
(iv) Sales = ₹ 1,800 crore

(v) Consumption of fixed capital = ₹ 20 crore
(vi) Purchase of intermediate products = ₹ 300 crore
(vii) Factor income to abroad = ₹ 10 crore
(viii) Exports = ₹ 200 crore

17. Calculate value added by firm A and firm B.
(i) Purchases by firm *A* = ₹ 200 crore
(ii) Exports of firm *B* = ₹ 300 crore
(iii) Sales by firm *A* = ₹ 600 crore
(iv) Closing stock of firm *A* = ₹ 50 crore
(v) Opening stock of firm *A* = ₹ 40 crore
(vi) Sales by firm *B* to general government = ₹ 800 crore
(vii) Opening stock of firm *B* = ₹ 30 crore
(viii) Closing stock of firm *B* = ₹ 60 crore
(ix) Purchases by firm *B* = ₹ 150 crore

18. Calculate sales
(i) NNP_{FC} = ₹ 5,000 crore
(ii) Net factor income to abroad = ₹ (–600) crore
(iii) Indirect taxes = ₹ 700 crore
(iv) Consumption of fixed capital = ₹ 200 crore
(v) Subsidies = ₹ 300 crore
(vi) Intermediate consumption = ₹ 800 crore
(vii) Excess of opening stock over closing stock =200 crore

19. Estimate the value of Net National Product at Factor Cost (NNP_{FC}), using the following information **[CBSE 2024]**

S.No.	Items	₹ (in crores)
(i)	Household Consumption Expenditure	1,200
(ii)	Business Fixed Investment Expenditure	800
(iii)	Government Final Consumption Expenditure	500
(iv)	Excess of Imports over Exports	100
(v)	Net Indirect Taxes	150
(vi)	Change in Inventory	(–) 50
(vii)	Consumption of Fixed Capital	200
(viii)	Net Factor Income from Abroad	80
(ix)	Public Fixed Investment	70

20. Find the missing value.
(i) Compensation of employees = ₹ 6,000 crore
(ii) Depreciation = ₹ 500 crore
(iii) Subsidies = ₹ 50 crore
(iv) Operating surplus = ?
(v) GNP_{FC} = ₹ 11,000 crore
(vi) Indirect taxes = ₹ 100 crore
(vii) Wages and salaries = ₹ 2,000 crore
(viii) Factor income from abroad = ₹ 1,100 crore
(ix) Factor income to abroad = ₹ 1,600 crore
(x) Mixed income of self-employed = ₹ 3,000 crore

21. Find the missing value.
(i) Wages and salaries = ₹ 18,000 crore
(ii) Consumption of fixed capital = ₹ 5,000 crore
(iii) Mixed income of self-employed = ₹ 4,000 crore
(iv) Net factor income from abroad = ₹ 5,000 crore
(v) Rent = ₹ 4,000 crore
(vi) Factor income to abroad = ₹ 2,000 crore
(vii) GNP_{MP} = ₹ 43,000 crore
(viii) Interest = ₹ 2,500 crore
(ix) Profit = ?

22. Calculate the value of National Income from the following data **[CBSE 2023]**

S.No.	Contents	₹ (in crores)
(i)	Rent and Royalties	1,300
(ii)	Net Indirect Taxes	200
(iii)	Wages and Salaries (in cash and in kind)	1,700
(iv)	Corporate Tax	400
(v)	Depreciation	400
(vi)	Retained Earnings	300
(vii)	Dividends	400
(viii)	Net Factor Income from Abroad	(–) 120
(ix)	Mixed Income of Self-employed	1,400
(x)	Change in Stock	(–) 200

Answers

If your answer matches with the answer given here then put (✓) in the box otherwise put (✗). In case you did not attempt the question leave the box blank.

Multiple Choice Questions

1. B	☐	2. B	☐
3. B	☐	4. A	☐
5. D	☐	6. A	☐
7. D	☐	8. D	☐
9. A	☐	10. B	☐
11. B	☐	12. C	☐
13. B	☐	14. B	☐
15. A	☐	16. A	☐
17. B	☐	18. C	☐
19. D	☐	20. B	☐
21. B	☐	22. A	☐
23. B	☐	24. B	☐
25. A	☐	26. C	☐
27. C	☐	28. C	☐
29. C	☐	30. B	☐
31. A	☐	32. B	☐
33. A	☐		
34. D	☐		
35. B	☐		

Your Score_________ *(No. of Correct Answers)*

Assertion-Reason Questions

1. A	☐	2. C	☐
3. C	☐	4. A	☐
5. B	☐	6. C	☐
7. B	☐	8. A	☐
9. D	☐	10. A	☐

Your Score_________ *(No. of Correct Answers)*

Correct/Incorrect Statements

1. C	☐	2. A	☐
3. C	☐	4. A	☐
5. A	☐	6. A	☐
7. B	☐	8. C	☐
9. C	☐	10. D	☐

Your Score_________ *(No. of Correct Answers)*

Case Based Questions

1. (iii) B ☐
   (iv) B ☐
2. (iii) B ☐

Your Score_________ *(No. of Correct Answers)*

Explanations

Multiple Choice Questions

1. (B) Goods used as raw materials or inputs in the production of other goods
2. (B) money flow
3. (B) Final goods are included in the calculation of Gross Domestic Product (GDP), while intermediate goods are excluded
4. (A) Capital goods are long-term investments used to produce other goods and services, enhancing productivity. Industrial machinery is a classic example of a capital good in manufacturing.
5. (D) Stocks are variables measured at a specific point in time, representing a quantity at a particular moment. Wealth and number of machines in a plant are stocks because they represent the value of assets or quantities at a specific point in time.
6. (A) Addition to machinery, factory buildings and equipment
7. (D) Addition of housing facilities
8. (D) Unexpected fall in sales resulting in excess unsold goods
9. (A) Interest earned by households on savings accounts
10. (B) The economic crisis led to severe downturns in output and employment levels, resulting in widespread hardship for individuals and families.

11. (B) Money flow
12. (C) Output, Disposition
13. (B) Counting the value of intermediate goods and the value of final goods in the GDP calculation
14. (B) The annual expenditure on healthcare services within a country
15. (A) In a closed economy (with no foreign trade), GDP (Gross Domestic Product) is equal to GNP (Gross National Product) because there are no international transactions influencing the difference between these two measures.
16. (A) Expenditure by households on goods and services for current consumption
17. (B) Investment expenditure includes spending by firms on capital goods such as machinery, equipment and factories, aimed at increasing future production capacity.
18. (C) Spending by the government on goods and services, as well as transfer payments
19. (D) Operating surplus includes corporate profits, proprietor's income and rental income.
20. (B) $GNP_{FC} = GDP_{FC} + NFIA$

$= 500 + 50 = ₹ 550$ billion

21. (B) Net production taxes are taxes minus subsidies on production, while net product taxes are taxes minus subsidies on products.
22. (A) Consumption expenditure, investment expenditure, government expenditure and net exports
23. (B) Gross National Product (GNP)
24. (B) By adjusting nominal GDP for changes in the price level using a base year
25. (A) It reflects changes in both the quantity of goods and services produced and changes in their prices over time
26. (C) An increase in the quantity of goods and services produced but a decrease in their prices
27. (C) Value Added = Revenue – Cost of Intermediate Goods

$= 50{,}000 - 20{,}000 = ₹ 30{,}000$

28. (C) GVA = Value of Output – Value of Intermediate Consumption

GVA = 100 – 20 = ₹ 80

NVA = GVA – Depreciation = 80 – 10 = ₹ 70

29. (C) NFIA = 200; Value of Factor Income to Abroad = 40

Factor Income from Abroad = NFIA + Factor Income to Abroad

= 200 + 40 = ₹ 240 crore

30. (B) (i) Value of Output = Value Added + Intermediate Consumption

= 2,000 + 2,000 = 4,000

(ii) Total Value of Output

= Value of Output of Farmer + Value of Output of Baker + Value of Output of Retail Seller

= 2,000 + 4,000 + 4,400 = 10,400

(iii) Intermediate Consumption

= Value of Output – Value Added

= 4,400 – 400 = 4,000

(iv) Total Value Added = Total Value of Output – Total Intermediate Consumption

= 10,400 – 6,000 = 4,400

31. (A) National Income = Consumption expenditure + Investment Expenditure + Government Expenditure + Net Exports
32. (B) (ii) (iii) (iv) (i)
33. (A) A-(i)
34. (D) (ii) (iv) (i) (iii)
35. (B) (iv) (iii) (i) (ii)

Assertion-Reason Questions

1. (A) Both Assertion (A) and Reason (R) are true and Reason (R) is the correct explanation of Assertion (A)
2. (C) The gross investment represents the total capital invested. Depreciation reduces the value of gross investment.
3. (C) Assertion (A) is true, but Reason (R) is false
4. (A) Both Assertion (A) and Reason (R) are true and Reason (R) is the correct explanation of Assertion (A)
5. (B) Both Assertion (A) and Reason (R) are true, but Reason (R) is not the correct explanation of Assertion (A)
6. (C) Assertion (A) is true, but Reason (R) is false
7. (B) Both Assertion (A) and Reason (R) are true, but Reason (R) is not the correct explanation of Assertion (A)

8. (A) Both Assertion (A) and Reason (R) are true and Reason (R) is the correct explanation of Assertion (A)

9. (D) A domestic territory in macroeconomics refers to the geographical area within a country's borders, including land, water and airspace.

10. (A) Both Assertion (A) and Reason (R) are true and Reason (R) is the correct explanation of Assertion (A)

Correct/Incorrect Statements

1. (C) Both statements are correct

2. (A) The purchase of new machinery by an automobile manufacturer to increase production capacity is an example of investment in capital goods.

3. (C) Both statements are correct

4. (A) Depreciation is considered an accounting concept.

5. (A) The factors of production may also save a portion of their income or spend it on goods and services produced by other entities besides firms, such as government services or imports.

6. (A) An unexpected fall in sales would lead to unplanned accumulation of inventories.

7. (B) Examples of transfer incomes included in the income method typically encompass payments made without the exchange of goods or services.

8. (C) Both statements are correct

9. (C) Both statements are correct

10. (D) Externalities refer to the unintended effects of economic activities on third parties, whether positive or negative, which are not accounted for in market transactions. GDP does not fully account for externalities such as pollution, which can impact well-being, leading to a potential overestimation of actual welfare.

Case Based Questions

1. (i) Sawmills (ii) Furniture

(iii) (B) It increases the GDP indirectly

(iv) (B) It produces intermediate goods

2. (i) rises

(ii) $\text{Real GDP} = \dfrac{\text{Nominal GDP}}{\text{GDP Deflator}} \times 100 = \dfrac{15{,}000}{125} \times 100$

$= ₹\ 12{,}000$ crore

(iii) (B) Assertion (A) is false and Reason (R) is true

(iv) GDP Deflator is a tool that shows changes in the price level of the economy over a given period of time.

Subjective Questions

1. The revenue from the sale of the car is included in national income because it represents the value of goods produced within the country's borders, regardless of the ownership of the producing entity.

2. Remittances sent by migrant workers back to their home country are included in national income as they represent earnings generated by domestic residents, even though the actual income is earned abroad.

3. Transfer payments are excluded from national income calculations because they do not reflect current production or income generated from productive activities. Instead, they are redistributions of income and do not contribute to the country's total output.

4. Non-market activities, such as household production and volunteer work, are typically excluded from national income calculations because they are difficult to measure accurately and may not have market values attached to them. However, they contribute to overall welfare and well-being.

5. While GDP is an important indicator of economic activity and prosperity, it does not directly measure overall welfare or well-being. Welfare encompasses a broader range of factors beyond just economic output, including income distribution, access to basic needs such as healthcare and education, environmental quality, and social cohesion. Therefore, an increase in GDP may not necessarily translate into improvements in these aspects of welfare.

e.g. If the increase in GDP is driven by activities that result in environmental degradation or income inequality, it may not lead to an equivalent increase in welfare. Similarly, if the benefits of economic growth are not equitably distributed across society, certain groups may not experience improvements in their welfare despite overall GDP growth.

6. All the goods which are used by producers in the production process are producer goods, this statement is correct.

We can categorise the good into intermediate and final goods on the basis of the following parameters

(i) Intermediate goods are single used producer goods whereas capital goods are used repeatedly during the production process.
(ii) Intermediate goods lose their identity during production process whereas capital goods don't lose their identity during production process.

7. The given statement is refuted as the disposition phase of circular flow of income includes expenditure on goods and services by the households.

There are three phases in a circular flow of income i.e. the first phase is comprised of production, the second phase is comprised of income generation or distribution of factor income and the third phase is the disposition phase.

8. The given image shows the circular flow of income. It is a macroeconomic model that illustrates the flow of money and resources throughout an economy. It shows how households and businesses interact through various economic activities. The model consists of four main phases

(i) **Production** This phase involves the creation of goods and services by firms. Firms utilise factors of production such as labour, capital and land to produce goods and services.
(ii) **Income** In this phase, factors of production are compensated for their contribution to the production process. This includes wages paid to labour, profits earned by entrepreneurs, rent paid for the use of land and interest earned on capital.
(iii) **Expenditure** Once households receive income, they use it to purchase goods and services produced by firms. Consumption represents the utilisation of goods and services for personal satisfaction and well-being.

These phases form a continuous cycle, as income generated from production flows back into consumption and investment, stimulating further economic activity. The circular flow of income highlights the interdependence of households and firms in generating and distributing income within an economy.

9. The impacts are as follows

(i) **GDP Growth** These infrastructure projects are expected to stimulate economic activity by improving connectivity, reducing transportation costs and attracting investments.

Enhanced transportation networks, such as highways, railways and ports under projects like Bharatmala and Sagarmala, can facilitate the movement of goods and services, leading to increased production and trade.

Similarly, the DMIC aims to develop industrial hubs along the Delhi-Mumbai corridor, promoting manufacturing and industrial output.

As a result, the contribution of these sectors to GDP is likely to expand, contributing to overall economic growth.

(ii) **Employment Generation** Infrastructure projects typically create employment opportunities across various sectors, including construction, manufacturing and services.

The development of smart cities and industrial corridors requires a workforce for planning, construction and maintenance activities.

Additionally, improved connectivity and infrastructure can attract investments and businesses, leading to job creation in ancillary industries. The resultant increase in employment levels can have a positive impact on household incomes and consumer spending, further fueling economic growth.

(iii) **Social Development** Beyond economic considerations, these projects have the potential to enhance social development indicators and overall welfare.

The Smart Cities Mission focuses on improving urban amenities, such as housing, water supply, sanitation and healthcare, which can enhance the quality of life for residents.

Similarly, investments in transportation infrastructure under Bharatmala and Sagarmala can improve accessibility to markets, healthcare facilities and educational institutions, particularly in rural and remote areas.

This accessibility can reduce disparities in access to essential services and contribute to social inclusion and human development.

While infrastructure projects like the Delhi-Mumbai Industrial Corridor (DMIC) and others mentioned can bring significant benefits, they may also have potential negative impacts on welfare.

Some of them are

(i) **Displacement and Social Disruption** Large-scale infrastructure projects often involve land acquisition and resettlement of communities. This can lead to displacement of people from their homes and disruption of social networks, impacting their livelihoods and well-being.

Adequate compensation, rehabilitation and resettlement policies are necessary to mitigate these adverse effects and ensure that affected communities are not left worse-off.

(ii) **Environmental Degradation** Infrastructure development can lead to environmental degradation, including deforestation, habitat destruction, air and water pollution and loss of biodiversity. These environmental impacts can harm human health, affect access to clean air and water, and degrade ecosystems that support livelihoods and cultural practices.

Sustainable development practices and environmental safeguards are essential to minimise these negative effects and promote long-term environmental sustainability.

(iii) **Income Inequality** Infrastructure projects may exacerbate income inequality if the benefits are not distributed equitably. e.g. Investments in urban infrastructure like smart cities may primarily benefit wealthier residents, leading to further marginalisation of low income communities.

It is crucial to ensure that infrastructure investments prioritise inclusive development and address the needs of all segments of society, particularly the marginalised and vulnerable.

10. (i) Sarah's groceries, such as milk and vegetables, fall under the category of non-durable goods. These goods are characterised by their short lifespan and are typically consumed or used up in a single use.

Non-durable goods play a significant role in everyday life, as they include essential items like food and household supplies that need regular replenishment.

Sarah's purchase of non-durable goods contributes to her immediate consumption needs, ensuring she has the necessary items for daily living.

(ii) The dinnerware items purchased by Sarah, such as crockery and utensils, belong to the category of semi-durable goods.

Unlike non-durable goods, semi-durable goods have a longer lifespan but do not last indefinitely.

They can be used repeatedly over a period of time before needing replacement. Sarah's investment in semi-durable goods reflects her desire for items that offer both functionality and longevity, contributing to her household's comfort and convenience over time.

Numerical Questions

11. $GDP_{FC} = NDP_{MP}$ + Consumption of Fixed Capital – (GST–Subsidies)

= 16,000 + 2,000 – (100 – 30)

= 16,000 + 2,000 – 70

= ₹ 17,930 crore

12. National Income/NNP_{FC} = GDP_{MP} – Current Replacement Cost + (–Net Factor Income to Abroad) – (Indirect Taxes – Subsidies)

= 43,500 – 1,200 + (– 600) – (500 – 700)

= 43,500 – 1,200 – 600 – (– 200)

= 43,500 – 1,800 + 200

= ₹ 41,900 crore

13. Domestic Income/NDP_{FC} = GNP_{MP} – Current Replacement Cost – Net Factor Income from Abroad – (Excise Duty + GST – Subsidies)

= 18,800 – 1,200 – 300 – (50 + 40 – 20)

= 18,800 – 1,500 – 70 = ₹ 17,230 crore

14. As per question

GDP_{MP} = ₹ 1,100 crore ; NFIA = ₹ 100 crore

NIT = ₹ 150 crore ; NNP_{FC} = ₹ 850 crore

$NNP_{FC} = GDP_{MP}$ – Depreciation + NFIA – NIT

850 = 1,100 – Depreciation + 100 – 150

∴ Depreciation = ₹ 200 crore

15. $NNP_{FC} = GDP_{MP}$ – Consumption of Fixed Capital + NFIA – (Indirect Taxes – Subsidies)

19,800 = 21,000 – 400 + NF1A – (400 – 200)

19,800 = 20,600 + NFIA –200

19,800 = 20,400 + NFIA

∴ NFIA = ₹ (–600) crore

16. NNP_{MP} = Sales + Change-in-stock – Purchase of Intermediate Products – Consumption of Fixed Capital + (Factor Income from Abroad – Factor Income to Abroad)

= 1,800 + 50 – 300 – 20 + (60 – 10)

= 1,850 – 320 + 50 = 1,900 – 320

= ₹ 1,580 crore

17. Value Added by firm A = Sales by Firm A + (Closing Stock of Firm A – Opening Stock of Firm B) – Purchases by Firm A

= 600 + (50 – 40) – 200

= ₹ 410 crore

Value Added by firm B = (Sales by Firm B to General Government + Exports of Firm B) + (Closing Stock of Firm B – Opening Stock of Firm B) – Purchases by Firm B.

= (800 + 300) + (60 – 30) – 150

= ₹ 980 crore

18. GDP_{MP} = NNP_{FC} + Dep. – NFIA + NIT

= 5,000 + 200 – 600 + (700 – 300)

= ₹ 5,000 crore

GDP_{MP} = Sales + (– Excess of Opening Stock over Closing Stock – Intermediate consumption)

5,000 = Sales + (– 200) – (800)

∴ Sales = ₹ 6,000 crore

19. NNP_{FC} = Household Consumption Expenditure + Government Final Consumption Expenditure + Business Fixed Investment Expenditure + Public Fixed Investment + Change in Inventory – Excess of Imports over Exports – Consumption of Fixed Capital + Net Factor Income from Abroad – Net Indirect Taxes

= 1,200 + 500 + 800 + 70 + (– 50) – 100 – 200 + 80 – 150

= ₹ 2,150 crore

Note *(iv) indicates net imports thus, it has been deducted.*

20. NDP_{FC} = GNP_{FC} – Dep. – (Factor Income from Abroad – Factor Income to Abroad)

= 11,000 – 500 – (1,100 – 1,600)

= ₹ 11,000 crore

NDP_{FC} = Compensation of Employees + Operating Surplus + Mixed Income of Self-employed

11,000 = 6,000 + Operating Surplus + 3,000

∴ Operating Surplus = ₹ 2,000 crore

21. NDP_{FC} = GNP_{MP} – Consumption of Fixed Capital – Net Factor Income from Abroad – NIT

= 43,000 – 5,000 – 5,000 – 3,000

= ₹ 30,000 crore

NDP_{FC} = Wages and Salaries + (Rent + Interest + Profit) + Mixed Income of Self-employed

30,000 = 18,000 + (4,000 + 2,500 + Profit) + 4,000

∴ Profit = 30,000 – 28,500 = ₹ 1,500 crore

22. NNP_{FC} = Wages and Salaries + Rent and Royalties + Corporate Tax + Retained Earnings + Dividends + Mixed Income of Self-employed + Net Factor Income from Abroad

= 1,700 + 1,300 + 400 + 300 + 400 + 1,400 + (–120)

= ₹ 5,380 crore

CHAPTER -2

Money and Banking

Types & Nos. of Questions

Multiple Choice Questions – 30
Assertion-Reason Questions – 10
Correct/Incorrect Statements – 8
Case Based Questions – 2 Cases, *each with four Questions*
Subjective Questions – 10

Trend Analysis

On the basis of analysis of last 2 years' papers, it is found that on an average 3 Multiple Choice Questions and 1 Short Answer Type Question are asked from this chapter. No case based question is asked but may be asked in coming exams.

Focus Topics of the Chapter

- Concept of Money
- Banking: Commercial Banks and Money Creation
- Central Bank

Multiple Choice Questions

No. of Questions : **30** Suggested Time : **45 Minutes**

Direction Each of the question given below is Multiple Choice Question (MCQ) i.e. there are Four Options/ Choices for answer, out of which ONLY ONE is correct. You have to select the correct option.
A response box is given with each option, mark (✓) in the box of the correct option. For each correct answer you will get 1 mark, while there is no penalty for incorrect answer or missed out questions.

1. Which of the following scenarios best exemplifies the barter system?
   (A) An individual buys groceries using a credit card ☐
   (B) A farmer exchanges a portion of his wheat for shoes from a local cobbler ☐
   (C) A customer purchases a car from a dealership using cash ☐
   (D) A company sells its products online and receives payments through a digital payment platform ☐

2. ……….. type of money is exemplified by items such as pearls and sea-shells, rather than by items whose monetary value exceeds their commodity value.
   (A) Metallic money ☐
   (B) Full-bodied money ☐
   (C) Commodity money ☐
   (D) Token coins ☐

3. Which term is used to describe the currency issued by the central bank, which serves as the basis for credit creation?
   (A) Commercial money ☐
   (B) Reserve money ☐
   (C) Market money ☐
   (D) Consumer money ☐

4. Which of the following options suits best for the following picture?

   (A) Fiduciary money ☐
   (B) Fiat money ☐
   (C) Bank money ☐
   (D) None of the above ☐

5. "The value of all goods and services can be expressed in monetary units."
   On the basis of the given statement, identify the function performed by money.
   (A) Medium of exchange ☐
   (B) Store of value ☐
   (C) Unit of account ☐
   (D) Means of standard of deferred payments ☐

6. Which function of money is highlighted in the following picture?

(A) Medium of exchange, store of value

(B) Store of value, unit of account

(C) Medium of exchange, unit of account

(D) Medium of exchange, standard of deferred payments

7. Which role of money is demonstrated when individuals hold onto currency or deposit it in savings accounts for future purchases or investments?

(A) Medium of exchange

(B) Unit of account

(C) Store of value

(D) Standard of deferred payment

8. Which of the following best describes the role of money in facilitating economic exchanges?

(A) Money is essential for individuals living on isolated islands

(B) Money eliminates the need for barter exchanges

(C) Money increases the search costs in barter exchanges

(D) Money is only necessary in large-scale transactions

9. How is the notion of a 'stock concept' elucidated within the framework of money supply analysis, emphasising its intricacies?

(A) It refers to the flow of money over a period of time

(B) It is concerned with the total volume of money at a specific point in time

(C) It signifies the rate at which money is circulated in the economy

(D) It represents the value of money in terms of goods and services

10. Which component is uniquely present in the M_2 measure of money supply, distinguishing it from the M_1 measure?

(A) Demand deposits of commercial banks

(B) Currency and coins with the public

(C) Other deposits with RBI

(D) Savings deposits with Post Office Saving Bank

11. "Mr. Sahotra borrowed funds from bank for purchasing a new house." From the above statement, identify the indicated function of money. *[CBSE 2024]*

(A) Medium of exchange

(B) Store of value

(C) Unit of account

(D) Standard of deferred payments

12. Find the correct option.

M_1 Measure of money supply

Currency and coins with public | Demand deposits | ____________

(A) Saving deposits with post office

(B) Net time deposits

(C) Other deposits with RBI

(D) Post office savings accounts

13. .... is a profit making financial entity that accepts both chequeable and non-chequeable deposits and provides various types of loans.

(A) Investment banks

(B) Central banks

(C) Commercial banks

(D) Credit unions

14. What motivates individuals to deposit their surplus funds in commercial banks rather than keeping them at home?

(A) Higher interest rates offered by banks on deposits

(B) Safer storage of funds in banks compared to home

(C) Greater accessibility to funds through online banking

(D) Lower risk of inflation eroding the value of deposited funds

15. Mr. Iqra Ansari a teacher was explaining in her class about various types of deposits with the commercial banks. She quoted that "These deposits form a part of M_1 measured of money supply and are payable or demand by the commercial banks."

Identify the types of deposits she was explaining about and choose the correct alternative. [CBSE 2023]

(i) Demand deposits (ii) Time deposits

(iii) Post office deposits

Codes

(A) Only (i) ☐ (B) Only (ii) ☐

(C) (i) and (ii) ☐ (D) (i), (ii) and (iii) ☐

16. Find the missing figures and choose the correct alternatives.

Round	Deposits	Loan (80%)	Reserve Ratio (20%)
I	1,000	800	200
II	800	...(i)...	160
	...	...	...
	...	...	...
Total	...(ii)...	...(iii)...	...(iv)...

(A) 640, 1000, 4000, 5000 ☐

(B) 960, 5000, 4000, 1000 ☐

(C) 640, 4000, 1000, 5000 ☐

(D) 640, 5000, 4000, 1000 ☐

17. The central bank can reduce the money supply in the economy by ...... the .... [CBSE 2024]

(A) increasing, bank rate ☐

(B) decreasing, cash reserve ratio ☐

(C) decreasing, bank rate ☐

(D) buying, government securities ☐

18. In the Indian economy, ... are issued by the Reserve Bank of India and acts as legal tender money. [CBSE 2023]

(i) coins of all denomination

(ii) currency notes of various dominations, except one rupee note

(iii) demand deposits

Codes

(A) Only (i) ☐ (B) Only (ii) ☐

(C) Only (iii) ☐ (D) (i) and (ii) ☐

19. "The RBI imposed supervisory restrictions on the Non-Banking Financial Company (NBFC) on 4th March, 2024 that followed an earlier inspection of the IIFL's financial position conducted on 31st March, 2023."

– Live Mint

Which of the following functions of a central bank is highlighted in the above news headline?

(A) Banker to the government ☐

(B) Authority of issuing currency notes ☐

(C) Supervision of all commercial banks and financial institutions ☐

(D) Clearing house ☐

20. What is the primary objective of the Statutory Liquidity Ratio (SLR) mandated by the Central Bank (RBI) for commercial banks?

(A) To restrict banks' lending capacity and curb inflationary pressures ☐

(B) To ensure banks maintain adequate liquidity for short-term obligations ☐

(C) To encourage banks to invest in long-term assets for sustainable growth ☐

(D) To maximise banks' profitability by diversifying their investment portfolios ☐

21. What phrase best captures the Reserve Bank of India's role in supplying urgent funds to commercial banks during periods of financial turmoil?

(A) Lender of first resort ☐

(B) Lender of last resort ☐

(C) Borrower of first resort ☐

(D) Borrower of last resort ☐

22. Identify the incorrect feature(s) of the money supply in an economy, from the following [CBSE 2024]

(i) It is measured during a period of time.
(ii) It includes stock of money held by the government of a nation.
(iii) It always represents the currency held with central bank of the nation.

Codes

(A) Only (i) ☐ (B) (ii) and (iii) ☐
(C) (i) and (ii) ☐ (D) (i), (ii) and (iii) ☐

23. How does the Reserve Bank of India (RBI) influence money supply through outright open market operations while buying the securities?

(A) Temporarily inject money without promise to withdraw later ☐
(B) Permanently inject money without promise to withdraw later ☐
(C) Temporarily withdraw money without promise to inject later ☐
(D) Permanently withdraw money without promise to inject later ☐

24. Which action by the Reserve Bank of India (RBI) would demonstrate a proactive approach towards supporting small businesses and encouraging entrepreneurship?

(A) Increasing the bank rate to curb inflationary pressures and stabilise the economy ☐
(B) Decreasing the bank rate to provide easier access to credit for small businesses ☐
(C) Maintaining a constant bank rate to ensure predictability in financial markets ☐
(D) Fluctuating the bank rate sporadically to maintain uncertainty and deter excessive borrowing ☐

25. Which of the following function of central bank is highlighted by the following picture?

(A) Custodian of foreign exchange reserves ☐
(B) Printing of currency ☐
(C) Banker to the government ☐
(D) Banker's bank ☐

26. Find the correct option for the values of A, B and C.

Deposits	Required Reserves (10%)	Excess Reserves (Loans)
1,000	100	900
...(i)...	90	810
810	91	...(ii)...
Total 10,000	...(iii)...	9,000

(A) 1,000, 729, 900 ☐
(B) 900, 1,000, 729 ☐
(C) 900, 729, 10,000 ☐
(D) 900, 729, 1,000 ☐

27. Match the following

Column I	Column II
A. Monetary system	(i) ₹ 500
B. Barter system	(ii) Universally accepted medium of exchange
C. Money supply	(iii) C-C economy
D. Credit money	(iv) Stock concept

Codes

	A	B	C	D	
(A)	(ii)	(iii)	(i)	(iv)	☐
(B)	(ii)	(iii)	(iv)	(i)	☐
(C)	(iii)	(ii)	(iv)	(i)	☐
(D)	(ii)	(iv)	(iii)	(i)	☐

28. Match the following

Column I	Column II
A. M_1	(i) Currency accepted by law
B. Fiat money	(ii) Total amount of money held by people at a point of time
C. Legal tender	(iii) Under the order from the government
D. Money supply	(iv) Currency, demand deposits with commercial banks

Codes

	A	B	C	D	
(A)	(iv)	(i)	(iii)	(ii)	☐
(B)	(iv)	(iii)	(ii)	(i)	☐
(C)	(iv)	(ii)	(i)	(iii)	☐
(D)	(iv)	(iii)	(i)	(ii)	☐

29. Match the following

	Column I		Column II
A.	Commercial bank	(i)	Loan to commercial bank to meet long-term needs
B.	Central bank	(ii)	1/LRR
C.	Money multiplier	(iii)	Custodian of foreign exchange reserves
D.	Bank rate	(iv)	Loan to public

Codes

	A	B	C	D	
(A)	(iv)	(iii)	(ii)	(i)	☐
(B)	(iv)	(ii)	(iii)	(i)	☐
(C)	(iv)	(iii)	(i)	(ii)	☐
(D)	(iii)	(iv)	(ii)	(i)	☐

30. Match the following

	Column I		Column II
A.	LRR = 20%	(i)	LRR = 12.5%
B.	Initial deposits = ₹ 200, Money multiplier = 4 times	(ii)	MM = 5 times
C.	Initial deposits	(iii)	Total deposits = ₹ 800
D.	Initial deposits = ₹ 200 crore, Total deposits = ₹ 1,600 crores	(iv)	Equal to total of required reserves

Codes

	A	B	C	D	
(A)	(ii)	(iv)	(iii)	(i)	☐
(B)	(ii)	(iii)	(iv)	(i)	☐
(C)	(iii)	(ii)	(iv)	(i)	☐
(D)	(ii)	(iii)	(i)	(iv)	☐

Assertion-Reason Questions

No. of Questions : **10** Suggested Time : **15 Minutes**

Direction Each of the question given below consist of the two statements; one labelled as **Assertion** (A) and other as **Reason** (R). List of common options applicable for each question is given below

(A) Both Assertion (A) and Reason (R) are true and Reason (R) is the correct explanation of Assertion (A)

(B) Both Assertion (A) and Reason (R) are true, but Reason (R) is not the correct explanation of Assertion (A)

(C) Assertion (A) is true, but Reason (R) is false

(D) Assertion (A) is false, but Reason (R) is true

You have to select the codes as *A*, *B*, *C* or *D* as your answer to the question by marking (✓) in the response box given against each option.

1. **Assertion (A)** Money serves as a facilitator of exchanges in a modern economy.

Reason (R) Without money, barter exchanges require a double coincidence of wants, which can be impractical and costly as the number of economic agents increases.

(A) ☐ (B) ☐ (C) ☐ (D) ☐

2. **Assertion (A)** Money serves as a store of value for individuals, allowing wealth to be stored for future use.

Reason (R) The value of money must not be sufficiently stable to perform its function as a store of value effectively.

(A) ☐ (B) ☐ (C) ☐ (D) ☐

3. **Assertion (A)** An increase in income leads to a rise in the demand for money.

Reason (R) The quantity of transactions to be made is directly influenced by income, thereby affecting the demand for money.

(A) ☐ (B) ☐ (C) ☐ (D) ☐

4. **Assertion (A)** Banks can loan out all the funds deposited with them without retaining any portion for repayment to depositors on demand.

Reason (R) Banks earn interest from the loans they make, so they aim to lend out the maximum possible amount of funds deposited with them.

(A) ☐ (B) ☐
(C) ☐ (D) ☐

5. **Assertion (A)** Demonetisation in India, implemented in November 2016, was solely aimed at improving tax compliance and reducing corruption.

Reason (R) Demonetisation resulted in long queues outside banks and ATM booths, causing a shortage of currency in circulation and adversely impacting economic activities.

(A) ☐ (B) ☐ (C) ☐ (D) ☐

6. **Assertion (A)** One of the primary functions of the central bank is to act as a banker to the government.

Reason (R) The central bank controls the money supply of the country through various methods such as bank rate adjustments, open market operations and variations in reserve ratios.

(A) ☐ (B) ☐ (C) ☐ (D) ☐

7. **Assertion (A)** Currency notes and coins derive their value from the guarantee provided by the issuing authority.

Reason (R) The value of currency notes and coins is based on the promise from the monetary authority, such as the Reserve Bank of India (RBI), to exchange them for goods and services.

(A) ☐ (B) ☐ (C) ☐ (D) ☐

8. **Assertion (A)** If the Reserve Bank of India (RBI) increases the reserve ratio from 20% to 25%, the money multiplier would decrease from 5 times to 4 times.

Reason (R) Increasing the reserve ratio reduces the amount of funds available for banks to lend, leading to a decrease in the money supply.

(A) ☐ (B) ☐ (C) ☐ (D) ☐

9. **Assertion (A)** Adjusting margin requirements is an effective tool for controlling the money supply in the economy.

Reason (R) By increasing margin requirements, the central bank can discourage lending by commercial banks, thus reducing the amount of money created through credit expansion.

(A) ☐ (B) ☐
(C) ☐ (D) ☐

10. **Assertion (A)** Both quantitative and qualitative tools are used by central banks to control the money supply in the economy.

Reason (R) Quantitative tools, such as changes in reserve requirements or open market operations, directly influence the quantity of money in circulation, while qualitative tools, such as moral suasion or changes in margin requirements, aim to influence the lending behaviour of commercial banks, indirectly affecting the money supply.

(A) ☐ (B) ☐ (C) ☐ (D) ☐

Correct/Incorrect Statements

No. of Questions : **8** Suggested Time : **15 Minutes**

Direction Each of the question given below consist of the two statements. List of common options applicable for each question is given below

(A) Both statements are correct
(B) Both statements are incorrect
(C) Statement I is correct and Statement II is incorrect
(D) Statement I is incorrect and Statement II is correct

You have to select the codes as *A*, *B*, *C* or *D* as your answer to the question by marking (✓) in the response box given against each option.

1. **Statement I** Countries are neglecting a transition towards a cashless economy, where financial transactions rely on digital information rather than physical bank notes or coins.

   Statement II In India, the government has implemented various initiatives such as Jan Dhan accounts, Aadhar enabled payment systems, e-Wallets and National Financial Switch (NFS) to promote financial inclusion and move towards a cashless society.

   (A) ☐ (B) ☐ (C) ☐ (D) ☐

2. **Statement I** Money's primary function as a medium of exchange facilitates transactions by eliminating the need for barter exchanges, which would be impractical in a large economy due to high transaction costs.

   Statement II Additionally, money serves as a convenient unit of account, allowing the value of goods and services to be expressed uniformly in monetary terms.

   (A) ☐ (B) ☐ (C) ☐ (D) ☐

3. **Statement I** Money supply is considered a stock concept in economics.

   Statement II Money supply represents the total stock of money available in an economy at a particular point in time, encompassing currency, demand deposits, and other liquid assets.

   (A) ☐ (B) ☐ (C) ☐ (D) ☐

4. **Statement I** Commercial banks play a crucial role in the economy by participating in the money creating system through their operations.

   Statement II The functioning of commercial banks involves accepting deposits from the public and providing loans to borrowers, with the profit generated from the interest rate spread between depositors and borrowers being a key source of revenue for the banks.

   (A) ☐ (B) ☐
   (C) ☐ (D) ☐

5. **Statement I** The modern banking system functions with central bank acting as intermediaries between individuals or firms with excess funds and those in need of funds.

   Statement II In the modern context, people prefer to keep their excess funds in banks due to the safety and convenience they offer, such as earning interest on deposits and facilitating transactions through cheques and debit cards.

   (A) ☐ (B) ☐ (C) ☐ (D) ☐

6. **Statement I** The value of money multiplier is determined by the reserve ratio prevailing in the monetary system.

   Statement II The process of credit creation directly relates to the value of reserve ratio.

   (A) ☐ (B) ☐
   (C) ☐ (D) ☐

7. **Statement I** Open market operations are a fiscal policy tool utilised by the central bank to regulate the money supply through the buying and selling of government bonds in the open market.

   Statement II The Cash Reserve Ratio (CRR) is a mandatory requirement set by the RBI, specifying the percentage of deposits that banks must maintain as cash reserves with themselves to prevent excessive lending.

   (A) ☐ (B) ☐ (C) ☐ (D) ☐

8. **Statement I** Money supply (M_1) in India does not include 'demand deposits' with commercial banks.

   Statement II Money supply (M_1), refers to assets available with the commercial banks during a particular period of time. *[CBSE 2023]*

   (A) ☐ (B) ☐ (C) ☐ (D) ☐

Case Based Questions

No. of Questions : **2** Suggested Time : **10 Minutes**

Direction This section contain 2 cases each having 4 questions of 1 mark each. You have to write the answer of each question based on the context of the related case.

Case 1 The Reserve Bank of India's Monetary Policy Dilemma

The Reserve Bank of India (RBI) is facing a challenging situation as it strives to strike a balance between controlling inflation and promoting economic growth. In recent months, India has experienced a surge in inflation due to rising food and fuel prices, while economic growth remains sluggish.

The RBI must formulate an effective monetary policy response to address these competing priorities. Amidst the inflationary pressures, the RBI is under pressure to raise interest rates to curb inflation and stabilise prices. However, raising interest rates could dampen investment and consumption, further slowing down economic growth.

On the other hand, keeping interest rates low to stimulate growth may exacerbate inflationary pressures. Additionally, the RBI is grappling with external factors such as volatile global oil prices and uncertainty in global financial markets. Fluctuations in oil prices could impact India's import bill and current account deficit, putting further strain on the economy.

The RBI faces challenges in communicating its monetary policy decisions effectively to the public and financial markets. Clear communication is essential to managing expectations and maintaining credibility, but conveying complex economic concepts in a way that is accessible to the general public can be a daunting task. As the RBI navigates these complexities, it must carefully weigh the trade-offs between inflation control and economic growth, considering both short-term challenges and long-term objectives for sustainable development.

Questions

(i) What dilemma is the Reserve Bank of India (RBI) facing in formulating monetary policy?

(A) Balancing fiscal deficit with current account deficit ☐

(B) Managing exchange rate stability amidst global volatility ☐

(C) Striking a balance between controlling inflation and promoting economic growth ☐

(D) Addressing unemployment while controlling inflation ☐

(ii) Raising interest rates could exacerbate .... by reducing investment and consumption, thus slowing down economic growth.

(iii) How does the uncertainties like pandemic Covid-19 contribute to the challenges faced by the RBI?

(A) Increases government revenue through higher taxes ☐

(B) Creates uncertainty in global financial markets ☐

(C) Boosts consumer confidence and spending ☐

(D) Disrupts supply chains and labour markets ☐

(iv) Clear communication helps in managing .... and .... towards informed decisions, thereby influencing the effectiveness of monetary policy interventions.

Case 2 Banking Sector Challenges

The banking sector in India is facing several challenges that impact its stability and growth. XYZ Bank, one of the leading private banks in India, is grappling with rising Non-performing Assets (NPAs) due to economic slowdowns and loan defaults by borrowers.

The bank's balance sheet has been adversely affected, leading to concerns among shareholders and regulators. In addition to NPAs, XYZ Bank is facing intense competition from both traditional and emerging players in the banking industry.

Fintech companies and digital payment platforms are disrupting the market with innovative products and services, posing a threat to traditional banking business models.

Moreover, regulatory compliance and governance issues have surfaced within XYZ Bank, leading to reputational risks and legal challenges. The bank is under scrutiny from regulatory authorities for alleged violations of banking regulations and corporate governance norms.

To address these challenges, XYZ Bank is undergoing a transformation process aimed at strengthening its risk management practices, enhancing customer experience and embracing digital technologies. The bank is investing in advanced analytics and artificial intelligence to improve credit risk assessment and streamline operations.

However, the road to recovery is fraught with obstacles. XYZ Bank must navigate regulatory hurdles, restore investor confidence and rebuild its reputation amidst growing competition and changing market dynamics.

Questions

(i) .... is one of the main challenges faced by XYZ Bank in the case study.

(ii) .... contributed to the intense competition faced by XYZ Bank.

(iii) What impact do rising Non-performing Assets (NPAs) have on XYZ Bank?

(A) Increased profitability ☐

(B) Adverse effects on the balance sheet ☐

(C) Improved asset quality ☐

(D) Expansion of loan portfolio ☐

(iv) How is XYZ Bank addressing its challenges?

(A) By ignoring regulatory compliance issues ☐

(B) By downsizing its operations ☐

(C) By investing in digital technologies and enhancing risk management practices ☐

(D) By reducing customer services ☐

Subjective Questions

Free Response Questions, Open-ended Questions etc.

No. of Questions : **10** Suggested Time : **50 Minutes**

1. "The multifaceted functions of money play a pivotal role in shaping the dynamics of modern economies." Defend/Refute.

2. As per the following news published in The Economic Times on 26th December, 2021: 'Reserve Bank of India has sold government securities worth ₹ 8,710 crore in the secondary market, over the last four weeks, to drain out excessive liquidity'.

   Identify the likely cause and the consequences behind, this type of action plan of the Reserve Bank.

3. ABC Bank, with a Legal Reserve Ratio (LRR) of 10%, receives initial deposits of ₹ 1,000. Calculate the potential increase in the money supply through the bank's lending activities.

4. There are two functions that can be interpreted from the following picture. Identify the following functions of RBI and explain them.

5. Based on the news headline, discuss the potential implications of the central bank's decision to raise interest rates on borrowers and economic growth.

   Evaluate the effects of higher interest rates on consumer spending, investment and inflation, considering the central bank's objectives controlling monetary policy.

6. "Open market operation by the Reserve Bank of India (RBI) helps in regulating money supply in the economy." Justify the given statement. *[CBSE 2024]*

7. "The process of credit creation by commercial banks comes to an end when the total of required reserve become equal to the initial deposits." With the help of a numerical example, prove that the given statement is true. *[CBSE 2023]*

8. Examine the comprehensive roles assumed by the Reserve Bank of India (RBI) as the apex financial institution, issue of currency and custodian of foreign exchange reserves and maintaining stability within the Indian economy.

9. Discuss the concept of credit creation within the banking system and its significance in the process of money supply expansion.

Explain how commercial banks create credit through the process of fractional reserve banking, highlighting the role of deposits, reserves and lending activities.

Furthermore, analyse the implications of credit creation for economic growth, inflation and financial stability, considering the multiplier effect and potential risks associated with excessive credit expansion.

10. **"Reserve Bank of India's Measures to Manage Money Supply Amid Economic Volatility"**

The Reserve Bank of India (RBI) has been actively implementing measures to manage the money supply amidst economic volatility in India.

With fluctuating economic indicators and global uncertainties, the RBI has adopted various strategies to ensure liquidity and stability in the financial markets.

One of the key initiatives undertaken by the RBI is the implementation of targeted Long-term Refinancing Operations (TLTROs). Through TLTROs, the central bank provides liquidity to specific sectors of the economy, such as agriculture, Small and Medium-sized Enterprises (SMEs) and infrastructure, to support their growth and development.

Additionally, the RBI has utilised Open Market Operations (OMOs) to adjust liquidity conditions in the banking system.

By buying and selling government securities, the RBI aims to influence short-term interest rates and maintain liquidity at desired levels.

Furthermore, the RBI has focused on enhancing regulatory oversight and risk management practices in the banking sector to prevent the build-up of Non-performing Assets (NPAs) and ensure financial stability. The central bank has introduced measures to strengthen corporate governance standards and improve transparency in financial reporting.

Moreover, the RBI has emphasised the importance of communication and transparency in its monetary policy decisions. By providing clear guidance on its policy stance and objectives, the central bank seeks to manage market expectations and maintain credibility in the financial markets.

Overall, the RBI's proactive measures aim to strike a balance between supporting economic growth and maintaining price stability amidst economic volatility in India.

(i) Discuss the role of Targeted Long-term Refinancing Operations (TLTROs) in managing liquidity and supporting specific sectors of the economy in India. How do TLTROs contribute to economic development and stability?

(ii) Evaluate the effectiveness of Open Market Operations (OMOs) as a tool for managing the money supply in India.

Answers

If your answer matches with the answer given here then put (✓) in the box otherwise put (✗). In case you did not attempt the question leave the box blank.

Multiple Choice Questions

1. B ☐	2. C ☐	13. C ☐	14. B ☐
3. B ☐	4. B ☐	15. A ☐	16. D ☐
5. C ☐	6. C ☐	17. A ☐	18. B ☐
7. C ☐	8. C ☐	19. C ☐	20. B ☐
9. B ☐	10. D ☐	21. B ☐	22. D ☐
11. D ☐	12. B ☐	23. B ☐	24. B ☐
		25. B ☐	26. D ☐

27. B ☐ 28. D ☐
29. A ☐ 30. B ☐

Your Score________ *(No. of Correct Answers)*

Assertion-Reason Questions

1. A ☐ 2. C ☐
3. A ☐ 4. D ☐
5. D ☐ 6. B ☐
7. A ☐ 8. A ☐
9. A ☐ 10. A ☐

Your Score________ *(No. of Correct Answers)*

Correct/Incorrect Statements

1. D ☐ 2. A ☐
3. A ☐ 4. A ☐
5. D ☐ 6. C ☐
7. D ☐ 8. B ☐

Your Score________ *(No. of Correct Answers)*

Case Based Questions

1. (i) C ☐ (iii) D ☐
2. (iii) B ☐ (iv) C ☐

Your Score________ *(No. of Correct Answers)*

Explanations

Multiple Choice Questions

1. (B) A farmer exchanges a portion of his wheat for shoes from a local cobbler
2. (C) Commodity money
3. (B) Reserve money
4. (B) Fiat money
5. (C) Unit of account
6. (C) Money serves as a medium of exchange by facilitating transactions between parties, allowing goods and services to be bought and sold using a universally accepted form of payment. Additionally, it acts as a unit of account, providing a standard measure for comparing the value of different goods and services.
7. (C) Store of value
8. (C) Money increases the search costs in barter exchanges
9. (B) It is concerned with the total volume of money at a specific point in time
10. (D) Savings deposits with Post Office Saving Bank
11. (D) Standard of deferred payments
12. (B) Net time deposits
13. (C) Commercial banks
14. (B) Safer storage of funds in banks compared to home
15. (A) Only (i)
16. (D) (i) Loan = 80% of Deposits = (0.80×800) = ₹ 640

 (ii) Total Deposits = Initial Deposits × Multiplier = $1{,}000 \times 5$ = ₹ 5,000
 (Multiplier = 1/LRR = 1/0.20)

 (iii) Total Loan = Total Deposits − Total Reserve = $5{,}000 - 1{,}000$ = ₹ 4,000

 (iv) Total Reserve = Initial Reserve × Multiplier = 200×5 = ₹ 1,000
17. (A) A higher bank rate makes borrowing more expensive for commercial banks, which in turn reduces their ability to lend to businesses and consumers, thereby decreasing the overall money supply in the economy.
18. (B) In the Indian economy, the Reserve Bank of India (RBI) issues currency notes of various denominations, except the one-rupee note, which is issued by the Government of India.
19. (C) Supervision of all commercial banks and financial institutions
20. (B) By requiring banks to hold a certain percentage of their net demand and time liabilities in the form of liquid assets, the SLR helps to ensure that banks have enough liquidity to meet their immediate liabilities and promotes the stability of the financial system.
21. (B) The phrase 'lender of last resort' best captures the Reserve Bank of India's role in supplying urgent funds to commercial banks during periods of financial turmoil.

This function ensures that banks have access to liquidity in emergencies, helping to maintain stability and confidence in the financial system.

22. (D) (i), (ii) and (iii)

23. (B) Permanently inject money without promise to withdraw later

24. (B) Decreasing the bank rate to provide easier access to credit for small businesses

25. (B) The central bank typically has the authority to print and issue currency within a country's jurisdiction. In most cases, the central bank is responsible for overseeing the production, distribution and regulation of physical currency, ensuring its authenticity and integrity.

26. (D) (i) Deposits = Excess Reserves + Required Reserves

= 810 + 90 = ₹ 900

(ii) Excess Reserves = Deposits – Deposits × 10%

= 810 – (810 × 10%)

= 810 – 81 = ₹ 729

(iii) Required Reserves = Deposits × 10%

= 10,000 × 10% = ₹ 1,000

27. (B) (ii) (iii) (iv) (i)

28. (D) (iv) (iii) (i) (ii)

29. (A) (iv) (iii) (ii) (i)

30. (B) (A) MM = 1/LRR = 1/20% = 1/0.20 = 5

(B) Total Deposits = Initial Deposits × Money Multiplier

= 200 × 4 = ₹ 800

(D) LRR =1 – 1,600 – 200/1,600 = 1 – 0.875

= 0.125 or 12.5%

Assertion-Reason Questions

1. (A) Both Assertion (A) and Reason (R) are true and Reason (R) is the correct explanation of Assertion (A)

2. (C) Assertion (A) is true, but Reason (R) is false

3. (A) Both Assertion (A) and Reason (R) are true and Reason (R) is the correct explanation of Assertion (A)

4. (D) While banks aim to lend out funds deposited with them to earn interest, they cannot loan out all funds without retaining a portion for repayment to depositors on demand, as this would lead to a liquidity crisis in case of mass withdrawals.

5. (D) Assertion (A) is false, but Reason (R) is true

6. (B) Both Assertion (A) and Reason (R) are true, but Reason (R) is not the correct explanation of Assertion (A)

7. (A) Both Assertion (A) and Reason (R) are true and Reason (R) is the correct explanation of Assertion (A)

8. (A) Both Assertion (A) and Reason (R) are true and Reason (R) is the correct explanation of Assertion (A)

9. (A) Both Assertion (A) and Reason (R) are true and Reason (R) is the correct explanation of Assertion (A)

10. (A) Both Assertion (A) and Reason (R) are true and Reason (R) is the correct explanation of Assertion (A)

Correct/Incorrect Statements

1. (D) Statement I is incorrect and Statement II is correct

2. (A) Both statements are correct

3. (A) Both statements are correct

4. (A) Both statements are correct

5. (D) Statement I is incorrect and Statement II is correct

6. (C) Statement I is correct and Statement II is incorrect

7. (D) Open market operations are a monetary policy tool.

8. (B) M_1 is the most liquid measure of money supply comprised of currency with public, demand deposits with commercial banks and other deposits with the RBI.

Case Based Questions

1. (i) (C) Striking a balance between controlling inflation and promoting economic growth

(ii) inflationary pressures

(iii) (D) Disrupts supply chains and labour markets

(iv) market expectations, guiding economic factors

2. (i) Rising Non-performing Assets (NPAs)

(ii) Emergence of fintech companies and digital payment platforms

(iii) (B) Adverse effects on the balance sheet
(iv) (C) By investing in digital technologies and enhancing risk management practices

Subjective Questions

1. The multifaceted functions of money play a pivotal role in shaping the dynamics of modern economies. This statement is defended.

   Firstly, as a medium of exchange, money facilitates transactions by serving as a universally accepted intermediary in the exchange of goods and services, thereby overcoming the limitations of barter systems and promoting specialisation and division of labour.

   Secondly, money functions as a unit of account, providing a standardised measure of value that allows individuals to compare the worth of different goods and services, enabling efficient pricing, accounting and economic calculations.

   Thirdly, money serves as a store of value, allowing individuals to preserve purchasing power over time by holding wealth in the form of money rather than perishable or rapidly depreciating assets.

2. The given instance where, Reserve Bank of India has sold government securities in the secondary market indicates towards inflation as a possible cause behind the action taken by RBI. By selling off the government securities, RBI withdraws money from circulation and thereby reducing the lending capacity of the commercial banks.

   In this process, the economy will experience contraction of credit, leading to reduction in consumption and investment demand. Consequently, the inflationary pressure in the economy will get eased out.

3. Given,
   Initial Deposits = ₹ 1,000
   Legal Reserve Ratio (LRR) = 10% = 0.10
   Using the formula for the money multiplier,
   Money Multiplier = 1/LRR = 1/0.10 = 10
   Now, to calculate the potential increase in the money supply
   Money Creation = Initial Deposits × Money Multiplier
   = 1,000 × 10 = ₹ 10,000

   Therefore, ABC Bank can potentially increase the money supply by ₹10,000 through its lending activities.

4. The functions of RBI interpreted in the given image are
   (i) **Banker's Bank** As a banker's bank central bank accepts deposits and lend loans to commercial banks whenever required. Central bank also regulates and supervises the commercial banks. Apart from this, it also performs the function of lender of the last resort and clearing house function for commercial banks.
   (ii) **Banker to the Government** As a banker to the government, central bank manages the accounts of the government, works as an agent by buying and selling of government securities and also advises on financial matters of the government.

5. The central bank's decision to raise interest rates is aimed at curbing inflationary pressures within the economy. Higher interest rates make borrowing more expensive, leading to reduced consumer spending and investment. As borrowing costs increase, businesses may scale back on expansion plans and investments, which can dampen economic growth in the short-term. Additionally, higher interest rates may lead to lower demand for big ticket items such as homes and automobiles, further impacting economic activity. On the flip side, higher interest rates can help control inflation by reducing aggregate demand and moderating price pressures.

   By discouraging excessive borrowing and spending, the central bank aims to achieve price stability and maintain the purchasing power of the currency over time.

   Overall, while the decision to raise interest rates may temporarily slow down economic growth, it serves the broader objective of controlling inflation and maintaining macroeconomic stability in the long-run.

   However, the exact impact on borrowers and economic growth will depend on various factors, including the magnitude of the interest rate hike, the responsiveness of consumers and businesses to higher borrowing costs and the overall state of the economy.

6. Open market operations are one of the primary monetary policy tools used by central bank to regulate the money supply and achieve macroeconomic objectives such as price stability, full employment and economic growth. Open market operations implies buying and selling of government securities in open market by the central bank.

   When the central bank buys government securities, it injects money into the financial system, increasing the money supply. Conversely, when the central bank sells government securities, it withdraws money from the financial system, reducing the money supply.

7. Reverse deposit ratio is the rate of interest at which commercial banks can park their surplus funds with the central bank for a short period of time. Increase in reverse deposit rate will reduce the credit supply and *vice-versa*.

   The following numerical example will make this clear

   Suppose the reverse deposit ratio is 3%. At this rate, commercial banks are willing to deposit ₹ 10 crore with the central bank out of total deposits of ₹ 50 crore. Assuming legal reserve ratio to be 10%, then

   $$\text{Money creation} = 40 \times \frac{1}{0.1} = ₹\ 400 \text{ crore}$$

   Now, reverse deposit ratio rises to 5% and at this rate commercial banks are willing to deposit ₹ 20 crore with the central bank out of total deposits of ₹ 50 crore.

   $$\text{Now, money creation} = 30 \times \frac{1}{0.1} = ₹\ 300 \text{ crore.}$$

   So, we see that as reverse deposit ratio rises, then credit creation falls.

8. The Reserve Bank of India (RBI) plays a multifaceted role as the apex financial institution, responsible for overseeing various aspects of the Indian economy.

   Firstly, as the sole authority entrusted with the issuance of currency, the RBI ensures the availability of an adequate supply of currency notes and coins to meet the demands of the economy.

   Secondly, the RBI serves as the custodian of India's foreign exchange reserves. These reserves play a crucial role in supporting the external value of the Indian rupee, stabilising exchange rates and meeting international payment obligations. The RBI manages the foreign exchange reserves prudently to safeguard against external shocks and maintain the country's external sector stability.

   Additionally, the RBI is tasked with maintaining stability within the Indian economy through its monetary policy framework. By setting interest rates, conducting open market operations and implementing regulatory measures, the RBI aims to achieve price stability, promote economic growth and manage inflation within the desired range.

   Through its monetary policy tools, the RBI influences money supply, credit availability and overall liquidity conditions in the economy, thereby shaping macroeconomic outcomes and fostering sustainable development.

9. Credit creation refers to the process by which commercial banks expand the money supply through lending activities. In a fractional reserve banking system, banks are required to hold only a fraction of their deposits as reserves, allowing them to lend out the remainder to borrowers.

   When a bank makes a loan, it creates new deposits in the borrower's account, effectively increasing the money supply in the economy. These newly created deposits can then be used for additional spending and investment, leading to further economic activity and growth.

   The significance of credit creation lies in its role in fueling economic expansion and development. By providing access to credit, banks enable individuals and businesses to finance consumption, investment and entrepreneurial ventures, stimulating economic growth and job creation.

   Moreover, credit creation contributes to the efficient allocation of resources within the economy, facilitating capital formation and productivity improvements over time.

   However, excessive credit creation can also pose risks to financial stability and macroeconomic balance. Rapid credit expansion may lead to asset bubbles, excessive leverage and unsustainable debt levels, potentially resulting in financial crises and economic downturns.

   Additionally, inflationary pressures may arise if credit growth outpaces the productive capacity of the economy, leading to rising prices and reduced purchasing power for consumers.

Overall, while credit creation plays a crucial role in driving economic activity and growth, it is essential for policymakers and regulators to monitor and manage credit expansion to mitigate risks and ensure the stability of the financial system.

Effective regulation and supervision of banks, prudent lending standards and macroeconomic policies aimed at maintaining price stability and sustainable growth are necessary to harness the benefits of credit creation while safeguarding against potential drawbacks.

10. (i) Role of TLTROs is as follows

(a) TLTROs provide targeted liquidity to specific sectors, such as agriculture, SMEs and infrastructure, to support their growth and development.

(b) By offering long-term funding at favourable rates, TLTROs encourage banks to lend to these sectors, thereby boosting investment and economic activity.

(c) TLTROs help address liquidity constraints faced by sectors facing funding challenges, contributing to overall economic stability and resilience.

(ii) Effectiveness of OMOs can be understood with the help of following points

(a) OMOs are effective in adjusting liquidity conditions in the banking system by buying and selling government securities.

(b) They help the central bank achieve its monetary policy objectives, such as controlling inflation, managing interest rates and stabilising financial markets.

(c) However, OMOs have limitations, such as their impact on long-term interest rates and their effectiveness in influencing broader economic variables like economic growth and employment.

(d) Additionally, the success of OMOs depends on various factors, including market conditions, investor sentiment, and the central bank's credibility and communication strategy.

CHAPTER -3

Determination of Income and Employment

Types & Nos. of Questions

Multiple Choice Questions – 30
Assertion-Reason Questions – 10
Correct/Incorrect Statements – 10
Case Based Questions – 2 Cases, *each with four Questions*
Subjective Questions – 8

Trend Analysis

On the basis of analysis of last 2 years' papers, it is found that on an average 4 Multiple Choice Questions and 1 Short Answer Type Question and 1 Case Based Question are asked from this chapter.

Focus Topics of the Chapter

- Concept of Aggregate Demand and Aggregate Supply
- Consumption and Saving Function
- Concept of Investment Multiplier
- Short-run Equilibrium in the Economy
- Equilibrium and Disequilibrium in the Economy
- Excess Demand and Deficient Demand

Multiple Choice Questions

No. of Questions : **30** Suggested Time : **45 Minutes**

Direction Each of the question given below is Multiple Choice Question (MCQ) i.e. there are Four Options/ Choices for answer, out of which ONLY ONE is correct. You have to select the correct option. A response box is given with each option, mark (✓) in the box of the correct option. For each correct answer you will get 1 mark, while there is no penalty for incorrect answer or missed out questions.

1. What leads to the parallel orientation of the Aggregate Demand (AD) curve and the consumption curve in macroeconomics?

(A) Difference between AD and consumption is investment which remains constant at all levels of income in short-run ☐

(B) Slope of AD and consumption is equal ☐

(C) Both (A) and (B) ☐

(D) Neither (A) nor (B) ☐

2. What situation arises in an economy when the demand for goods and services exceeds the economy's ability to produce them at current prices?

(A) Deflation ☐ (B) Recession ☐

(C) Inflation or excess demand ☐

(D) Stagflation ☐

3. Which of the following scenarios is most likely to lead to excess demand in an economy?

(A) A decrease in consumer confidence leading to decreased spending ☐

(B) A increase in government spending on infrastructure projects ☐

(C) A decrease in exports due to a global economic downturn ☐

(D) A decrease in wages leading to lower disposable income ☐

4. Which of the following measures is typically used to control excess demand in an economy?

(i) Decreasing taxes to stimulate consumer spending.

(ii) Increasing government spending on public projects.

(iii) Tightening monetary policy by raising interest rates

(iv) Implementing expansionary fiscal policy to boost aggregate demand.

Codes

(A) Only (iii) ☐

(B) (ii) and (iii) ☐

(C) Only (iv) ☐

(D) (i) and (iv) ☐

5. In a scenario, where deficient demand is causing sluggish economic growth and high unemployment, which policy action would be most effective for policy makers to stimulate aggregate demand?

(A) Decreasing interest rates to encourage borrowing and investment ☐

(B) Implementing austerity measures to reduce government debt ☐

(C) Increasing taxes to decrease consumer spending ☐

(D) Cutting government spending to reduce budget deficits ☐

6. Based on the diagram below, what does the point of intersection between the Aggregate Demand (AD) and Aggregate Supply (AS) curves represent?

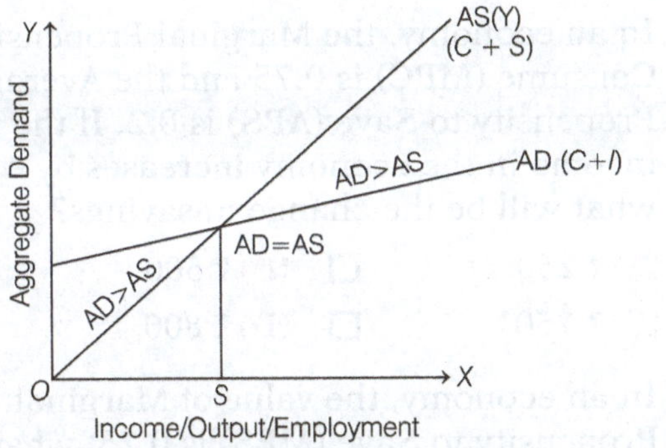

(A) Equilibrium level of income and output ☐
(B) Full employment level of income ☐
(C) Cyclical unemployment ☐
(D) Recessionary gap ☐

7. Referring to the diagram given below, what does the distance between AD and consumption curve indicate?

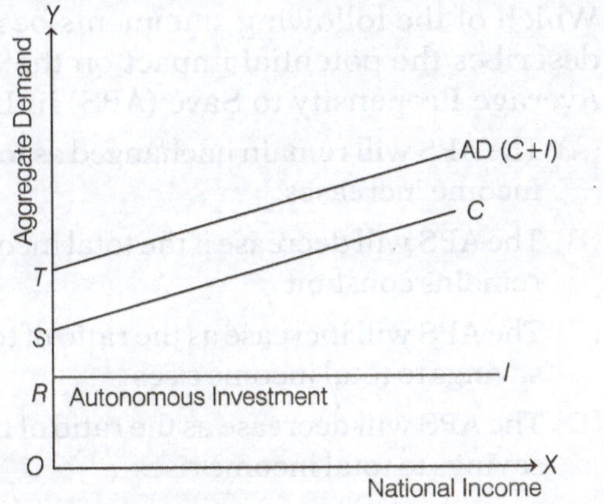

(A) Slopes are equal ☐
(B) Parametric shift ☐
(C) Deflation ☐ (D) Inflation ☐

8. If a straight line consumption function makes a positive intercept at the y-axis, it implies that the marginal propensity to consume .... and average propensity to consume ..... as the level of income rises. *[CBSE 2024]*

(A) remains constant, rises ☐
(B) falls, falls ☐
(C) rises, rises ☐
(D) remains constant, falls ☐

9. Suppose in a hypothetical economy, the income rises from ₹ 5,000 crore to ₹ 6,000 crore. As a result, the consumption expenditure rises from ₹ 4,000 crore to ₹ 4,600 crore. Marginal propensity to consume in such a case would be ....

(A) 0.8 ☐ (B) 0.4 ☐
(C) 0.2 ☐ (D) 0.6 ☐

10. If Autonomous Consumption (C) is greater than zero, it indicates that the National Income (NI) of the economy will be

(i) rising (ii) falling
(iii) zero (iv) constant

Codes

(A) (i) and (ii) ☐ (B) (i) and (iii) ☐
(C) Only (i) ☐ (D) All of these ☐

11. From the given table, identify that level of income, where Average Propensity to Save (APS) becomes zero. *[CBSE 2024]*

Income (₹ in crores)	0	50	100	200	300	400
Consumption (₹ in crores)	50	75	100	150	200	250

(A) 50 ☐ (B) 100 ☐
(C) 200 ☐ (D) 0 ☐

12. Arrange the following in the correct sequential order, if the government of a nation is trying to curtail the situation of inflationary gap. *[CBSE 2024]*

(i) Decrease in disposable income
(ii) Increase in taxes
(iii) Decrease in aggregate demand

Codes

(A) (i), (ii), (iii) ☐ (B) (iii), (ii), (i) ☐
(C) (ii), (iii), (i) ☐ (D) (ii), (i), (iii) ☐

13. Which concept in macroeconomics quantifies the responsiveness of consumption expenditure to changes in disposable income over a specific period?

(A) The ratio of incremental consumption to corresponding changes in savings ☐
(B) The fraction of total income designated for consumption after tax deductions ☐
(C) The ratio of change in consumption expenditure to change in aggregate income ☐
(D) The proportion of total savings directly influenced by changes in consumption patterns ☐

14. Which of the following statements accurately describes the Aggregate Demand (AD) curve in macroeconomics?

(A) The AD curve illustrates the relationship between level of income and the expenditure on the goods and services demanded by households, firms and the government ☐
(B) The AD curve shows the relationship between the money supply and the interest rate in an economy ☐
(C) The AD curve represents the relationship between the level of output and the price level, holding all other factors constant ☐
(D) The AD curve depicts the relationship between consumption and disposable income in an economy ☐

15. If increase in national income is equal to savings, the value of marginal propensity to consume would be .... *[CBSE 2023]*

(A) equal to unity ☐
(B) greater than one ☐
(C) less than one ☐
(D) equal to zero ☐

16. If Marginal Propensity to Save (MPS) is 0.25 and initial change in investment is ₹ 250 crore, then the final change in income would be ....

(A) ₹ 1,000 crore ☐
(B) ₹ 1,200 crore ☐
(C) ₹ 500 crore ☐
(D) ₹ 3,500 crore ☐

17. In an economy, the Marginal Propensity to Consume (MPC) is 0.75 and the Average Propensity to Save (APS) is 0.2. If the total income in the economy increases by ₹ 1,000, what will be the change in savings?

(A) ₹ 250 ☐ (B) ₹ 500 ☐
(C) ₹ 750 ☐ (D) ₹ 800 ☐

18. In an economy, the value of Marginal Propensity to Save (MPS) is 0.25, what will be the value of increase in income, if investments increased by ₹ 200 crores? *[CBSE 2023]*

(A) ₹ 200 crore ☐ (B) ₹ 150 crore ☐
(C) ₹ 1,000 crore ☐ (D) ₹ 800 crore ☐

19. "India's household savings can potentially rise by 2.7% by 2030." – Economic Times

Which of the following statements best describes the potential impact on the Average Propensity to Save (APS) in India?

(A) The APS will remain unchanged as total income increases ☐
(B) The APS will decrease if the total income remains constant ☐
(C) The APS will increase as the ratio of total savings to total income rises ☐
(D) The APS will decrease as the ratio of total savings to total income rises ☐

20. Break-even point is a point where

(A) APC = 1 ☐
(B) APS = 0 ☐
(C) Both (A) and (B) ☐
(D) Neither (A) nor (B) ☐

21. Identify the correct statements regarding shifts in equilibrium in an economy.

(i) Injections boost the flow of income and cause a positive multiplier effect.
(ii) Withdrawals reduce the flow of income and cause a negative multiplier effect.
(iii) Investment is considered as an injection, while savings is treated as a withdrawal from the circular flow.

Codes

(A) (i) and (ii) ☐ (B) (ii) and (iii) ☐
(C) (i) and (iii) ☐ (D) All of these ☐

22. What is 'paradox' referred to as the 'paradox of thrift' in macroeconomics?

(A) An increase in the proportion of income saved by individuals leads to a decrease or no change in total savings in the economy ☐
(B) An increase in the proportion of income spent by individuals leads to a decrease or no change in total consumption in the economy ☐
(C) An increase in government spending leads to a decrease or no change in overall investment in the economy ☐
(D) An increase in interest rates leads to a decrease or no change in borrowing and lending activities in the economy ☐

23. Identify the relationship between the Marginal Propensity to Consume (MPC) and the Multiplier (K) in macroeconomics.

(A) The multiplier is maximum when MPC is 1 and minimum when MPC is 0 ☐
(B) The multiplier is maximum when MPC is 0 and minimum when MPC is 1 ☐
(C) The multiplier is minimum when MPC is 0 and maximum when MPC is 1 ☐
(D) The multiplier is minimum when MPC is 1 and maximum when MPC is 0 ☐

24. During a recessionary period, with deficient demand causing high unemployment rates, which policy measure should the government prioritise to stimulate economic activity?

(A) Decreasing interest rates to encourage investment and consumption ☐
(B) Implementing austerity measures to reduce budget deficits ☐
(C) Increasing taxes to decrease disposable income and discourage spending ☐
(D) Cutting government spending to reduce aggregate demand ☐

25. Suppose for a given economy,

$$S = -60 + 0.1Y$$
$$I = ₹\ 4{,}000 \text{ crore}$$

(where S = Saving Function, Y = National Income and I = Investment Expenditure) equilibrium level of income would be ……… crore.

(A) ₹ 4,000 ☐ (B) ₹ 40,000 ☐
(C) ₹ 40,600 ☐ (D) ₹ 60,400 ☐

26. Which of the following highlights the fact related to ex-post and ex-ante measures in macroeconomics?

(A) Ex-post measures focus on forecasted economic indicators, while ex-ante measures analyse actual economic outcomes ☐
(B) Ex-ante measures involve predicting economic variables, while ex-post measures evaluate realised economic data ☐
(C) Ex-post measures assess future economic trends, while ex-ante measures evaluate historical economic performance ☐
(D) Ex-ante measures refer to government policies, while ex-post measures pertain to consumer behaviour in the market ☐

27. Match the following

Column I	Column II
A. Aggregate demand	(i) $\frac{C}{Y}$
B. Break-even point	(ii) $\frac{\Delta C}{\Delta Y}$
C. Average propensity to consume	(iii) Y = C
D. Marginal propensity to consume	(iv) C + I

Codes

	A	B	C	D	
(A)	(iv)	(iii)	(i)	(ii)	☐
(B)	(iv)	(i)	(iii)	(ii)	☐
(C)	(iv)	(iii)	(ii)	(i)	☐
(D)	(iv)	(ii)	(i)	(iii)	☐

28. Match the following

	Column I	Column II
A.	C > Y	(i) Aggregate supply
B.	Y > C	(ii) Positive savings
C.	C + S	(iii) Dissavings
D.	APS = 1	(iv) Income = Savings

Codes

	A	B	C	D
(A)	(iii)	(i)	(ii)	(iv)
(B)	(iii)	(ii)	(iv)	(i)
(C)	(iii)	(ii)	(i)	(iv)
(D)	(iii)	(iv)	(i)	(ii)

29. Match the following

	Column I	Column II
A.	MPC = MPS	(i) Autonomous consumption = 60
B.	MPC	(ii) $K = \infty$
C.	MPC = 0	(iii) Ranges between 0 to 1
D.	C = 60 + 0.5Y	(iv) K = 2

Codes

	A	B	C	D
(A)	(iv)	(ii)	(iii)	(i)
(B)	(iv)	(iii)	(i)	(ii)
(C)	(iii)	(iv)	(i)	(ii)
(D)	(iv)	(iii)	(ii)	(i)

30. Match the following

	Column I	Column II
A.	Inflation	(i) Increased to control inflation
B.	Bank rate	(ii) Rise in general price level
C.	Deflation	(iii) Fall in disposable income
D.	Increase in taxes	(iv) Fall in income, output and employment

Codes

	A	B	C	D
(A)	(ii)	(i)	(iii)	(iv)
(B)	(ii)	(iii)	(i)	(iv)
(C)	(ii)	(i)	(iv)	(iii)
(D)	(ii)	(iv)	(iii)	(i)

Assertion-Reason Questions

No. of Questions : **10** Suggested Time : **15 Minutes**

Direction Each of the question given below consist of the two statements; one labelled as **Assertion** (A) and other as **Reason** (R). List of common options applicable for each question is given below

(A) Both Assertion (A) and Reason (R) are true and Reason (R) is the correct explanation of Assertion (A)

(B) Both Assertion (A) and Reason (R) are true, but Reason (R) is not the correct explanation of Assertion (A)

(C) Assertion is true, but Reason is false

(D) Assertion is false, but Reason is true

You have to select the codes as *A, B, C or D* as your answer to the question by marking (✓) in the response box given against each option.

1. **Assertion (A)** The slope of the consumption curve is positive, indicating that consumption increases with increase in income but at a decreasing rate.

Reason (R) After reaching a certain level, individuals tend to save a portion of their income rather than allocating it entirely to consumption.

(A) ☐ (B) ☐ (C) ☐ (D) ☐

2. **Assertion (A)** The saving curve intersects the vertical axis at a point representing autonomous consumption.

Reason (R) At zero level of income, saving is equal to autonomous consumption, resulting in a starting point for the saving curve on the negative y-axis.

(A) ☐ (B) ☐ (C) ☐ (D) ☐

3. **Assertion (A)** Before break-even point, APC is greater than 1.

Reason (R) At initial level, consumption is greater than income.

(A) ☐ (B) ☐ (C) ☐ (D) ☐

4. **Assertion (A)** At the break-even level of income, the value of Average Propensity to Consume (APC) is zero.

Reason (R) Sum of Average Propensity to Consume (APC) and Average Propensity to Save (APS) is always equal to the one.

[CBSE 2023]

(A) ☐ (B) ☐ (C) ☐ (D) ☐

5. **Assertion (A)** Deficient demand in an economy is solely caused by a decrease in propensity to consume.

Reason (R) Factors such as higher taxes, reduced government expenditure, lower investment, increased imports, and decreased exports collectively contribute to a decrease in aggregate demand, leading to deficient demand in the economy.

(A) ☐ (B) ☐ (C) ☐ (D) ☐

6. **Assertion (A)** The cost of borrowing money for financing an investment does not affect the volume of investment.

Reason (R) There exists an inverse relationship between Return on Investment (RoI) and the volume of investment. At a high RoI, the investment spending will be less and *vice-versa*.

(A) ☐ (B) ☐ (C) ☐ (D) ☐

7. **Assertion (A)** The 45° line in Keynesian economics, represents the relationship between aggregate supply and aggregate demand.

Reason (R) The 45° line has a slope of one and bisects the 90° angle formed by the two axis.

(A) ☐ (B) ☐
(C) ☐ (D) ☐

8. **Assertion (A)** In the saving-investment (S-I) approach, the equilibrium level of income is determined solely by the equality of planned saving and planned investment.

Reason (R) The investment curve (I) is not parallel to the x-axis due to the varying nature of investment decisions, while the saving curve (S) slopes upwards, indicating that as the income rises, saving also rises.

(A) ☐ (B) ☐
(C) ☐ (D) ☐

9. **Assertion (A)** The working of the multiplier is based on the principle that an increase in investment leads to a proportional increase in income through subsequent rounds of spending.

Reason (R) As individuals receive additional income, they spend a portion of it on consumption, which in turn increases the income of others, creating a chain reaction of spending and further income generation.

(A) ☐ (B) ☐
(C) ☐ (D) ☐

10. **Assertion (A)** As an advisor in the fiscal policy of government, you have decided to increase the taxes and reduce the government spending to correct the situation of excess demand in an economy.

Reason (R) By implementing such measures, the government aims to reduce disposable income and overall aggregate demand, thereby curbing inflationary pressures and bringing the economy back to a sustainable level of growth.

(A) ☐
(B) ☐
(C) ☐
(D) ☐

Correct/Incorrect Statements

No. of Questions : **10** Suggested Time : **15 Minutes**

Direction Each of the question given below consist of the two statements. List of common options applicable for each question is given below

(A) Both statements are correct
(B) Both statements are incorrect
(C) Statement I is correct and Statement II is incorrect
(D) Statement I is incorrect and Statement II is correct

You have to select the codes as *A, B, C* or *D* as your answer to the question by marking (✓) in the response box given against each option.

1. **Statement I** Aggregate Supply (AS) refers to the actual output of goods and services produced in an economy during a given time period.

Statement II National income (Y) is calculated as the sum of consumption expenditure (C) and investment (I), where consumption (C) represents the expenditure on goods and services by households and Investment (I) represents the expenditure on capital goods by businesses.

(A) ☐ (B) ☐ (C) ☐ (D) ☐

2. **Statement I** Consumption and savings are the components of national output of an economy.

Statement II Higher level of income often leads to lower savings. *[CBSE 2024]*

(A) ☐ (B) ☐ (C) ☐ (D) ☐

3. **Statement I** The induced consumption shows the direct relation between consumption and income.

Statement II With a certain increase in income, induced consumption also increases. *[CBSE 2023]*

(A) ☐ (B) ☐ (C) ☐ (D) ☐

4. **Statement I** Autonomous consumption is denoted by $\overline{C}$ and shows the consumption which is independent of income.

Statement II The induced component of consumption, cY shows the dependence of consumption on income.

(A) ☐ (B) ☐ (C) ☐ (D) ☐

5. **Statement I** At the break-even point, the Average Propensity to Save (APS) is equal to 1, indicating that saving equals national income.

Statement II As income increases, the Average Propensity to Consume (APC) declines steadily because the portion of income allocated to consumption decreases.

(A) ☐ (B) ☐ (C) ☐ (D) ☐

6. **Statement I** The equilibrium output in an economy, determined by the equality of total output (Y) and Aggregate Demand (AD), always signifies full employment of resources.

Statement II Full employment level of income is achieved when all factors of production are fully employed in the production process and equilibrium at the point of equality of Y and AD guarantees full employment of resources.

(A) ☐ (B) ☐ (C) ☐ (D) ☐

7. **Statement I** Increasing the bank rate, repo rate and reverse repo rate are all qualitative instruments used by the central bank to contract credit and decrease aggregate demand during deflationary situations.

Statement II Open market operations involve the sale and purchase of securities by the central bank, directly impacting the level of money supply in the economy and increasing purchasing power.

(A) ☐ (B) ☐ (C) ☐ (D) ☐

8. **Statement I** The equilibrium in the economy occurs when ex-ante aggregate demand equals ex-ante aggregate supply.

Statement II If planned spending (AD) exceeds planned output (AS), the (C+I) curve lies above the 45° line, indicating that consumers and firms are collectively purchasing more goods than firms intend to produce.

This results in a situation where planned inventory falls below the desired level, prompting firms to increase production to restore inventory to its desired level.

(A) ☐ (B) ☐ (C) ☐ (D) ☐

9. **Statement I** Inventory investment can occur due to two reasons i.e. planned inventory investment, where firms decide to keep stocks for various reasons and unplanned inventory investment, which happens when sales differ from the planned level, leading firms to add to or run down existing inventories.

Statement II If the ex-ante demand for final goods falls short of the output of final goods that producers have planned to produce, there will be no unintended accumulation of inventories.

(A) ☐ (B) ☐ (C) ☐ (D) ☐

10. **Statement I** The investment multiplier of an economy represents the ratio of the total increment in equilibrium value of final goods output to the initial increment in autonomous expenditure.

Statement II The size of the investment multiplier depends on the value of the Marginal Propensity to Consume (MPC), i.e. with a larger MPC leading to an increase in the multiplier.

(A) ☐ (B) ☐ (C) ☐ (D) ☐

Case Based Questions

No. of Questions : 2   Suggested Time : **10 Minutes**

Direction This section contains 2 cases each having 4 questions of 1 mark each. You have to write the answer of each question based on the context of the related case.

Case 1 From the following image given below, answer the questions

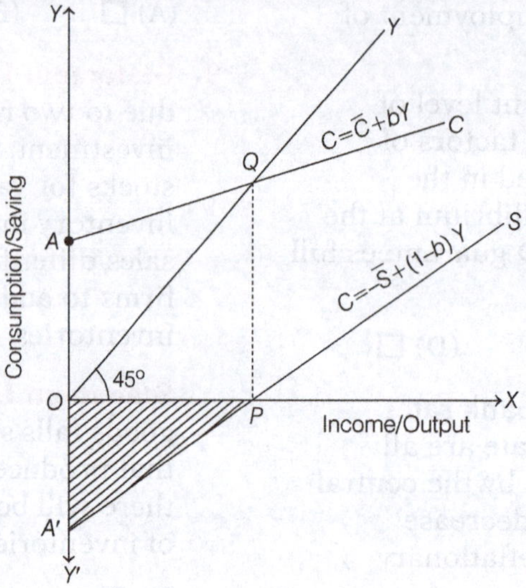

Questions

(i) The consumption which is independent of income is highlighted through

(A) OP ☐

(B) OA′ ☐

(C) OA ☐

(D) OQ ☐

(ii) The break-even level of income is highlighted by .... in the image.

(iii) What is being highlighted by the shaded area?

(A) Positive savings as Y > C ☐

(B) Negative savings as C > Y ☐

(C) Break-even point as C= Y ☐

(D) None of the above ☐

(iv) The functional relationship between the consumption expenditure and the income is known as ....

Case 2 A country is experiencing a period of economic downturn characterised by high unemployment and low levels of output and income. The government is concerned about addressing these issues and restoring economic stability.

To tackle the situation, the government implements various policies and measures aimed at stimulating aggregate demand and promoting economic growth. The government initiates infrastructure development projects, such as building new roads and bridges, to boost investment and create job opportunities.

Additionally, it reduces taxes on consumers and businesses to increase disposable income and encourage spending and investment. Furthermore, the central bank lowers interest rates to make borrowing cheaper, thus promoting investment and consumption.

Despite these efforts, the economy continues to face challenges, including persistent unemployment and sluggish growth. The government and policy-makers are analysing the situation and considering further interventions to revitalise the economy and achieve full employment and sustainable economic growth.

Questions

(i) The primary objective of the government's infrastructure development projects in the country is ....

(ii) How does the reduction in taxes on consumers and businesses affect the economy?

(A) It decreases disposable income and leads to higher savings ☐

(B) It increases disposable income and encourages spending and investment ☐

(C) It has no impact on aggregate demand ☐

(D) It reduces government revenue ☐

(iii) The purpose of lowering interest rates by the central bank is ....

(iv) Despite the implemented policies, the economy of the country continues to face challenges.

Which of the following is a likely reason for this?

(A) Excessive government intervention ☐

(B) Lack of infrastructure development projects ☐

(C) High levels of consumer spending ☐

(D) Persistent unemployment and sluggish growth ☐

Subjective Questions

Free Response Questions, Open-ended Questions etc.

No. of Questions : **8** Suggested Time : **65 Minutes**

1. In an economy planned spending is greater than planned output. Explain all the changes that will take place in the economy.

2. For a hypothetical economy, assuming there is an increase in the Marginal Propensity to Consume (MPC) from 80% to 90% and change in investment to be ₹ 1,000 crore.

Using the concept of investment multiplier, calculate the increase in income due to change in marginal propensity to consume. *[CBSE 2023]*

3. Assuming that increase in investment is ₹ 1,000 crore and marginal propensity to consume is 0.9, explain the working of multiplier.

4. "With the objective to correct deflation, Reserve Bank of India may decrease the bank rate."

Discuss the rationale behind the step taken by the Reserve Bank of India (RBI). *[CBSE 2024]*

5. Given that national income is ₹ 80 crore and consumption expenditure is ₹ 64 crore, find out average propensity to save.

When income rises to ₹ 100 crore and consumption expenditure to ₹ 78 crore, what will be the average propensity to consume and marginal propensity to consume?

6. 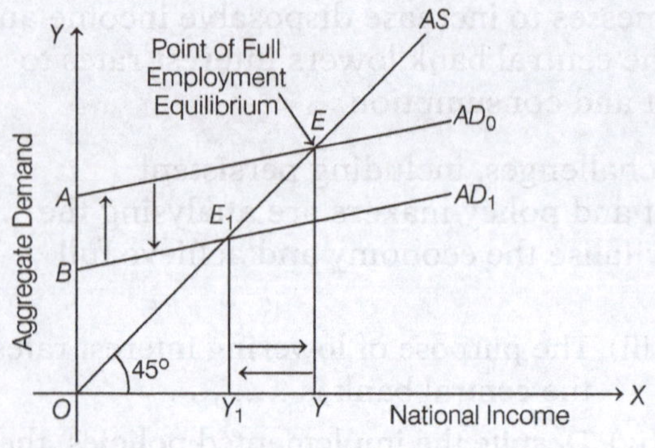

Identify the situation represented in the above curve and highlight any two qualitative measures that can be taken by RBI to correct the situation.

7. As per the news headline given below, explain the reason for this decision of RBI. Suggest any two measures which can be adopted to tackle the situation.

8. On 30th September, 2022, the Reserve Bank of India (RBI) raised repo rate for the fourth time in a row. The Monetary Policy Committee (MPC) decided to raise the policy rate by 50 basis points (1 basis point = 1/100th of a percent). After this announcement, the new repo rate stands at 5.9%, while the reverse repo rate continues to stand at 3.35%.

Commercial banks borrow money from the central bank, when there is a shortage of funds. With the surge in the repo rate, borrowings by general public will become costlier. This is because, as RBI hikes its repo rate, it becomes costly for the banks to borrow short-term funds from the central bank.

As a result, the banks hike the rates at which customers borrow money from them to compensate for the hike in the repo rate. This happens because banks offer loans to retail consumers at an interest rate which is generally, directly proportional to the repo rate.

The increase of 0.50 percent in repo rate will lead to a higher interest rates on loans for borrowers, implying that the Equated Monthly Instalments (EMIs) for repaying the existing loans will also increase. *[CBSE 2023]*

(i) State the meaning of repo rate and reverse repo rate.

(ii) In order to bring down the rate of inflation, outline and discuss the step taken by the Monetary Policy Committee of Reserve Bank of India.

Answers

If your answer matches with the answer given here then put (✓) in the box otherwise put (✗). In case you did not attempt the question leave the box blank.

Multiple Choice Questions

1. C ☐
2. C ☐
3. B ☐
4. A ☐
5. D ☐
6. A ☐
7. A ☐
8. D ☐
9. D ☐
10. C ☐
11. B ☐
12. D ☐
13. C ☐
14. A ☐
15. D ☐
16. A ☐
17. A ☐
18. D ☐

19. C ☐ 20. C ☐
21. D ☐ 22. A ☐
23. A ☐ 24. A ☐
25. C ☐ 26. B ☐
27. A ☐ 28. C ☐
29. D ☐ 30. C ☐

Your Score__________ *(No. of Correct Answers)*

Assertion-Reason Questions

1. A ☐ 2. A ☐
3. A ☐ 4. D ☐
5. D ☐ 6. D ☐
7. D ☐ 8. C ☐
9. A ☐ 10. A ☐

Your Score__________ *(No. of Correct Answers)*

Correct/Incorrect Statements

1. D ☐ 2. C ☐
3. A ☐ 4. A ☐
5. D ☐ 6. B ☐
7. D ☐ 8. A ☐
9. C ☐ 10. A ☐

Your Score__________ *(No. of Correct Answers)*

Case Based Questions

1. (i) C ☐
(iii) B ☐
2. (ii) B ☐
(iv) D ☐

Your Score__________ *(No. of Correct Answers)*

Explanations

Multiple Choice Questions

1. (C) Both (A) and (B)

2. (C) Inflation or excess demand

3. (B) A increase in government spending on infrastructure projects

4. (A) Only (iii)

5. (D) Cutting government spending to reduce budget deficits

6. (A) Equilibrium level of income and output

7. (A) The distance between the Aggregate Demand (AD) curve and the consumption curve indicates that their slopes are equal. This means that the difference between total spending (AD) and consumption remains constant across different levels of income.

8. (D) The positive intercept indicates initial consumption even with no income, so MPC remains constant. As income rises, the portion of income spent on consumption decreases, leading to a falling APC.

9. (D) $\text{MPC} = \dfrac{\text{Change in Consumption}}{\text{Change in Income}} = \dfrac{600}{1{,}000} = 0.6$

10. (C) Only (i)

11. (B) 100

12. (D) (ii), (i), (iii)

13. (C) The ratio of change in consumption expenditure to change in aggregate income

14. (A) The AD curve illustrates the relationship between level of income and the expenditure on the goods and services demanded by households, firms and the government

15. (D) equal to zero

16. (A) $K = \dfrac{1}{\text{MPS}} \Rightarrow \dfrac{1}{0.25} \Rightarrow 4$

Also, $K = \dfrac{\Delta Y}{\Delta I} \Rightarrow 4 = \dfrac{\Delta Y}{250} \Rightarrow \Delta Y = ₹\,1{,}000$ crore

17. (A) The change in savings can be calculated using the Marginal Propensity to Save (MPS), which is derived from the MPC. MPS is calculated as 1 – MPC.

Given that MPC is 0.75, MPS would be 1 – 0.75 = 0.25. If the total income increases by ₹ 1,000, the change in savings is calculated as 0.25 × 1,000 = ₹ 250.

18. (D) MPS = 0.25

Investment Multiplier = 1/MPS = 1/0.25 = 4

$\text{MPS} = \Delta S/\Delta Y$; $4 = \Delta S/200$

$\therefore \Delta S = ₹\,800$ crore

19. (C) As household savings rise by 2.7% by 2030, the total savings (S) will increase. If the total income (Y) remains constant or rises at a slower rate, the APS, which is the ratio of total savings to total income, will increase.

20. (C) Both (A) and (B)

21. (D) All of these

22. (A) An increase in the proportion of income saved by individuals leads to a decrease or no change in total savings in the economy
23. (A) The multiplier is maximum when MPC is 1 and minimum when MPC is 0
24. (A) Decreasing interest rates is a common monetary policy tool used to stimulate economic activity during a recession.

    Lower interest rates reduce the cost of borrowing, which encourages businesses to invest and consumers to spend, thereby increasing aggregate demand and reducing unemployment.
25. (C) Equilibrium income is attained where $S = I$

$$-60 + 0.1Y = 4{,}000$$
$$0.1Y = 4{,}060$$
$$\therefore \quad Y = 4{,}060/0.1 = ₹\ 40{,}600$$

26. (B) Ex-ante measures involve predicting economic variables, while ex-post measures evaluate realised economic data
27. (A) (iv) (iii) (i) (ii)
28. (C) (iii) (ii) (i) (iv)
29. (D) (iv) (iii) (ii) (i)
30. (C) (ii) (i) (iv) (iii)

Assertion-Reason Questions

1. (A) Both Assertion (A) and Reason (R) are true and Reason (R) is the correct explanation of Assertion (A)
2. (A) Both Assertion (A) and Reason (R) are true and Reason (R) is the correct explanation of Assertion (A)
3. (A) Both Assertion (A) and Reason (R) are true and Reason (R) is the correct explanation of Assertion (A)
4. (D) Assertion (A) is false, but Reason (R) is true
5. (D) Assertion (A) is false, but Reason (R) is true
6. (D) Assertion (A) is false, but Reason (R) is true
7. (D) Assertion (A) is false, but Reason (R) is true
8. (C) Assertion (A) is true, but Reason (R) is false
9. (A) Both Assertion (A) and Reason (R) are true and Reason (R) is the correct explanation of Assertion (A)
10. (A) Both Assertion (A) and Reason (R) are true and Reason (R) is the correct explanation of Assertion (A)

Correct/Incorrect Statements

1. (D) Aggregate Supply (AS) refers to the total quantity of goods and services that producers in an economy are willing and able to supply at a given price level during a specified period.
2. (C) Statement I is correct and Statement II is incorrect
3. (A) Both statements are correct
4. (A) Both statements are correct
5. (D) At the break-even point, the Average Propensity to Save (APS) is equal to 0, indicating that saving equals zero.
6. (B) Both statements are incorrect
7. (D) Increasing the bank rate, repo rate and reverse repo rate are quantitative instruments used by the central bank to tighten credit and reduce aggregate demand during inflationary periods.
8. (A) Both statements are correct
9. (C) If the ex-ante demand for final goods falls short of the output of final goods that producers have planned to produce, there will be an unintended accumulation of inventories.
10. (A) Both statements are correct

Case Based Questions

1. (i) (C) Consumption which is independent of income refers to autonomous consumption. This represents the portion of consumption expenditure that does not vary with changes in income levels.

   (ii) OP

   (iii) (B) Negative savings as C > Y

   (iv) consumption function
2. (i) to boost investment and create job opportunities

   (ii) (B) It increases disposable income and encourages spending and investment

   (iii) to make borrowing cheaper and promote investment and consumption

   (iv) (D) Persistent unemployment and sluggish growth

Subjective Questions

1. If in an economy, planned spending, i.e. aggregate demand is greater than the planned output i.e. aggregate supply then the following changes will take place in the economy.

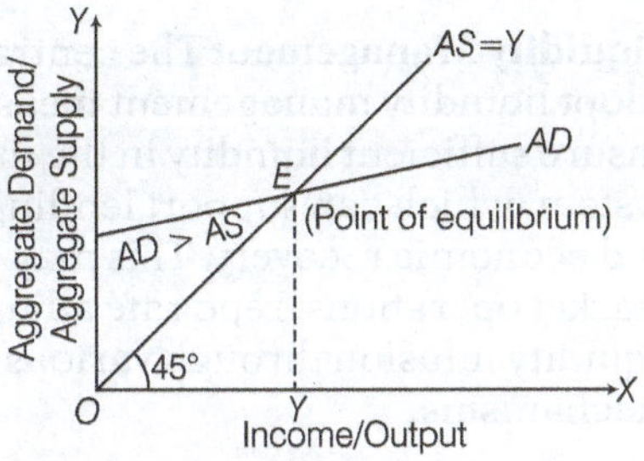

AD and AS curves

(i) Since the aggregate demand exceeds aggregate supply, therefore the existing stocks of the producers will be sold out.

(ii) To rebuild the desired stocks, so as to be able to meet the demand, the producers would plan greater production.

(iii) This decision of producers will increase the level of aggregate supply, till the point it converges with aggregate demand, as is shown in the diagram given above.

2. MPC increases from 0.80 to 0.90. Accordingly, investment multiplier will increase from $5\left(\frac{1}{0.2}\right)$ to $10\left(\frac{1}{0.1}\right)$. Therefore, income will increase by

$$\Rightarrow \quad K = \frac{\Delta Y}{\Delta I}$$

$$\Rightarrow \quad 10 = \frac{\Delta Y}{1{,}000}$$

$$\Delta Y = ₹10{,}000$$

3. Investment multiplier or simply the multiplier is measured as a ratio between change in output or income and change in investment.

Symbolically, Investment Multiplier (K)

$$= \frac{\text{Change in Income } (\Delta Y)}{\text{Change in Investment } (\Delta I)}$$

Also, there is a direct relationship between investment multiplier and Marginal Propensity to Consume (MPC). Multiplier can also be estimated by using the following formula

$$K = \frac{1}{1 - \text{MPC}}$$

So, if MPC = 0.9, then $K = \frac{1}{1-0.9}$

$$= \frac{1}{0.1} = 10$$

Now, if the investment increases by ₹ 1,000 crore, then increase in income can be computed by substituting the values in the following formula

$$K = \frac{\Delta Y}{\Delta I} \Rightarrow 10 = \frac{\Delta Y}{1{,}000}$$

$\Rightarrow$ Change in Income (ΔY) = ₹10,000 crore

So, if investment increases by ₹ 1,000 crore and MPC = 0.9, then in such an instance, income will increase by ₹ 10,000 crore.

4. Deflation or deficit demand is a situation wherein aggregate demand falls short of aggregate supply at the full employment level. This leads to a fall in output, employment and income. To deal with this situation, the RBI may decrease the bank rate so that the credit creation capacity of the commercial banks gets increased. As a result, the aggregate demand, purchasing power and money supply in the economy will be increased which are necessary to control the situation of deficient demand.

5. Here, in first condition, Income (Y) = ₹ 80 crore

Consumption (C) = ₹ 64 crore

Hence, Savings (S) = Y − C = 80 − 64 = ₹ 16 crore

Now, Average Propensity to Save (APS) $= \frac{S}{Y}$

$$= \frac{16}{80} = 0.20$$

Again, when income and consumption expenditure rises,

New Income (Y) = ₹ 100 crore; Change in Income (ΔY) = ₹20 crore (100 − 80)

New Consumption (C) = ₹ 78 crore

Change in Consumption (ΔC) = ₹14 crore (78 − 64)

So, Average Propensity to Consume (APC)

$$= \frac{C}{Y} = \frac{78}{100} = 0.78$$

And, Marginal Propensity to Consume (MPC)

$$= \frac{\Delta C}{\Delta Y} = \frac{14}{20} = 0.70$$

6. The given curve highlights the situation of deficient demand. If equilibrium level of output is less than the full employment of output, it is due to the fact that demand is not enough to employ all factors of production. This situation is called the situation of deficient demand. It leads to decline in prices in the long-run.

Qualitative measures control the situation of deficient demand include

(i) **Margin Requirement** It refers to the difference between the amount of loan taken and value of collateral offered.

During deficient demand, margin requirement is reduced so that more loan can be offered to people.

(ii) **Credit Rationing** In this, central bank controls the credit limits of the commercial bank. During deficient demand, central bank withdraws credit rationing and promote commercial banks to create credit.

7. The Reserve Bank of India's decision to maintain the status quo on the policy repo rate may be driven by several factors. One possible reason could be the need to assess the current economic situation carefully before making any changes to the interest rates. Additionally, the RBI might want to monitor inflationary pressures, global economic trends and domestic growth indicators before adjusting the policy rate.

To tackle the situation, the RBI could consider implementing measures such as

(i) **Forward Guidance** The RBI can provide clear communication regarding its future monetary policy intentions, which can help manage market expectations and guide economic behaviour.

(ii) **Liquidity Management** The central bank can adopt liquidity management measures to ensure sufficient liquidity in the financial system, which can support lending activities and economic recovery. This may include open market operations, repo rate adjustments or liquidity infusion through various mechanisms.

8. (i) **Repo Rate** It refers to the rate at which commercial banks borrow from the central bank for their short-term needs ranging from 1-14 days against approved government securities.

Reverse Repo Rate It refers to the rate at which commercial banks can park their excess reserves with the central bank and can withdraw at any point in time.

(ii) In order to bring down the inflation rate, the monetary policy committee raises the above key rate i.e. the repo rate and reverse repo rate. With the increase in repo rate, credit becomes expensive for commercial banks and hence commercial banks raise the rate of interest on the loans. This will discourage people from taking loans and fall in the money supply. Also, a rise in the reverse repo rate will leave commercial banks with less money to offer loans and advances leading to a fall in money supply and control the inflation.

CHAPTER -4

Government Budget and The Economy

Types & Nos. of Questions

Multiple Choice Questions – 30
Assertion-Reason Questions – 10
Correct/Incorrect Statements – 8
Case Based Questions – 2 Cases, *each with four Questions*
Subjective Questions – 8

Trend Analysis

On the basis of analysis of last 2 years' papers, it is found that on an average 1 Multiple Choice Question and 1 Long Answer Type Question (Statement Based and Graph Based) are asked from this chapter.

Focus Topics of the Chapter

- Concept of Government Budget
- Components: Revenue Budget and Capital Budget
- Measures of Budget Deficit

Multiple Choice Questions

No. of Questions : **30** Suggested Time : **45 Minutes**

Direction Each of the question given below is Multiple Choice Question (MCQ) i.e. there are Four Options/ Choices for answer, out of which ONLY ONE is correct. You have to select the correct option.

A response box is given with each option, mark (✓) in the box of the correct option. For each correct answer you will get 1 mark, while there is no penalty for incorrect answer or missed out questions.

1. Which of the following statements best describes the government budget in the context of constitutional requirements?

(A) The government budget is a legally binding document that outlines the allocation of funds for specific government programmes and projects ☐

(B) The government budget is a statement of government's financial position at a particular point in time ☐

(C) The government budget is a plan that is subject to approval by the legislative body, as mandated by the constitution ☐

(D) The government budget is an accounting tool used to track government revenues and expenditures for transparency purposes ☐

2. "In the Annual Budget 2022-23, the Government of India set-up disinvestment targets of ₹ 65,000 crore."
Such proceeds from disinvestment can be classified as ...... receipts in the government budget as it leads to ...... of the government. *[CBSE 2023]*

(A) capital, decrease in assets ☐

(B) revenue, increase in assets ☐

(C) capital, increase in liabilities ☐

(D) revenue, decrease in liabilities ☐

3. The budget that relates to the current financial year only is included in the .... and the one that is concerned with the assets and liabilities of the government is called ....

(A) revenue budget, capital budget ☐

(B) capital budget, revenue budget ☐

(C) surplus budget, deficit budget ☐

(D) balances budget, unbalanced budget ☐

4. What critical role does the stabilisation function of the government budget play in managing economic fluctuations, particularly concerning income and employment levels?

(A) By maximising government revenue through taxation ☐

(B) By adjusting aggregate demand to correct fluctuations in income and employment ☐

(C) By regulating the distribution of income within society ☐

(D) By reducing government expenditure on public services ☐

5. Which of the following can be put in the category of revenue receipts in government budget?

(A) Proceeds from the sale of government assets ☐

(B) Interest earned on government investments ☐

(C) Taxes and duties collected by the government ☐

(D) Borrowings from domestic and foreign sources ☐

6. In order to tackle the problem of rising general price level in an economy, government may come up with a surplus budget to achieve the budget objective of .... *[CBSE 2023]*

(i) reallocation of resources

(ii) price stability

(iii) redistribution of income

Codes

(A) Only (i) ☐
(B) Only (ii) ☐
(C) Only (iii) ☐ (D) (i) and (ii) ☐

7. "Budget is used as an important policy instrument to combat flucuations in an economy." In the light of above lines, identify the related objective of government budget.

(A) Allocation of resources ☐
(B) Stablisation of price ☐
(C) Growth of the economy ☐
(D) Redistribution of income ☐

8. From the following image, identify the incorrect statement.

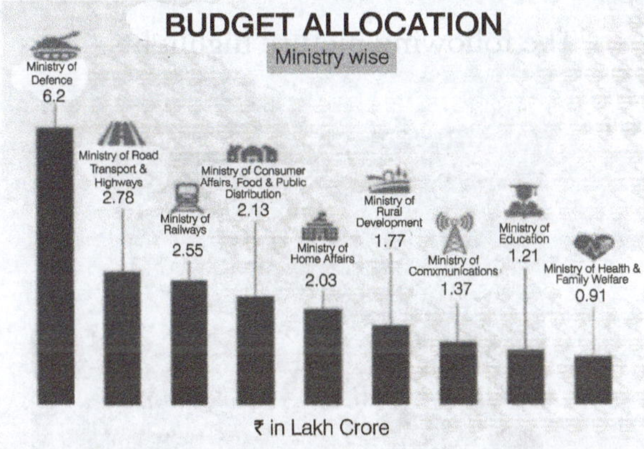

(A) Budget has allocated the maximum funds to ministry of defence ☐
(B) Ministry of railways has been allocated more funds than ministry of consumer affairs by 0.42 lakh crores ☐
(C) The government is focusing on building roads and highways that contributes to strong infrastructure ☐
(D) Ministry of education has got more funds than ministry of rural development as education is one of the most important components of human capital formation ☐

9. Which of the following objective of government budget is required according to the following picture?

(A) Allocation of resources ☐
(B) Redistribution of income and wealth ☐
(C) Stabilisation function ☐
(D) GDP growth ☐

10. The Government of India has decided to vaccinate the adult population of India (with Covaxin/Covishield), without any charge. This would be categorised as ....

(A) revenue nature income ☐
(B) capital nature expenditure ☐
(C) revenue nature expenditure ☐
(D) capital nature income ☐

11. Among the following statements, which one signifies a revenue receipt for the government?

(A) Proceeds from the sale of government owned land ☐
(B) Interest earned on government investments ☐
(C) Loans obtained from international financial institutions ☐
(D) Funds received from the sale of government bonds ☐

12. Identify the incorrect statement in context of revenue expenditure.

(A) Revenue expenditure is expenditure incurred for purposes other than the creation of physical or financial assets of the central government ☐
(B) These relates to those expenses incurred for the normal functioning of the government departments ☐

(C) Expenditure on interest payments, expenditure on mid day meal programmes is a revenue expenditure ☐

(D) Revenue expenditure either creates an asset or reduces any liability ☐

13. "The government of a developing country is implementing a major infrastructure project to improve transportation networks across the country. The project involves the construction of new highways, bridges and public transportation systems to enhance connectivity and facilitate economic growth."

In the above paragraph, which type of expenditure is focused for economic growth?

(A) Revenue ☐ (B) Capital ☐

(C) Financial ☐ (D) Economical ☐

14. Repayment of borrowing is a .... expenditure whereas interest paid on borrowings is .... expenditure.

(A) revenue, capital ☐

(B) capital, revenue ☐

(C) revenue, revenue ☐

(D) capital, capital ☐

15. Identify the incorrect statements.

(i) The government may spend an amount equal to the revenue it collects. This is known as a balanced budget.

(ii) When tax collection exceeds the required expenditure, the budget is said to be in surplus.

(iii) The most uncommon feature is the situation when expenditure exceeds revenue. This is when the government runs a surplus budget.

Codes

(A) Only (i) ☐

(B) Only (ii) ☐

(C) Only (iii) ☐

(D) (i), (ii) and (iii) ☐

16. What is the consequence of using capital receipts to cover revenue deficit?

(A) It leads to a decrease in government liabilities ☐

(B) It results in a decrease in future interest payments ☐

(C) It creates inflationary pressure in the economy ☐

(D) It reduces the need for future borrowings ☐

17. Which of the following is an example of non-debt creating capital receipts?

(A) Borrowing from RBI ☐

(B) Recovery of loans ☐

(C) Borrowing from abroad ☐

(D) Proceeds from the sale of government securities ☐

18. The following picture highlights.

(i) The government receipts are less than the expenditures ☐

(ii) The amount recovered from tax is not enough to meet out the necessary expenses like expenditure on education, health, etc ☐

(iii) Government is able to made easy access of education and health to the people

Codes

(A) Only (i) ☐

(B) Only (ii) ☐

(C) Both (i) and (ii) ☐

(D) (i), (ii) and (iii) ☐

19. An individual who get benefits from a public good, such as a clean and well-maintained public park, without contributing towards its upkeep or maintenance is described as ………… .

(A) consumer ☐ (B) producer ☐
(C) free-rider ☐ (D) contributor ☐

20. "Union Budget 2024: Here is how revenue, fiscal and primary deficit impacts the Indian economy." – The Economic Times

What are the main sources of financing revenue deficit for the Indian economy?

(A) Borrowings ☐
(B) Deficit financing ☐
(C) Both (A) and (B) ☐
(D) None of the above ☐

21. If a person passed away without a valid will and no heirs could be located to inherit the person's estate, in such cases, the state government may claim the deceased person's property. Amount recovered from this property will be categorised under …… head of non-tax revenue receipt.

(A) interest ☐
(B) special assessment ☐
(C) escheat ☐ (D) gifts and grants ☐

22. What is the revenue deficit if a government has revenue expenditure of ₹ 500 million and revenue receipts of ₹ 400 million?

(A) ₹ 100 million ☐ (B) ₹ 400 million ☐
(C) ₹ 900 million ☐ (D) ₹ 1 billion ☐

23. Which of the following strategies can be employed to mitigate revenue deficit and promote fiscal sustainability?

(i) Reduce revenue expenditure
(ii) Increase revenue receipts

Codes

(A) Only (i) ☐
(B) Only (ii) ☐
(C) Both (i) and (ii) ☐
(D) Neither (i) nor (ii) ☐

24. Which of the following is correct in context of fiscal deficit?

(A) The difference between the government's total expenditure and its total receipts, including borrowing ☐
(B) The difference between the government's total revenue and its total expenditure, excluding borrowing ☐
(C) The difference between the government's total revenue and its total expenditure, including borrowing ☐
(D) The difference between the government's total expenditure and its total receipts, excluding borrowing ☐

25. Find out the fiscal deficit, if a government has

- Total budget expenditure of ₹ 800 crore,
- Total budget receipts (excluding borrowings) of ₹ 600 crore,
- Revenue expenditure of ₹ 500 crore,
- Capital expenditure of ₹ 300 crore,
- Revenue receipts of ₹ 400 crore and
- Capital receipts (excluding borrowings) of ₹ 200 crore.

(A) ₹ 100 crore ☐ (B) ₹ 200 crore ☐
(C) ₹ 300 crore ☐ (D) ₹ 400 crore ☐

26. Which of the following represents a significant negative outcome of fiscal deficit?

(A) Enhanced government spending efficiency ☐
(B) Expansion of public services ☐
(C) Escalation of national debt burden ☐
(D) Stimulation of economic growth ☐

27. Match the following

Column I	Column II
A. Allocation of resources	(i) Establishment of SEZs
B. Distribution of income and wealth	(ii) Surplus budget during inflation
C. Economic stability	(iii) High taxes from rich sections
D. Reducing regional disparities	(iv) Profit maximisation with social welfare

Codes

	A	B	C	D	
(A)	(iv)	(iii)	(ii)	(i)	☐
(B)	(iv)	(iii)	(i)	(ii)	☐
(C)	(iv)	(ii)	(iii)	(i)	☐
(D)	(iv)	(i)	(ii)	(iii)	☐

28. Match the following

Column I	Column II
A. Revenue receipts	(i) Building roads
B. Revenue expenditure	(ii) Recovery of loan
C. Capital receipts	(iii) Escheat
D. Capital expenditure	(iv) Interest on loans

Codes

	A	B	C	D	
(A)	(iii)	(iv)	(i)	(ii)	☐
(B)	(iii)	(ii)	(iv)	(i)	☐
(C)	(iii)	(iv)	(ii)	(i)	☐
(D)	(iii)	(ii)	(i)	(iv)	☐

29. Match the following

Column I	Column II
A. Impact and incidence of tax lie on same person	(i) Special assessment
B. Non-debt capital receipt	(ii) Direct tax
C. Tax revenue receipt	(iii) Disinvestment
D. Non-tax revenue receipt	(iv) GST

Codes

	A	B	C	D	
(A)	(ii)	(i)	(iv)	(iii)	☐
(B)	(ii)	(iv)	(iii)	(i)	☐
(C)	(ii)	(iii)	(i)	(iv)	☐
(D)	(ii)	(iii)	(iv)	(i)	☐

30. Match the following

Column I	Column II
A. Revenue deficit	(i) Estimated government receipts < Estimated government expenditure
B. Fiscal deficit	(ii) FD – Interest payments
C. Primary deficit	(iii) Revenue expenditure – Revenue receipts
D. Deficit budget	(iv) Total expenditure – Total receipts excluding borrowings

Codes

	A	B	C	D	
(A)	(iii)	(ii)	(iv)	(i)	☐
(B)	(iii)	(iv)	(ii)	(i)	☐
(C)	(iii)	(i)	(ii)	(iv)	☐
(D)	(iii)	(iv)	(i)	(ii)	☐

Assertion-Reason Questions

No. of Questions : **10** Suggested Time : **15 Minutes**

Direction Each of the question given below consist of the two statements; one labelled as **Assertion** (A) and other as **Reason** (R). List of common options applicable for each question is given below

(A) Both Assertion (A) and Reason (R) are true and Reason (R) is the correct explanation of Assertion (A)
(B) Both Assertion (A) and Reason (R) are true, but Reason (R) is not the correct explanation of Assertion (A)
(C) Assertion (A) is true, but Reason (R) is false
(D) Assertion (A) is false, but Reason (R) is true

You have to select the codes as *A, B, C* or *D* as your answer to the question by marking (✓) in the response box given against each option.

1. **Assertion (A)** The government budget is a constitutional requirement in India.

   Reason (R) It outlines the actual revenue and expenditure for a specific period, typically a fiscal year.

   (A) ☐ (B) ☐
   (C) ☐ (D) ☐

2. **Assertion (A)** The division of the government budget into revenue and capital accounts allows for a better understanding of the short-term and long-term financial implications of budgetary decisions.

   Reason (R) While the revenue account focuses on current financial transactions, the capital account encompasses investments in assets and liabilities with long-term benefits.

   (A) ☐ (B) ☐ (C) ☐ (D) ☐

3. **Assertion (A)** The redistribution function of the government budget aims to ensure a fair distribution of income in the society.

   Reason (R) Personal disposable income refers to the portion of private income that households can spend before government taxes.

   (A) ☐ (B) ☐ (C) ☐ (D) ☐

4. **Assertion (A)** Capital receipts of the government are classified into tax and non-tax revenues, with tax revenues comprising direct and indirect taxes.

   Reason (R) The redistribution objective of the government is achieved through progressive income taxation, where higher incomes are subjected to higher tax rates and through proportional taxation on corporate profits.

   (A) ☐ (B) ☐
   (C) ☐ (D) ☐

5. **Assertion (A)** Capital receipts of the government include money obtained from loans and the sale of assets, which can be either debt creating or non-debt creating.

   Reason (R) Loans taken by the government create liabilities, while the sale of government assets reduces its total financial assets.

   (A) ☐ (B) ☐
   (C) ☐ (D) ☐

6. **Assertion (A)** Public goods provided by the government, such as national defense and public parks, offer benefits that are non-rivalrous and non-excludable.

   Reason (R) Unlike private goods, the consumption of public goods by one individual does not diminish their availability to others, allowing multiple individuals to benefit simultaneously.

   (A) ☐ (B) ☐
   (C) ☐ (D) ☐

7. **Assertion (A)** Budgetary deficit occurs when a government's total expenditures exceed its total revenues within a fiscal year.

   Reason (R) Budgetary deficit indicates that the government is spending more money than it is earning, leading to a shortfall that needs to be financed through borrowing or other means.

   (A) ☐ (B) ☐ (C) ☐ (D) ☐

8. **Assertion (A)** Revenue deficit is a component of fiscal deficit and indicates that a significant portion of government borrowing is utilised for consumption expenditure rather than investment.

   Reason (R) Fiscal deficit represents the total borrowing requirements of the government from all sources, including both revenue and capital expenditures.

   (A) ☐ (B) ☐
   (C) ☐ (D) ☐

9. **Assertion (A)** Fiscal deficit can lead to a debt trap due to the cycle of borrowing to repay previous loans, ultimately hampering economic growth.

Reason (R) Increased borrowing to finance fiscal deficit results in higher interest payments, leading to a rise in revenue expenditure and contributing to a vicious circle of debt accumulation.

(A) ☐ (B) ☐ (C) ☐ (D) ☐

10. **Assertion (A)** The primary deficit measures the fiscal imbalance resulting from current expenditures exceeding revenues, excluding interest payments.

Reason (R) Net interest liabilities, included in the calculation of gross primary deficit, consist of interest payments minus interest receipts on net domestic lending.

(A) ☐ (B) ☐ (C) ☐ (D) ☐

Correct/Incorrect Statements

No. of Questions : **8** Suggested Time : **15 Minutes**

Direction Each of the question given below consist of the two statements. List of common options applicable for each question is given below

(A) Both statements are correct
(B) Both statements are incorrect
(C) Statement I is correct and Statement II is incorrect
(D) Statement I is incorrect and Statement II is correct

You have to select the codes as *A, B, C* or *D* as your answer to the question by marking (✓) in the response box given against each option.

1. **Statement I** There may be times when demand exceeds available output under conditions of high employment and thus may give rise to inflation. In such situations, restrictive conditions may be needed to reduce demand.

Statement II The intervention of the government whether to expand demand or reduce it constitutes the redistribution function.

(A) ☐ (B) ☐
(C) ☐ (D) ☐

2. **Statement I** The receipts and expenditures shown in the budget, are not the actual figures, but the estimated values for the coming fiscal year. Fiscal year is taken from 1st April to 31st March.

Statement II Budget is prepared by government at all levels, i.e. central government, state government and local government, prepares its respective annual budget.

(A) ☐ (B) ☐
(C) ☐ (D) ☐

3. **Statement I** Capital expenditure is expenditure incurred for purposes other than the creation of physical or financial assets of the central government.

Statement II Interest payments, salaries and pensions are some examples of capital expenditure of the government.

(A) ☐ (B) ☐
(C) ☐ (D) ☐

4. **Statement I** Payment of interest on loans is a revenue expenditure as it neither creates assets nor reduces liabilities.

Statement II Revenue expenditures are recurring in nature as such expenditures are incurred on day-to-day activities.

(A) ☐ (B) ☐
(C) ☐ (D) ☐

5. **Statement I** When the government incurs a revenue deficit, it implies that the government is dissaving and is using up the savings of the other sectors of the economy to finance a part of its consumption expenditure.

Statement II Since a major part of revenue expenditure is committed expenditure, it cannot be reduced. Often the government reduces productive capital expenditure or welfare expenditure. This would mean lower growth and adverse welfare implications.

(A) ☐ (B) ☐ (C) ☐ (D) ☐

6. **Statement I** By borrowing, the government does not transfer the burden of reduced consumption on future generations.

Statement II A high fiscal deficit may not necessarily lead to inflation if it is accompanied by increased demand and greater output.

(A) ☐ (B) ☐ (C) ☐ (D) ☐

7. **Statement I** Revenue deficit implies higher inflation in the economy.

Statement II Fiscal deficit implies increased foreign dependence on the economy.

(A) ☐ (B) ☐
(C) ☐ (D) ☐

8. **Statement I** Primary deficit can be reduced by increasing fiscal deficit.

Statement I Fiscal deficit can be reduced by increasing public expenditure.

(A) ☐ (B) ☐
(C) ☐ (D) ☐

Case Based Questions

No. of Questions : 2 Suggested Time : **10 Minutes**

Direction This section contains 2 cases each having 4 questions of 1 mark each. You have to write the answer of each question based on the context of the related case.

Case 1 Government Unveils Ambitious Budget to Revitalise Economy Amidst Pandemic Fallout

In a bid to navigate the economic challenges posed by the ongoing Covid-19 pandemic, the Government of India has unveiled an ambitious budget aimed at revitalising the economy and fostering inclusive growth. The budget presented by finance minister focuses on key areas such as healthcare, infrastructure, education and job creation.

One of the central pillars of the budget is healthcare reform, with significant allocations towards strengthening the healthcare infrastructure, procuring vaccines and bolstering the public health system to combat future health crises effectively. Investments in healthcare are seen as crucial to building resilience against pandemics and ensuring the well-being of citizens.

Furthermore, the budget prioritises infrastructure development, with a particular emphasis on transportation, energy and digital connectivity projects. These investments are expected to stimulate economic activity, create employment opportunities and enhance productivity across various sectors.

Education emerges as another key area of focus, with measures to improve access to quality education, skill development initiatives and investments in research and innovation. The government aims to equip the youth with the necessary skills and knowledge to thrive in a rapidly evolving global economy.

Additionally, the budget outlines measures to support Small and Medium-sized Enterprises (SMEs), including tax incentives, credit support and regulatory reforms to promote entrepreneurship and facilitate business growth. SMEs are recognised as engines of economic growth and job creation, particularly in the post-pandemic recovery phase. In conclusion, the government's budget for the fiscal year reflects a comprehensive strategy to address the socio-economic impacts of the pandemic and steer the country towards sustainable development and prosperity.

Questions

(i) What is the central focus of the Indian government's budget, as highlighted in the article?

(A) Strengthening the defense sector ☐

(B) Revitalising the economy amidst the pandemic fallout ☐

(C) Investing in luxury infrastructure projects ☐

(D) Enhancing diplomatic relations with neighbouring countries ☐

(ii) .... sector receives significant allocations in the budget to combat future health crises effectively.

(iii) What is the main objective of investing in infrastructure development projects?

(A) To stimulate economic activity and create employment opportunities ☐

(B) To promote tourism and hospitality sector ☐

(C) To boost luxury real estate market ☐

(D) To fund overseas projects ☐

(iv) .... measures are outlined in the budget to support Small and Medium-sized Enterprises (SMEs).

Case 2 The government of Country X faces a persistent budgetary deficit, where expenditures consistently surpass revenue collection. Despite attempts to curtail spending and enhance revenue streams, the deficit persists, challenging fiscal stability.

To address this, the government has instituted measures to narrow the deficit and restore fiscal health. However, challenges persist as expenditure on administration and maintenance remains high, exacerbating the deficit. Moreover, the reliance on borrowings and deficit financing further compounds the issue.

Efforts to mitigate the deficit include reducing non-essential expenditure, enhancing revenue through tax reforms and promoting fiscal responsibility. Nevertheless, tackling the deficit remains a complex task, requiring concerted efforts to balance fiscal prudence with socio-economic needs.

Questions

(i) The government's revenue deficit arises when its .... exceed its ....

(ii) Fiscal deficit is calculated as total budget expenditure minus total budget receipts excluding ....

(iii) Which of the following is a measure to reduce revenue deficit?

(A) Increasing government expenditure ☐

(B) Reducing subsidies ☐

(C) Decreasing tax revenue ☐

(D) Expanding non-developmental expenditure ☐

(iv) What is the implication of primary deficit?

(A) Indicates the extent of government borrowing for interest payments ☐

(B) Reflects the financial burden on citizens ☐

(C) Reflects the extent of current government policy adding to future burdens ☐

(D) Indicates the excess of total expenditure over revenue receipts ☐

Subjective Questions

Free Response Questions, Open-ended Questions etc.

No. of Questions : 8 **Suggested Time : 60 Minutes**

1. Interpret the image given below and discuss the highlighted objective of the government budget.

2. Suppose a country is experiencing high unemployment rates and sluggish economic growth. As an economic advisor to the government, propose a set of fiscal policy measures that could be implemented to stimulate economic activity and create employment opportunities while maintaining fiscal sustainability.

3. With valid reasons, classify the following into capital receipts or revenue receipts of the government *[CBSE 2024]*
   (i) Dividend received by the government from a Maharatan company.
   (ii) Receipts of the government from sale of shares of a Public Sector Undertaking (PSU) in open market.
   (iii) Debt cleared by Sri Lanka Government to the Indian Government.

4. Compare and contrast the implications of fiscal deficit and revenue deficit on the economy and discuss how each deficit affects key economic indicators such as inflation, growth and external debt.

5. Explain the potential consequences of a persistent fiscal deficit on a country's economy in simple terms.

   How might it affect future generations, the government's ability to provide essential services and overall economic stability?

6. "The government budget serves as a comprehensive financial plan outlining expected revenues and expenditures for the upcoming fiscal year, impacting various aspects of the economy."

   How does the government budget influence economic decision-making and resource allocation within a country?

   Provide examples to illustrate its significance in shaping economic policies and priorities.

7. Study the given picture carefully.

   Sources of State and Local Government Tax Revenues for a Financial Year

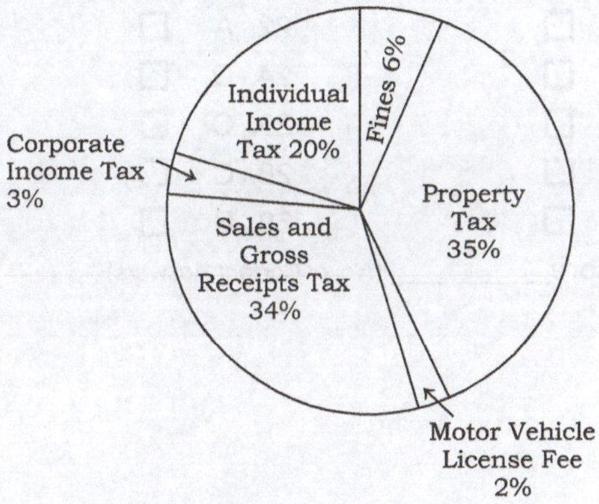

Answer the following questions based on common knowledge and picture

(i) Categorise the given items in the picture into tax/non-tax receipts.

(ii) "Government has started spending more on providing free services like education and health to the poor."

In the light of above statement, explain how the government can use the budgetary policy in reducing 'inequalities of income'. *[CBSE 2023]*

8. According to the data released by the Controller General of Accounts (CGA) fiscal deficit during April-August was at 109.3% of the annual target estimated in the budget. In absolute terms, the fiscal deficit was at ₹ 8,70,347 crore. It stood at 78.7% of Budget Estimates (BE) in the corresponding period of the last fiscal.

Fiscal deficit or the gap between expenditure and revenue had breached the annual target in July. The government had pegged fiscal deficit for 2020-21 at ₹ 7.96 lakh crore or 3.5 percent of GDP in the budget presented by Finance Minister Nirmala Sitharaman in February.

Source *The Economic Times, 30th September, 2020*

(i) Explain any three implications of fiscal deficit.

(ii) Briefly explain how the fiscal deficit of the government can be reduced.

Answers

If your answer matches with the answer given here then put (✓) in the box otherwise put (✗). In case you did not attempt the question leave the box blank.

Multiple Choice Questions

1. C ☐	2. A ☐
3. A ☐	4. B ☐
5. C ☐	6. B ☐
7. B ☐	8. D ☐
9. B ☐	10. C ☐
11. B ☐	12. D ☐
13. B ☐	14. B ☐
15. C ☐	16. C ☐
17. B ☐	18. C ☐
19. C ☐	20. C ☐
21. C ☐	22. A ☐
23. C ☐	24. D ☐
25. B ☐	26. C ☐
27. A ☐	28. C ☐
29. D ☐	30. B ☐

Your Score__________ *(No. of Correct Answers)*

Assertion-Reason Questions

1. C ☐	2. A ☐
3. C ☐	4. D ☐
5. B ☐	6. A ☐
7. A ☐	8. A ☐
9. A ☐	10. A ☐

Your Score__________ *(No. of Correct Answers)*

Correct/Incorrect Statements

1. C ☐	2. A ☐
3. B ☐	4. A ☐
5. A ☐	6. D ☐
7. A ☐	8. B ☐

Your Score__________ *(No. of Correct Answers)*

Case Based Questions

1. (i) B ☐	(iii) A ☐
2.(iii) B ☐	(iv) C ☐

Your Score__________ *(No. of Correct Answers)*

Explanations

Multiple Choice Questions

1. (C) The government budget is a plan that is subject to approval by the legislative body, as mandated by the constitution
2. (A) capital, decrease in assets
3. (A) The budget that relates to the current financial year only is included in the revenue budget, which covers day-to-day expenses like salaries and subsidies.

   The capital budget, on the other hand, concerns the government's assets and liabilities, including long-term investments in infrastructure and equipment.
4. (B) By adjusting aggregate demand to correct fluctuations in income and employment
5. (C) Taxes and duties collected by the government
6. (B) Only (ii)
7. (B) The government budget serves as a crucial policy instrument to combat fluctuations in the economy, primarily aiming at stabilising prices.

   Through fiscal measures like taxation and spending, the budget endeavours to mitigate inflationary pressures or economic downturns, ensuring stability in price levels for sustainable economic growth.
8. (D) Ministry of education has got more funds than ministry of rural development as education is one of the most important components of human capital formation
9. (B) Redistribution of income and wealth refers to the process by which resources, whether monetary or asset-based, are reallocated within a society to reduce disparities among its members.
10. (C) Vaccinating the adult population of India without charge is categorised as revenue nature expenditure because it involves ongoing operational costs for providing public services without creating long-term assets or reducing liabilities.
11. (B) Interest earned on government investments
12. (D) The revenue expenditure is incurred for day-to-day expenses and does not create assets or reduce liabilities.
13. (B) Capital expenditure involves investment in physical or financial assets, such as infrastructure projects like constructing highways and bridges, aimed at fostering economic growth.
14. (B) Capital expenditure involves the acquisition of assets or the reduction of liabilities, such as repaying borrowings, while revenue expenditure pertains to day-to-day expenses incurred by the government.
15. (C) When expenditure exceeds revenue, it results in a budget deficit. A surplus budget occurs when revenue exceeds expenditure.
16. (C) It creates inflationary pressure in the economy
17. (B) When the government recovers loans that it had extended previously, it constitutes a non-debt creating capital receipt because it does not involve borrowing but rather the retrieval of funds lent out earlier.
18. (C) Both (i) and (ii)
19. (C) free-rider
20. (C) Both (A) and (B)
21. (C) escheat
22. (A) Revenue Deficit = 500 (Revenue Expenditure) – 400 (Revenue Receipts) = ₹ 100 million
23. (C) Both (i) and (ii)
24. (D) The difference between the government's total expenditure and its total receipts, excluding borrowing
25. (B) Fiscal Deficit = Total Budget Expenditure – Total Budget Receipts (Excluding borrowings)

    = 800 – 600 = ₹ 200 crore
26. (C) Escalation of national debt burden
27. (A) (iv) (iii) (ii) (i)
28. (C) (iii) (iv) (ii) (i)
29. (D) (ii) (iii) (iv) (i)
30. (B) (iii) (iv) (ii) (i)

Assertion-Reason Questions

1. (C) Assertion (A) is true, but Reason (R) is false
2. (A) Both Assertion (A) and Reason (R) are true and Reason (R) is the correct explanation of Assertion (A)
3. (C) Assertion (A) is true, but Reason (R) is false
4. (D) The capital receipts of the government are not classified into tax and non-tax revenue; rather, they include borrowings and disinvestment proceeds.
5. (B) Both Assertion (A) and Reason (R) are true, but Reason (R) is not the correct explanation of Assertion (A)
6. (A) Both Assertion (A) and Reason (R) are true and Reason (R) is the correct explanation of Assertion (A)
7. (A) Both Assertion (A) and Reason (R) are true and Reason (R) is the correct explanation of Assertion (A)
8. (A) Both Assertion (A) and Reason (R) are true and Reason (R) is the correct explanation of Assertion (A)
9. (A) Both Assertion (A) and Reason (R) are true and Reason (R) is the correct explanation of Assertion (A)
10. (A) Both Assertion (A) and Reason (R) are true and Reason (R) is the correct explanation of Assertion (A)

Correct/Incorrect Statements

1. (C) The redistribution function of the government budget typically involves policies and measures aimed at reducing income and wealth disparities within society, such as progressive taxation, social welfare programmes and targeted public spending.
2. (A) Both statements are correct
3. (B) The capital expenditure refers to spending incurred for the creation or acquisition of physical or financial assets that provide long-term benefits.

   Interest payments, salaries and pensions are examples of revenue expenditure, as they involve current expenses related to the operation of government activities.
4. (A) Both statements are correct
5. (A) Both statements are correct
6. (D) The government borrowing can transfer the burden of reduced consumption onto future generations, as it may lead to higher debt levels and interest payments that future taxpayers may need to address.
7. (A) Both statements are correct
8. (B) Primary deficit is calculated as fiscal deficit minus interest payments, so increasing fiscal deficit without addressing interest payments would likely result in a higher primary deficit. Increasing public expenditure may lead to an increase in fiscal deficit rather than a reduction.

Case Based Questions

1. (i) (B) Revitalising the economy amidst the pandemic fallout

   (ii) Healthcare

   (iii) (A) To stimulate economic activity and create employment opportunities

   (iv) Credit support and regulatory reforms
2. (i) expenditures revenue receipts

   (ii) borrowings

   (iii) (B) By reducing subsidies, the government can lower its expenditure, thereby narrowing the gap between revenue receipts and expenditures, which contributes to reducing the revenue deficit.

   (iv) (C) Reflects the extent of current government policy adding to future burdens

Subjective Questions

1. The given image highlights that government should focus on reducing inequalities through its redistribution function.

   Government can reduce the inequalities by charging high taxes from rich sections of the society and distribute this amount in the form of subsidies to poor people. This will help government to achieve its objective.

2. Fiscal policy measures to stimulate economic activity and employment may include increased government spending on infrastructure projects, tax cuts to boost consumer spending and targeted subsidies to support struggling industries. These measures should be complemented by monetary policy actions to ensure price stability and financial stability.

3. (i) Dividends received are revenue receipts as these receipts neither create any liabilities nor reduce any assets of the government. Also, these receipts are recurring in nature.
   (ii) Receipts of the government from the sale of shares of PSU are capital receipts as it reduces the assets of the government. Also, these receipts are non-recurring in nature.
   (iii) Debt cleared by Sri Lanka Government is a capital receipt as it reduces the assets of the government. This receipt is non-recurring in nature.

4. Fiscal deficit refers to the excess of total government expenditure over total revenue (excluding borrowing), while revenue deficit refers to the excess of revenue expenditure over revenue receipts.

   Fiscal deficit can lead to inflation and external debt accumulation, while revenue deficit indicates inefficient use of resources and can hinder investment in productive assets.

5. A persistent fiscal deficit happens when a country spends more money than it earns. It arises when government total expenditure is more than the government total receipts excluding borrowings. This can lead to several problems for the economy. Firstly, it can burden future generations with debt.

   Secondly, when the government keeps borrowing money, it might not have enough left to provide essential services like healthcare, education and infrastructure.

   Lastly, persistent fiscal deficits can make the economy unstable. When the government borrows too much, it can lead to higher interest rates and inflation. This can make it harder for businesses to borrow money, invest and grow.

   Overall, a persistent fiscal deficit can have serious consequences for a country's economy, affecting both present and future generations.

6. The government budget significantly influences economic decision-making and resource allocation within a country by delineating the expected revenues and expenditures for the fiscal year.

   e.g. Through budgetary allocations, the government can prioritise sectors such as healthcare, education, infrastructure and defense, reflecting its policy objectives and societal needs.

   Moreover, the budget serves as a tool for fiscal policy implementation, enabling the government to stimulate or restrain economic activity through taxation, expenditure and borrowing measures.

   Additionally, the budget signals the government's commitment to fiscal discipline, influencing investor confidence, market expectations and overall economic stability.

   Overall, the government budget plays a pivotal role in shaping economic policies, allocating resources efficiently and driving economic development.

7. (i) Tax receipts – Individual income tax, corporate income tax, sales and gross receipt tax, property tax.

   Non-tax receipts – Fines, motor vehicle license fee.

   (ii) Reducing inequality is a major objective of government's budget especially in developing country like India, where inequality of income and wealth is very high.

   Government uses its financial tools of taxation and subsidies to enhance equal distribution of income and wealth. In order to ensure equity of income, progressive tax structure is followed in India, which imposes higher burden of taxes on higher income group and lesser burden on lower income group.

   Also, those who earn below a substantial limit are exempted from payment of taxes.

   The additional income generated from higher income group is re-distributed by the government in the form of subsidies to the poor sections of the society, to ensure the objective of welfare.

   LPG subsidy is a good example of such re-distribution of income.

8. (i) A high fiscal deficit can have the following implications

(a) **Inflation** The primary source of borrowings for the government is the central bank. The government borrows from the central bank through deficit financing, which is the printing of new currency.
This leads to an increase in money circulation in the economy thus leading to inflation.

(b) **Burden of Debt on Future Generations** A mounting debt poses a very large burden on the future generations, who become liable to repay the existing obligations i.e. the principal amount and the interest.

(c) **Increased Risk of Debt-trap** Higher borrowings mean a larger amount of interest payments, which contributes to the revenue expenditures. The revenue deficit will rise. The fiscal deficit will then rise further, for which borrowings will have to be made again. This vicious cycle goes on and spirals the economy into a debt-trap.

(ii) A fiscal deficit is a difference between a government's total revenue and expenses in a given fiscal year. It indicates the extent to which a government relies on borrowing to finance its spending. A fiscal deficit can be funded by issuing government bonds, increasing taxes, or running down foreign exchange reserves.

CHAPTER -5

Foreign Exchange Rate and Balance of Payments

Types & Nos. of Questions

Multiple Choice Questions	-	32
Assertion-Reason Questions	-	10
Correct/Incorrect Statements	-	10
Case Based Questions	-	2 Cases, *each with four Questions*
Subjective Questions	-	8

Trend Analysis

On the basis of analysis of last 2 years' papers, it is found that on an average 2 Multiple Choice Questions and 1 Short Answer Type Question (Statement Based) are asked from this chapter. No case based question is asked but may be asked in coming exams.

Focus Topics of the Chapter

- Types of Foreign Exchange Rate
- Determination of Exchange Rate in a Free Market
- Components of Balance of Payments
- Equilibrium and Disequilibrium in Balance of Payments

Multiple Choice Questions

No. of Questions : **32** Suggested Time : **45 Minutes**

Direction Each of the question given below is Multiple Choice Question (MCQ) i.e. there are Four Options/ Choices for answer, out of which ONLY ONE is correct. You have to select the correct option. A response box is given with each option, mark (✓) in the box of the correct option. For each correct answer you will get 1 mark, while there is no penalty for incorrect answer or missed out questions.

1. Identify the correct reason(s) that may affect the demand for foreign exchange in an economy.

(i) Imports of visibles
(ii) Exports of invisibles
(iii) Remittances by residents working abroad
(iv) Purchase of assets abroad

Codes

(A) (i) and (ii) ☐ (B) (ii) and (iii) ☐
(C) (iii) and (iv) ☐ (D) (i) and (iv) ☐

2. A rise in price of foreign currency will lead to

(A) increase in exports ☐
(B) increase in imports ☐
(C) fall in imports ☐ (D) Both (A) and (C) ☐

3. Which of the following scenarios can lead to or represents an appreciation of the domestic currency?

(A) A decrease in the value of exports due to decreased global demand ☐
(B) An increase in the value of imports due to rising domestic consumer spending ☐
(C) A decrease in the exchange rate from 1 USD = 70 INR to 1 USD = 75 INR ☐
(D) An increase in foreign investment inflows due to higher interest rates in the domestic economy ☐

4. Which of the following factors is most likely to trigger a decline in the value of a domestic currency?

(A) Increased demand for domestic goods and services in foreign markets ☐
(B) Decrease in domestic interest rates relative to foreign interest rates ☐
(C) Reduction in government spending leading to a decrease in the budget deficit ☐
(D) Strengthening of the domestic economy due to increased exports ☐

5. How does an increase in income abroad affect the demand for domestic exports?

(A) It decreases demand for domestic exports ☐
(B) It increases demand for domestic exports ☐
(C) It has no effect on the demand for domestic exports ☐
(D) It causes fluctuations in the demand for domestic exports ☐

6. What is the relationship between a country's currency depreciation and the growth of its aggregate demand relative to the rest of the world?

(A) Currency depreciation occurs when a country's aggregate demand grows faster than the rest of the world's ☐
(B) Currency appreciation occurs when a country's aggregate demand grows faster than the rest of the world's ☐
(C) Currency depreciation occurs when a country's aggregate demand grows at the same rate as the rest of the world's ☐
(D) Currency depreciation is not influenced by the growth of a country's aggregate demand ☐

7. Identify the correct sequence.
(i) Demand for foreign currency increases
(ii) Depreciation of domestic currency
(iii) Imports increases
(iv) Demand curve shifts rightward

Codes
(A) (i), (ii), (iii), (iv) ☐
(B) (iv), (ii), (iii), (i) ☐
(C) (ii), (iv), (i), (iii) ☐
(D) (iii), (i), (iv), (ii) ☐

8. Which of the following statements best describes a characteristic of a fixed exchange rate system?
(A) Exchange rates are determined by supply and demand in the foreign exchange market ☐
(B) Central banks intervene regularly to adjust the exchange rate based on economic conditions ☐
(C) Currencies are pegged to a specific value against another currency or a basket of currencies ☐
(D) Exchange rates are allowed to fluctuate freely in response to market forces ☐

9. Suppose, the price of one UK Pound (£) has increased from ₹ 70 to ₹ 80, owing to market forces.
This means that value of Indian currency (₹) has ... . *[CBSE 2023]*
(A) appreciated ☐ (B) depreciated ☐
(C) revalued ☐ (D) devalued ☐

10. In the context of exchange rate systems, which of the following represents a critical weakness of a flexible exchange rate regime?
(A) Limited effectiveness in stabilising currency values during periods of economic turbulence ☐
(B) Increased susceptibility to speculative activities and currency market manipulations ☐
(C) Reduced attractiveness for international investors due to heightened exchange rate uncertainty ☐
(D) Higher likelihood of trade imbalances and disruptions in international commerce ☐

11. Find the odd one out in context of foreign exchange market.
(A) The market in which national currencies are traded for one another is known as the foreign exchange market ☐
(B) The major participants in the foreign exchange market are commercial banks, foreign exchange brokers and other authorised dealers and monetary authorities ☐
(C) The market gives an opportunity to shift the purchasing power to rest of the world ☐
(D) Facilitating the transfer of goods and services across international borders ☐

12. What is being indicated by the following picture?

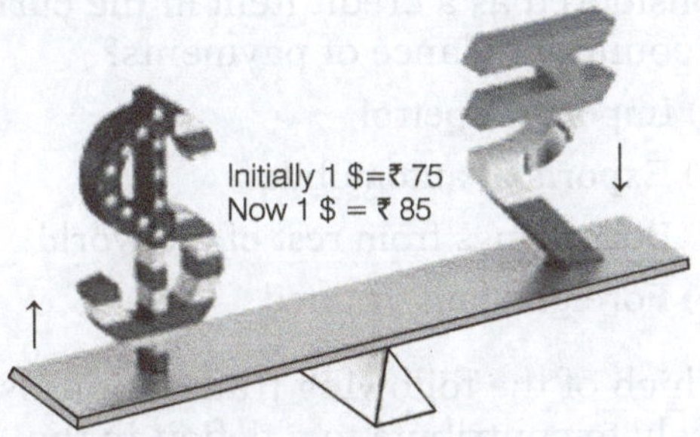

(A) Appreciation of domestic currency ☐
(B) Depreciation of domestic currency ☐
(C) Either (A) or (B) ☐
(D) None of the above ☐

13. India is exporting the pearls and precious stones to USA. This export will be recorded in ………… account of balance of payments of India.
(A) current account ☐
(B) capital account ☐
(C) financial account ☐
(D) reserve account ☐

14. There has been an increase in the exports of petroleum products by India to other countries. This will result in
(A) BoP surplus ☐
(B) BoP deficit ☐
(C) BoT surplus ☐
(D) BoT deficit ☐

15. Which of the following statements is incorrect in context of BoP?
(A) In balance of payments, repayment of loans by Indian government to Russian government will be indicated as debit item ☐
(B) Remittances received from abroad will be recorded as credit item of BoP ☐
(C) Deficit in balance of trade will lead to deficit in BoP ☐
(D) Foreign investments are recorded in capital account of BoP ☐

16. Which of the following transactions will be considered as a credit item in the current account of balance of payments?
(A) Imports of petrol ☐
(B) Exports of automobiles ☐
(C) Borrowings from rest of the world ☐
(D) Foreign loans granted ☐

17. Which of the following transactions is most likely to contribute to a deficit in the balance of payments?
(A) Increase in tourism revenue from foreign visitors ☐
(B) Repayment of foreign loans and interest ☐
(C) Surge in foreign direct investment inflows ☐
(D) Growth in remittances from nationals working abroad ☐

18. Which condition determines the equilibrium rate of exchange in an economy?
(i) When the supply of domestic currency equals the demand for foreign currency
(ii) When the supply of foreign currency equals the demand for domestic currency
(iii) When the supply of foreign exchange equals the demand for foreign exchange
(iv) When the supply of domestic currency exceeds the demand for foreign currency

Codes
(A) Only (iii) ☐ (B) Only (iv) ☐
(C) (i) and (ii) ☐ (D) (ii) and (iv) ☐

19. The Indian government has implemented policies to liberalise and simplify regulations governing foreign investment in various sectors of the economy. These reforms have included raising FDI caps, easing entry restrictions and streamlining approval processes for foreign investors. By making it easier for foreign companies to invest in India, the government aims to attract more FDI inflows, stimulate economic growth, create jobs and enhance technology transfer and infrastructure development.
In context of the above case, which one is true?
(A) Increase in foreign investments which will lead to capital account deficit ☐
(B) Increase in foreign investments which will lead to capital account surplus ☐
(C) Increase in foreign investments which will lead to outflow of foreign currency ☐
(D) Increase in foreign investments which will lead to increase in unilateral transfers ☐

20. Indian government has recently taken loan from Japan. This will be recorded in .... side of .... account of BoP.
(A) credit, capital ☐
(B) credit, current ☐
(C) debit, capital ☐
(D) debit, current ☐

21. Identify, which of the following is not a source of demand for foreign exchange for Indian economy? [CBSE 2024]

(A) Import of goods and services ☐
(B) Remittances by foreigners living in India to their families abroad ☐
(C) Indian tourists visiting foreign countries ☐
(D) Loans from Rest of the World (RoW) ☐

22. If a country experiences a surge in imports due to increased consumer demand for foreign luxury goods, what type of item in the balance of payments does this represent?
(A) Accommodating ☐
(B) Autonomous ☐
(C) Transfer ☐ (D) Investment ☐

23. As per the Reserve Bank of India (RBI) press report, dated 22nd June, 2022.

"Net Foreign Portfolio Investment (FPI) recorded an outflow of US$15.2 billion mainly from the equity market."

The above transaction will be recorded in the ...... account on ...... side of balance of payments account of India. *[CBSE 2023]*
(A) current, credit ☐
(B) current, debit ☐
(C) capital, credit ☐ (D) capital, debit ☐

24. A country experiences a persistent deficit in its balance of payments. Which of the following scenarios could best explain this situation, considering both autonomous and accommodating items?
(A) The government implements austerity measures to reduce public spending, leading to decreased imports and a trade surplus ☐
(B) Foreign investors withdraw their investments due to uncertainty in the domestic economy, exacerbating the deficit in the financial account ☐
(C) The central bank intervenes in the foreign exchange market to prevent the domestic currency from appreciating, despite underlying market pressures ☐
(D) Rising global demand for the country's exports drives an increase in export earnings, resulting in a surplus in the current account ☐

25. Assuming that, the following data is given for an imaginary economy

Items \ Year	2020 (₹ in crore)	2021 (₹ in crore)
Exports of visibles	1,000	1,100
Imports of visibles	800	850

The balance of trade from 2020 to 2021 ...... by ₹ ...... crore. *[CBSE 2023]*
(A) increased, 200 ☐
(B) decreased, 200 ☐
(C) increased, 50 ☐
(D) decreased, 50 ☐

26. The BoP status of an economy affects the foreign exchange rate. In this context, how does a surplus in the balance of payments affect the foreign exchange rate of a country's currency?
(A) It causes the currency to appreciate due to increased demand in the foreign exchange market ☐
(B) It leads to depreciation of the currency as domestic goods become less competitive in international markets ☐
(C) It has no impact on the foreign exchange rate, as it is determined solely by government interventions ☐
(D) It causes volatility in the foreign exchange rate, making it unpredictable for investors and businesses ☐

27. The transactions which are recorded under the term 'errors and omissions' in the Balance of Payments (BoP) refer to
(A) mistakes made by government agencies in recording international transactions ☐
(B) unrecorded transactions that occur in the economy and are not captured in the BoP accounts ☐

(C) adjustments made by central banks to correct discrepancies in the BoP data ☐

(D) inaccuracies in exchange rate calculations used to convert foreign currency transactions into domestic currency equivalents ☐

28. What is best depicted by the following picture?

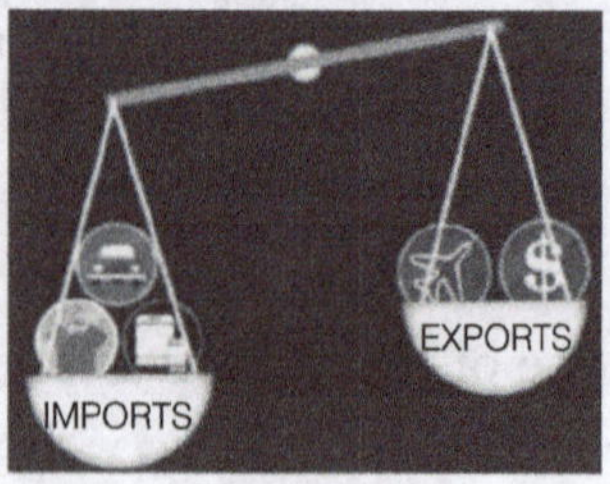

(A) BoP deficit ☐

(B) BoP current account deficit ☐

(C) BoP capital account deficit ☐

(D) None of the above ☐

29. Identify the missing values.

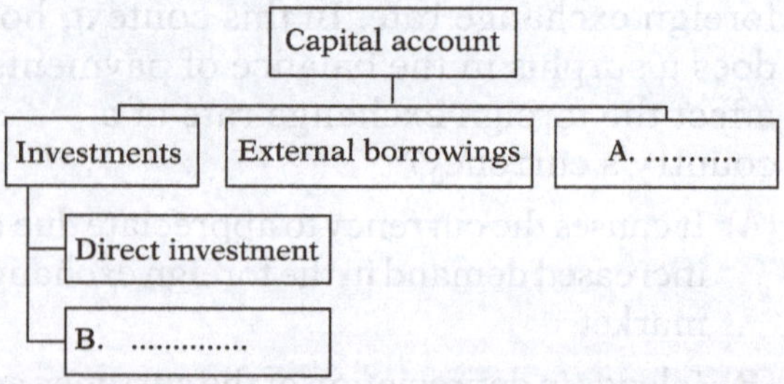

(A) External assistance, Portfolio investment ☐

(B) Portfolio investment, External assistance ☐

(C) Commercial borrowings, Portfolio investments ☐

(D) Commercial borrowing, External assistance ☐

30. Match the following

Column I	Column II
A. Tourism to rest of the world	(i) Supply for foreign currency
B. Investments from abroad	(ii) Flexible exchange rate
C. Exchange rate through market forces	(iii) Dirty floating
D. Managed floating	(iv) Demand for foreign currency

Codes

	A	B	C	D	
(A)	(iv)	(i)	(ii)	(iii)	☐
(B)	(iv)	(ii)	(i)	(iii)	☐
(C)	(iv)	(iii)	(ii)	(i)	☐
(D)	(iv)	(i)	(iii)	(ii)	☐

31. Match the following

Column I	Column II
A. Balance of trade	(i) Remittances from abroad
B. Accommodating items	(ii) Profit motive
C. Autonomous items	(iii) Correct BoP surplus or deficit
D. Unilateral transfers	(iv) Exports and imports of goods

Codes

	A	B	C	D	
(A)	(iv)	(ii)	(iii)	(i)	☐
(B)	(iv)	(iii)	(ii)	(i)	☐
(C)	(iv)	(iii)	(i)	(ii)	☐
(D)	(iv)	(i)	(ii)	(iii)	☐

32. Match the following

Column I	Column II
A. Exports of goods	(i) Capital account, debit side
B. Import of technical services	(ii) Current account, credit side
C. Investments from rest of the world	(iii) Capital account, credit side
D. Borrowings to abroad	(iv) Current account, debit side

Codes

	A	B	C	D	
(A)	(ii)	(iii)	(iv)	(i)	☐
(B)	(ii)	(iv)	(i)	(iii)	☐
(C)	(ii)	(iv)	(iii)	(i)	☐
(D)	(ii)	(i)	(iii)	(iv)	☐

Assertion-Reason Questions

No. of Questions : **10** Suggested Time : **15 Minutes**

Direction Each of the question given below consist of the two statements; one labelled as **Assertion** (A) and other as **Reason** (R). List of common options applicable for each question is given below

(A) Both Assertion (A) and Reason (R) are true and Reason (R) is the correct explanation of Assertion (A)
(B) Both Assertion (A) and Reason (R) are true, but Reason (R) is not the correct explanation of Assertion (A)
(C) Assertion (A) is true, but Reason (R) is false
(D) Assertion (A) is false, but Reason (R) is true

You have to select the codes as *A, B, C* or *D* as your answer to the question by marking (✓) in the response box given against each option.

1. **Assertion (A)** The exchange rate of a country's currency is influenced by the demand and supply of foreign currency.

Reason (R) An increase in the demand for foreign currency relative to its supply, leads to an appreciation of the domestic currency, while a decrease in demand or an increase in supply results in an depreciation of the domestic currency.

(A) ☐ (B) ☐ (C) ☐ (D) ☐

2. **Assertion (A)** If there is rise in income abroad, domestic exports will rise and supply curve of foreign currency will shift rightward.

Reason (R) Rise in exports will lead to fall in foreign exchange rate and there will be depreciation of domestic currency.

(A) ☐ (B) ☐ (C) ☐ (D) ☐

3. **Assertion (A)** Due to depreciation of foreign currency, there will be fall in domestic exports.

Reason (R) Foreigners will have to pay more domestic currency to purchase the same quantity of domestic product.

(A) ☐ (B) ☐ (C) ☐ (D) ☐

4. **Assertion (A)** The foreign exchange market facilitates the conversion of one currency into another and determines exchange rates.

Reason (R) It serves as a platform for international trade, investment, speculation and central bank interventions, influencing the flow of capital and impacting a country's economy.

(A) ☐ (B) ☐ (C) ☐ (D) ☐

5. **Assertion (A)** The revenue generated from international tourism will be recorded in balance of invisibles.

Reason (R) This will increase inflow of foreign currency and hence will be recorded as debit item of BoP.

(A) ☐ (B) ☐ (C) ☐ (D) ☐

6. **Assertion (A)** A surplus current account means that the nation is a lender to other countries.

Reason (R) This means that the country is earning more than it is spending internationally. As a result, the country accumulates net foreign assets, making it a lender to other countries.

(A) ☐ (B) ☐
(C) ☐ (D) ☐

7. **Assertion (A)** Borrowings from abroad are component of capital account of BoP.

Reason (R) Interest on borrowings is the component of current account of BoP.

(A) ☐ (B) ☐ (C) ☐ (D) ☐

8. **Assertion (A)** Many new MNCs have been established due to an initiative 'Make in India' taken by the Indian government which has led to decrease in foreign direct investment.

Reason (R) This will lead to change in assets of the economy and hence will be recorded in capital account of BoP.

(A) ☐ (B) ☐ (C) ☐ (D) ☐

9. **Assertion (A)** A surplus on BoP is indicated by excess of autonomous receipts over autonomous payments.

Reason (R) The decrease in official reserves is indicated by negative sign in BoP.

(A) ☐ (B) ☐ (C) ☐ (D) ☐

10. **Assertion (A)** Shares of a foreign company purchased by an Indian is the part of portfolio investment.

Reason (R) Acquisition of an Indian company by a foreign company will be recorded under capital account and credit side of BoP.

(A) ☐ (B) ☐ (C) ☐ (D) ☐

Correct/Incorrect Statements

No. of Questions : **10** Suggested Time : **15 Minutes**

Direction Each of the question given below consist of the two statements. List of common options applicable for each question is given below

(A) Both statements are correct
(B) Both statements are incorrect
(C) Statement I is correct and Statement II is incorrect
(D) Statement I is incorrect and Statement II is correct

You have to select the codes as *A, B, C* or *D* as your answer to the question by marking (✓) in the response box given against each option.

1. **Statement I** Depreciation of domestic currency occurs when the value of domestic currency decreases in relation to the value of foreign currency.

Statement II Revaluation is the rise in the value of domestic currency in relation to foreign currency as planned by Central Bank in a situation when exchange rate is not determined by market forces of demand and supply.

(A) ☐ (B) ☐
(C) ☐ (D) ☐

2. **Statement I** A rise in price of foreign exchange will increase the cost of purchasing a foreign good. This reduces demand for imports and hence demand for foreign exchange also decreases, other things remaining constant.

Statement II A rise in price of foreign exchange will reduce the foreigner's cost while purchasing products from India, other things remaining constant. This increases India's exports and hence supply for foreign exchange may increase.

(A) ☐ (B) ☐ (C) ☐ (D) ☐

3. **Statement I** The exchange rate which is determined by the market forces of demand and supply is known as floating exchange rate.

Statement II Increase in exchange rate implies that the price of foreign currency (dollar) in terms of domestic currency (rupees) has increased. This is called appreciation of domestic currency (rupees) in terms of foreign currency (dollars).

(A) ☐ (B) ☐ (C) ☐ (D) ☐

4. **Statement I** Devaluation is said to occur, when the government decreases the exchange rate (thereby, making domestic currency costlier) in a fixed exchange rate system.

Statement II The major advantage of flexible exchange rate is that movements in the exchange rate automatically take care of the surpluses and deficits in the BoP.

(A) ☐ (B) ☐ (C) ☐ (D) ☐

5. **Statement I** An increase in foreign income leads to increase in exports and increases domestic output. It also improves the trade balance.

Statement II Trade deficits need not be alarming if the country invests the borrowed funds yielding a rate of growth higher than the interest rate.

(A) ☐ (B) ☐ (C) ☐ (D) ☐

6. **Statement I** Export of financial services by India will be recorded on credit side of current account.

Statement II Foreign Direct Investments in India will be recorded on credit side of capital account.

(A) ☐ (B) ☐ (C) ☐ (D) ☐

7. **Statement I** The Balance of Payments (BoP) record the transactions in goods, services and assets within the country and between the residents of a country with the rest of the world for a specified time period, typically a year.

Statement II There are two main accounts in the BoP, i.e. the current account and the capital account.

(A) ☐ (B) ☐

(C) ☐ (D) ☐

8. **Statement I** Dividends received by a domestic company from its overseas subsidiaries would be recorded in the balance of invisibles as a component of income.

Statement II BoP current account records all such transactions that will bring change in the assets and liabilities status of the economy.

(A) ☐ (B) ☐

(C) ☐ (D) ☐

9. **Statement I** The capital account in the Balance of Payments (BoP) records international transactions involving assets, such as foreign direct investment and portfolio investment.

Statement II On the credit side of the BoP capital account, outflows of capital, such as domestic investment abroad, repayment of foreign loans and acquisition of foreign assets, are recorded, leading to a decrease in the country's external assets.

(A) ☐ (B) ☐ (C) ☐ (D) ☐

10. **Statement I** Deficit in capital account arises when capital inflows are greater than capital outflows, whereas surplus in capital account arises when capital inflows are lesser than capital outflows.

Statement II BoP always balances when official reserves account is a part of capital account and therefore Current account balance + Capital account balance = Zero.

(A) ☐ (B) ☐

(C) ☐ (D) ☐

Case Based Questions

No. of Questions : **2** Suggested Time : **10 Minutes**

Direction This section contain 2 cases each having 5 questions of 1 mark each. You have to write the answer of each question based on the context of the related case.

Case 1 Interest Rates and the Exchange Rate

In the short-run, another factor that is important in determining exchange rate movements is the interest rate differential i.e. the difference between interest rates between countries. There are huge funds owned by banks, multinational corporations and wealthy individuals which move around the world in search of the highest interest rates.

If we assume that government bonds in country A, pays 8 per cent rate of interest whereas equally safe bonds in county B yield 10 per cent, the interest rate differential is 2 per cent. Investors from country A will be attracted by the high interest rates in country B and will buy the currency of country B selling their own currency.

At the same time investors in country B will also find investing in their own country more attractive and will therefore demand less of country A's currency. This means that the demand curve for country A's currency will shift to the left and the supply curve will shift to the right causing a depreciation of country A's currency and an appreciation of country B's currency.

Thus, a rise in the interest rates at home often leads to an appreciation of the domestic currency. Here, the implicit assumption is that no restrictions exist in buying bonds issued by foreign governments.

Quetions

(i) The primary reason for investors from country A buying the currency of country B is.............. .

(ii) How does an increase in interest rates in country B affect the demand for country A's currency, according to the passage?

(A) It decreases the demand for country A's currency ☐

(B) It increases the demand for country A's currency ☐

(C) It has no effect on the demand for country A's currency ☐

(D) It causes the demand for country A's currency to fluctuate unpredictably ☐

(iii) What effect does the movement of funds in search of higher interest rates have, on the exchange rate between country A and country B?

(A) It causes the exchange rate to remain constant ☐

(B) It causes the exchange rate to appreciate for country A's currency and depreciate for country B's currency ☐

(C) It causes the exchange rate to depreciate for country A's currency and appreciate for country B's currency ☐

(D) It has no effect on the exchange rate between the two countries ☐

(iv) .... is the implicit assumption regarding investing in foreign government bonds.

Case 2 India's Balance of Payments (BoP) data for the latest quarter reflects several key trends in the country's international financial transactions. In the third quarter of the fiscal year 2023-24, India's current account deficit widened due to increased in imports of crude oil and gold, while exports showed moderate growth.

However, the capital account surplus expanded, driven by higher Foreign Direct Investment (FDI) inflows and robust portfolio investment. The Reserve Bank of India (RBI) continued to build its foreign exchange reserves, bolstering the country's external position amid global economic uncertainties.

Questions

(i) What was the primary factor contributing to the widening of India's current account deficit in the latest BoP data?

(A) Increased exports ☐

(B) Rising imports of crude oil and gold ☐

(C) Decrease in foreign direct investment ☐

(D) Appreciation of the Indian rupee ☐

(ii) …….. account experienced an expansion in surplus in India's BoP data for the third quarter of fiscal year 2023-24.

(iii) What contributed to the growth of India's capital account surplus in the latest BoP data?

(A) Decrease in foreign direct investment ☐

(B) Lower portfolio investment ☐

(C) Higher foreign direct investment and robust portfolio investment ☐

(D) Decline in remittances from abroad ☐

(iv) ……….. was mentioned in the case study as actively building foreign exchange reserves.

Subjective Questions

Free Response Questions, Open-ended Questions etc.

No. of Questions : 8 **Suggested Time : 60 Minutes**

1. In a flexible exchange rate system, the foreign exchange rate is primarily determined by market forces of supply and demand. Defend/ Refute. Also, explain the sources that lead to the demand and supply of foreign currency.

2. "Under the flexible exchange rate system, the central bank does not intervene in the foreign exchange market." Justify the statement, giving valid arguments. *[CBSE 2023]*

3. "Trade deficit must exist, if a country is facing situation of Current Account Deficit (CAD)." Defend or refute the above mentioned statement with valid arguments. *[CBSE 2024]*

4. Identify the type of statement in which transactions between the residents and rest of the world are recorded.

State the components of BoP capital account with example.

5. Which type of exchange rate system is depicted in the given image? Explain.

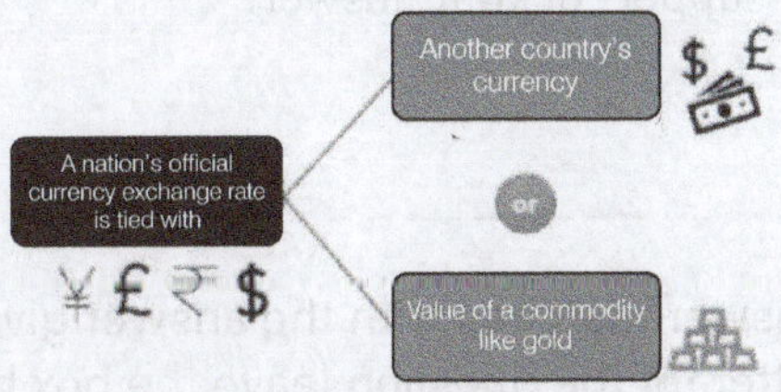

6. "Current account deficit in an economy must be financed by a corresponding capital account surplus."

Do you agree with the given statement? Give valid reason(s) in support of your answer.

7. India's Current Account Balance (CAB) recorded a surplus of US$ 19.8 billion (3.9 per cent of GDP) in Q1 of 2020-21 on top of a surplus of US$ 0.6 billion (0.1 per cent of GDP) in the preceding quarter, i.e., Q4 of 2019-20; a deficit of US$ 15.0 billion (2.1 per cent of GDP) was recorded a year ago [i.e. Q1 of 2019-20].

The surplus in the current account in Q1 of 2020-21 was on account of a sharp contraction in the trade deficit to US$ 10.0 billion due to steeper decline in merchandise imports relative to exports on a year-on-year basis. Net services receipts remained stable, primarily on the back of net earnings from computer services.

Private transfer receipts, mainly representing remittances by Indians employed overseas, amounted to US$ 18.2 billion, a decline of 8.7 per cent from their level a year ago. Net foreign portfolio investment was US$ 0.6 billion as compared with US$ 4.8 billion in Q1 of 2019-20 as net purchases in the equity market were offset by net sales in the debt segment.

With repayments exceeding fresh disbursals, external commercial borrowings to India recorded net outflow of US$ 1.1 billion in Q1 of 2020-21 as against an inflow of US$ 6.0 billion a year ago.

(i) Can a surplus in BoT account be sufficient to cover a deficit in BoP account? Explain with valid reasons.

(ii) Investments from abroad are a part of which transaction of BoP? Give reason in support of your answer.

8. India's Balance of Payments (BoP) reflects a complex interplay of economic factors influenced by domestic policies and global trends. In the latest data, India recorded a widening current account deficit due to increased imports of crude oil and electronics, while exports saw moderate growth.

The capital account surplus expanded, driven by higher Foreign Direct Investment (FDI) inflows and robust portfolio investment.

The Reserve Bank of India (RBI) continued to build its foreign exchange reserves, bolstering the country's external position amid global economic uncertainties.

However, concerns emerged over the sustainability of the deficit and the need for policy measures to address structural imbalances and promote export led growth.

(i) Elaborate the factors contributing to the widening current account deficit in India's balance of payments.

What are the implications of a widening current account deficit for India's economy and what policy measures could be adopted to address it?

(ii) How important is the role of Foreign Direct Investment (FDI) and portfolio investment in India's capital account surplus?

Discuss the potential benefits and challenges associated with a growing capital account surplus and propose strategies to leverage foreign investment for sustainable economic development in India.

Answers

If your answer matches with the answer given here then put (✓) in the box otherwise put (✗). In case you did not attempt the question leave the box blank.

Multiple Choice Questions

1. D ☐ 2. D ☐ 3. D ☐ 4. B ☐ 5. B ☐ 6. A ☐ 7. D ☐ 8. C ☐ 9. B ☐ 10. A ☐ 11. D ☐ 12. B ☐ 13. A ☐ 14. C ☐

15. C ☐ 16. B ☐
17. B ☐ 18. A ☐
19. B ☐ 20. A ☐
21. D ☐ 22. B ☐
23. D ☐ 24. C ☐
25. D ☐ 26. A ☐
27. B ☐ 28. B ☐
29. A ☐ 30. A ☐
31. B ☐ 32. C ☐

Your Score______ *(No. of Correct Answers)*

Assertion-Reason Questions

1. C ☐ 2. C ☐
3. A ☐ 4. A ☐
5. C ☐ 6. A ☐

7. B ☐ 8. D ☐
9. C ☐ 10. B ☐

Your Score______ *(No. of Correct Answers)*

Correct/Incorrect Statements

1. A ☐ 2. A ☐
3. C ☐ 4. D ☐
5. A ☐ 6. A ☐
7. D ☐ 8. C ☐
9. C ☐ 10. D ☐

Your Score______ *(No. of Correct Answers)*

Case Based Questions

1. (ii) A ☐ (iii) C ☐
2. (i) B ☐ (iii) C ☐

Your Score______ *(No. of Correct Answers)*

Explanations

Multiple Choice Questions

1. (D) (i) and (iv)
2. (D) A rise in the price of foreign currency will lead to an increase in exports because it makes the country's goods relatively cheaper for foreign buyers. Conversely, it will result in a fall in imports because foreign goods become relatively more expensive for domestic consumers.
3. (D) An increase in foreign investment inflows due to higher interest rates in the domestic economy
4. (B) Decrease in domestic interest rates relative to foreign interest rates
5. (B) When income abroad increases, it usually leads to higher purchasing power among consumers in foreign markets. This, in turn, can result in increased demand for goods and services produced domestically, leading to higher exports.
6. (A) Currency depreciation occurs when a country's aggregate demand grows faster than the rest of the world's
7. (D) (iii), (i), (iv), (ii)
8. (C) Currencies are pegged to a specific value against another currency or a basket of currencies
9. (B) When the price of one UK Pound (£) increases from ₹ 70 to ₹ 80, it means that more Indian Rupees are needed to purchase one Pound. This indicates a decrease in the value of the Indian currency relative to the Pound, reflecting currency depreciation.
10. (A) Limited effectiveness in stabilising currency values during periods of economic turbulence
11. (D) Option (D) is different because it talks about the purpose of the foreign exchange market, while the other options focus on various aspects of the market itself or its effects on currency value and balance of payments data.
12. (B) Depreciation of domestic currency
13. (A) The current account captures transactions related to trade in goods and services, as well as income flows between residents and non-residents.
14. (C) When there is an increase in exports of petroleum products by a country, it contributes to a surplus in the Balance of Trade (BoT). This surplus reflects that the value of exports, in this case, petroleum products, exceeds the value of imports, thereby indicating a positive trade balance.
15. (C) Deficit in balance of trade will lead to deficit in BoP
16. (B) When a country exports goods, such as automobiles, it earns foreign currency, which is considered a credit in the current account as it contributes to the country's income from abroad.
17. (B) Repayment of foreign loans and interest
18. (A) Only (iii)

19. (B) Increase in foreign investments which will lead to capital account surplus

20. (A) When the Indian government takes a loan from Japan, it represents an inflow of capital into the country.

In the Balance of Payments (BoP), such inflows of capital are recorded on the credit side of the capital account, indicating an increase in the country's liabilities to the rest of the world.

21. (D) Loans from Rest of the World (RoW)

22. (B) Autonomous transactions are those that occur without any specific corresponding transactions or actions by the government or central bank.

23. (D) The outflow of Foreign Portfolio Investment (FPI) from the equity market represents a capital transaction. In the balance of payments account of India, this transaction will be recorded in the capital account on the debit side since it indicates a reduction in the country's financial assets held by foreign investors.

24. (C) The central bank intervenes in the foreign exchange market to prevent the domestic currency from appreciating, despite underlying market pressures

25. (D) Balance of Trade = Exports of Visible – Imports of Visible

For the year 2020

Balance of Trade = 1,000 – 800 = ₹ 200 crore

For the year 2021

Balance of Trade = 1,100 – 850 = ₹ 250 crore

The change in the balance of trade from 2020 to 2021 = 200 crore – 250 crore = ₹ – 50 crore

26. (A) It causes the currency to appreciate due to increased demand in the foreign exchange market

27. (B) unrecorded transactions that occur in the economy and are not captured in the BoP accounts

28. (B) A current account deficit in the Balance of Payments (BoP) occurs when a country's imports of goods, services and transfers exceed its exports.

29. (A) External assistance, Portfolio investment

30. (A) (iv) (i) (ii) (iii)

31. (B) (iv) (iii) (ii) (i)

32. (C) (ii) (iv) (iii) (i)

Assertion-Reason Questions

1. (C) Assertion (A) is true, but Reason (R) is false
2. (C) An increase in exports typically leads to an appreciation of the domestic currency, as it increases the demand for the domestic currency in the foreign exchange market.
3. (A) Both Assertion (A) and Reason (R) are true and Reason (R) is the correct explanation of Assertion (A)
4. (A) Both Assertion (A) and Reason (R) are true and Reason (R) is the correct explanation of Assertion (A)
5. (C) Assertion (A) is true, but Reason (R) is false
6. (A) Both Assertion (A) and Reason (R) are true and Reason (R) is the correct explanation of Assertion (A)
7. (B) Both Assertion (A) and Reason (R) are true, but Reason (R) is not the correct explanation of Assertion (A)
8. (D) The establishment of New Multinational Corporations (MNCs) due to initiatives like 'Make in India' would likely increase Foreign Direct Investment (FDI).
9. (C) Assertion (A) is true, but Reason (R) is false
10. (B) Both Assertion (A) and Reason (R) are true, but Reason (R) is not the correct explanation of Assertion (A)

Correct/Incorrect Statements

1. (A) Both statements are correct
2. (A) Both statements are correct
3. (C) An increase in the exchange rate implies a depreciation of the domestic currency (rupees) as it now costs more rupees to buy the same amount of foreign currency (dollars).
4. (D) Devaluation means the government decreases the value of the domestic currency, making it cheaper.
5. (A) Both statements are correct
6. (A) Both statements are correct
7. (D) Balance of Payments (BoP) records transactions between residents of a country and the rest of the world, not within the country.
8. (C) BoP current account records transactions in goods, services, income and current transfers, not those that change the assets and liabilities status, as these are recorded in the capital account.

9. (C) Capital outflows are recorded on the debit side of the BoP capital account.

10. (D) A deficit in the capital account arises when capital outflows exceed capital inflows and a surplus arises when capital inflows exceed capital outflows.

Case Based Questions

1. (i) country B offers higher interest rates on government bonds compared to country A
   (ii) (A) It decreases the demand for country A's currency
   (iii) (C) It causes the exchange rate to depreciate for country A's currency and appreciate for country B's currency
   (iv) There are no restrictions in place on buying bonds issued by foreign governments
2. (i) (B) Rising imports of crude oil and gold
   (ii) Capital account
   (iii) (C) Higher foreign direct investment and robust portfolio investment
   (iv) Reserve Bank of India (RBI)

Subjective Questions

1. The statement is defended. In a flexible exchange rate system, the foreign exchange rate is primarily determined by market forces of supply and demand.

   The exchange rate is determined at the intersection point of demand and supply of foreign currency.

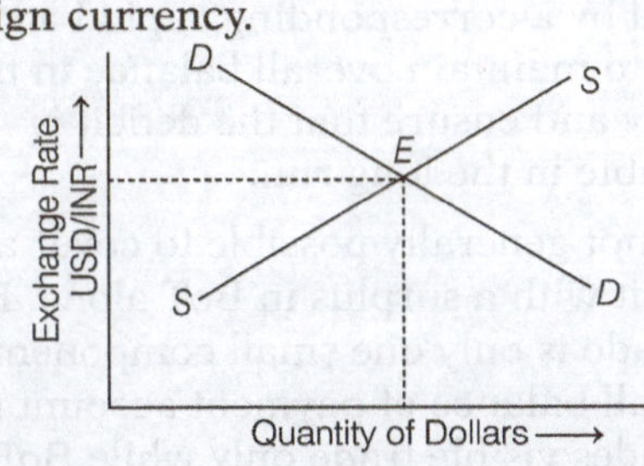

   The demand curve of foreign currency is downward sloping due to inverse relationship between foreign exchange rate and demand for foreign currency.

   The supply curve of foreign currency is upward sloping due to positive relationship between foreign exchange rate and supply for foreign currency.

   Sources of demand for foreign currency
   (i) Imports
   (ii) Tourism to rest of the world
   (iii) Educational/Medical services from abroad
   (iv) Foreign direct investments

   Sources for supply of foreign currency
   (i) Exports
   (ii) Tourism from rest of the world
   (iii) Educational/Medical services to abroad
   (iv) Investments from abroad

2. True, under flexible exchange rate system, foreign exchange rate is determined by the market forces of demand and supply.

   Intersection of demand for foreign exchange and supply of foreign exchange determines the rate without any government intervention.

3. The given statement is refuted. A current account deficit does not necessarily imply a trade deficit, but it often includes a trade deficit as one of its components. A current account deficit can arise from deficits in other components such as services, income and transfers, even if a country maintains a trade surplus.

   A country facing a current account deficit typically imports more goods and services, receives less income from abroad or has fewer transfers from abroad than it exports, earns or receives in transfers.

   Therefore, it is common to see a trade deficit when a country is facing a current account deficit, but it is not mandatory as other factors also contribute to the overall current account balance.

4. The type of statement referring to transactions between residents and the rest of the world is related to the Balance of Payments (BoP) framework. In BoP accounting, transactions between residents and the rest of the world are recorded in both the current account and the capital account.

   The components of the BoP capital account include

   (i) **Foreign Investment** It includes investment made by the residents of a country in rest of the world or by the residents of rest of the world in the domestic country.

   Foreign investment can be of the following types
   (a) Foreign Direct Investment (FDI)
   (b) Foreign Portfolio Investment (FPI)

   (ii) **Borrowings** Borrowings to and from abroad also affect the assets and liabilities status of the country and are therefore recorded in capital account.

Borrowings can be further categorised as follows

(a) External commercial borrowing

(b) External assistance

(iii) **Other Components** The other components of capital account include the following

(a) **NRI Deposits** It refers to deposits held by Non-resident Indians (NRIs) in India. It should be remembered that only deposits held by NRIs in the domestic economy to be considered as a component of capital account.

(b) **Banking Capital** It refers to foreign assets held by the commercial banks.

(c) **Short-term Trade Credit** It refers to purchases made in the international market without paying for them immediately.

5. Fixed exchange rate system is depicted in the given image.

In a fixed exchange rate system, the value of a country's currency is pegged or fixed to the value of another currency, a basket of currencies, or some other standard like gold. Here are its features

(i) **Centralised Control** The government or central bank actively intervenes in the foreign exchange market to maintain the fixed value of the currency.

(ii) **Stability** Fixed exchange rates provide stability and predictability for international trade and investment by eliminating exchange rate fluctuations.

(iii) **Limited Autonomy** Countries operating under fixed exchange rates have limited autonomy in monetary policy, as they must adjust their domestic policies to maintain the fixed rate.

(iv) **Reserves** Governments need to hold substantial foreign currency reserves to intervene in the currency market and defend the fixed rate.

(v) **Fixed Parity** Exchange rates are set at a fixed parity or rate and deviations from this rate are corrected through government intervention.

6. Yes, I agree with the given statement. A current account deficit in an economy represents an excess of imports over exports, meaning that the country is spending more on foreign goods and services than it is earning from its exports.

To finance this deficit, the country needs to attract capital from abroad, which typically results in a corresponding surplus in the capital account.

It is because of the following points

(i) **Capital Inflows to Finance the Deficit** When a country runs a current account deficit, it needs to attract capital from foreign investors to cover the shortfall.

This capital can come in the form of Foreign Direct Investment (FDI), portfolio investment or loans from international financial institutions. These inflows are recorded in the capital account as a surplus.

(ii) **Balancing the Accounts** The balance of payments must ultimately balance, meaning that the current account deficit must be offset by a surplus in the capital account and *vice versa*.

If there is a deficit in one account, there must be a surplus in the other to ensure that the overall balance remains zero.

(iii) **Maintaining External Balance** A capital account surplus indicates that the country is successful in attracting foreign investment to finance its current account deficit.

This helps maintain external balance and ensures that the deficit does not lead to unsustainable levels of debt or currency depreciation.

Therefore, a current account deficit is typically financed by a corresponding capital account surplus to maintain overall balance in the economy and ensure that the deficit is sustainable in the long run.

7. (i) It is not generally possible to cover a BoP deficit with a surplus in BoT alone. Balance of trade is only one small component of the overall balance of payment account that includes visible trade only while BoP is comprised of invisible items as well as capital transfer. So, it is not possible to cover the deficit of BoP with a surplus in BoP.

(ii) Investment received from abroad impacts the assets of the country thus, is recorded in the capital account of BoP.

Further, as the investment is received from abroad, it will increase the inflow of currency from abroad and thus be recorded on the credit side.

8. (i) The widening current account deficit in India's balance of payments can be attributed to several factors, including increased imports of crude oil and electronics, changes in global commodity prices and shifts in domestic consumption patterns.

The widening deficit has implications for India's economy, including pressure on the rupee exchange rate, inflationary pressures and dependence on external financing.

To address the deficit, policy measures could focus on promoting export diversification, enhancing domestic manufacturing capabilities and reducing import dependence through import substitution and energy efficiency measures.

(ii) Foreign Direct Investment (FDI) and portfolio investment play a crucial role in India's capital account surplus, contributing to economic growth, technology transfer and job creation.

Challenges such as policy uncertainty, bureaucratic red tape and infrastructure bottlenecks may deter investment inflows. Leveraging foreign investment for sustainable development requires measures to improve ease of doing business, enhance infrastructure and address skill shortages.

Additionally, promoting sectors with high FDI potential, such as manufacturing, infrastructure and services, can stimulate investment inflows and contribute to India's economic growth.

PART B

Indian Economic Development

Note

Note

CHAPTER - 1

Indian Economy on The Eve of Independence

Types & Nos. of Questions

Multiple Choice Questions	–	25
Assertion-Reason Questions	–	8
Correct/Incorrect Statements	–	10
Case Based Questions	–	2 Cases, *each with four Questions*
Subjective Questions	–	5

Trend Analysis

On the basis of analysis of last 2 years' papers, it is found that on an average 3 Multiple Choice Questions are asked from this chapter. No case based question is asked but may be asked in coming exams.

Focus Topics of the Chapter

- State of Indian Economy on the Eve of Independence
- Sectors of Indian Economy on the Eve of Independence

Multiple Choice Questions

No. of Questions : **25** Suggested Time : **40 Minutes**

Direction Each of the question given below is Multiple Choice Question (MCQ) i.e. there are Four Options/Choices for answer, out of which ONLY ONE is correct. You have to select the correct option. A response box is given with each option, mark (✓) in the box of the correct option. For each correct answer you will get 1 mark, while there is no penalty for incorrect answer or missed out questions.

1. Most studies did find that the country's growth of aggregate real output during the first half of the twentieth century was .... coupled with a meagre .... growth in per capita output per year.

(A) less than 0.5%, 2% ☐

(B) less than 2%, 0.5% ☐

(C) more than 2%, 0.5% ☐

(D) more than 2%, 5% ☐

2. The economic policies pursued by the colonial government in India were concerned more with the ....

(A) protection and promotion of the economic interests of the Indian economy ☐

(B) protection and promotion of the economic interests of the Britain ☐

(C) protection and promotion of the economic interests of both Indian economy and Britain ☐

(D) protection and promotion of the economic interests of the other countries ☐

3. Before India gained independence, the agricultural sector experienced significant stagnation.

Despite various factors that could potentially boost productivity, such as investment in technology, agricultural facilities and advanced infrastructural developments, the primary cause of this stagnation was related to a specific policy implemented by the British colonial administration.

Which policy could have contributed most to the stagnation in India's agricultural sector during this period?

(A) Investment in technology ☐

(B) Investment in agriculture facilities ☐

(C) Advanced infrastructural facilities ☐

(D) Land settlement system ☐

4. "Indian agriculture under British rule suffered from low productivity and neglected investment in infrastructure, finds study." **Source** *The Hindu*

How did Indian agriculture fare during British colonial rule?

(A) Flourished due to modern farming techniques ☐

(B) Suffered from low productivity and lack of investment ☐

(C) Experienced a boom in export of agricultural products ☐

(D) Achieved self-sufficiency in food production ☐

5. Which of the following is not true about foreign trade during the colonial rule? *[CBSE 2023]*

(A) India suffered from large trade deficit ☐

(B) Restrictive policies of commodity production, were followed ☐

(C) Britain maintained a monopoly control over India's exports and imports ☐

(D) India because an exporter of primary products and an importer of finished consumer goods ☐

6. The impact of Britishers in the Indian economy led to

(i) low agricultural sector

(ii) modernised industrial sector

(iii) prevalence of rampant poverty

Codes
(A) Only (i) (B) (i) and (ii)
(C) (ii) and (iii) (D) (i) and (iii)

7. The cotton textile mills, mainly dominated by ...., while the jute mills dominated by the ....
(A) foreigners, Indians
(B) Indians, foreigners
(C) Indians, Indians
(D) foreigners, foreigners

8. Under the British Rule, commercialisation of agriculture resulted in shifting of agricultural production from .... crops to .... crops. [CBSE 2024, 23]
(A) cash, food (B) cotton, jute
(C) food, cash (D) jute, food

9. "Industrial sector's contribution to pre-independence India's GDP minimal, agriculture remains backbone."
Source *Financial Express*

What was the industrial sector's contribution to India's Gross Domestic Product (GDP) on the eve of independence?
(A) Dominant, leading India's economic growth
(B) Minimal, with agriculture remaining the backbone of the economy
(C) Moderate, alongside a booming services sector
(D) Negligible, as public sector enterprises held sway

10. During the British rule in India, Indian agricultural output witnessed stagnation due to .... [CBSE 2023]
(A) decline in handicrafts
(B) drain of Indian wealth
(C) land settlement
(D) introduction of railways

11. On the basis of the given image, which year is regarded as the year of great divide?

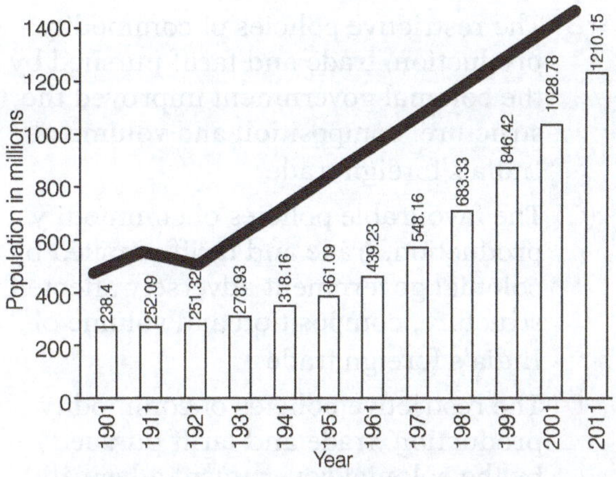

(A) 1901 (B) 1911
(C) 1921 (D) 1931

12. During British colonial rule in India, the economic policies were designed to integrate India into the British global trade network. What role did India primarily serve in this trade system?
(A) Importer of primary products
(B) Exporter of finished products
(C) Exporter of primary products
(D) Importer of raw materials

13. "Policies brought up by the Britishers resulted into a fundamental change in the structure of the Indian economy." This change was ....
(A) transforming India into supplier of raw materials and consumer of finished industrial products from Britain
(B) transforming the India into supplier of finished products and consumer of raw materials
(C) transforming the Britain into supplier of raw materials and consumer of finished industrial products from India
(D) transforming the Britain into supplier of raw materials and finished industrial products both

14. Choose the correct statement from the following.
(A) The favourable policies of commodity production, trade and tariff pursued by the colonial government improved the structure, composition and volume of India's foreign trade

(B) The restrictive policies of commodity production, trade and tariff pursued by the colonial government improved the structure, composition and volume of India's foreign trade ☐

(C) The favourable policies of commodity production, trade and tariff pursued by the colonial government adversely affected the structure, composition and volume of India's foreign trade ☐

(D) The restrictive policies of commodity production, trade and tariff pursued by the colonial government adversely affected the structure, composition and volume of India's foreign trade ☐

15. Identify, which of the following indicates the adverse impact of British rule in India.

(A) Introduction of communication networks in India ☐

(B) Change in composition of India's foreign trade ☐

(C) Introduction of modern administrative system in India ☐

(D) Introduction of railways in India ☐

16. Which of the following is incorrect statement in context of introduction of railways in India by Britishers?

(A) It enabled people to undertake long distance travel and thereby break geographical and cultural barriers ☐

(B) It fostered commercialisation of Indian agriculture which adversely affected the self-sufficiency of the village economies in India ☐

(C) The volume of India's exports had fallen and its benefit was accrued to the Indian people ☐

(D) The social benefits, which the Indian people gained owing to the introduction of the railways, were thus outweighed by the country's huge economic loss ☐

17. Which of the following is incorrect statement?

(A) Foreign trade was oriented to feed the Industrial Revolution in Britain ☐

(B) The social and economic challenges before the country were enormous ☐

(C) The inland waterways, at times, also proved uneconomical as in the case of the coast canal on the Orissa coast ☐

(D) Another striking aspect of occupational structure was the reducing regional variation ☐

18. Arrange the following in chronological order.

(i) Year of great divide
(ii) Opening of suez canal
(iii) Introduction of railways
(iv) First official census

Codes

(A) (iii), (ii), (i), (iv) ☐
(B) (iii), (ii), (iv), (i) ☐
(C) (iii), (iv), (ii), (i) ☐
(D) (iii), (i), (iv), (ii) ☐

19. Based on the image, what type of infrastructure is depicted?

(A) Modern railway station ☐
(B) Colonial-era road ☐
(C) Inland waterway ☐
(D) Electric telegraph station ☐

20. Observe the image given below and choose the correct statement(s).

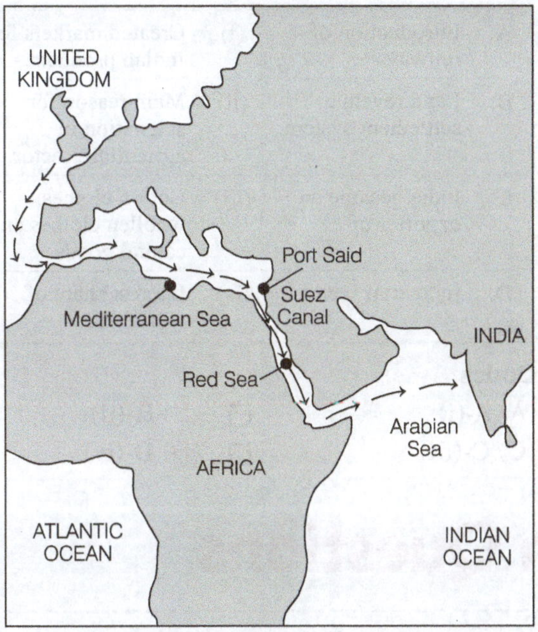

(i) Canal was used as highway between India and Britain.
(ii) It reduced the cost of transportation.
(iii) It made access to the Indian market difficult.

Codes

(A) Only (i) ☐
(B) Only (ii) ☐
(C) Both (i) and (ii) ☐
(D) Both (i) and (iii) ☐

21. On the basis of the given image, choose the incorrect option.

Occupational Structure during Colonial Period

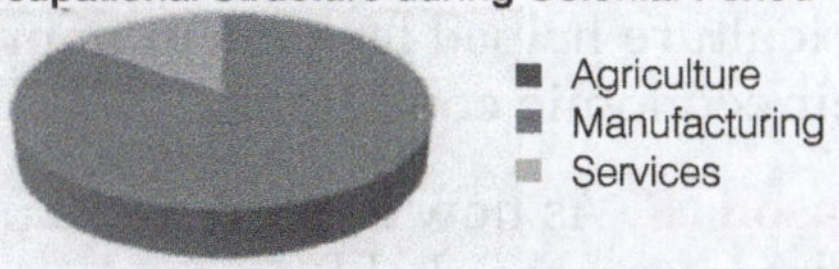

(A) The agricultural sector accounted for the largest share of workforce, which usually remained at a high of 70-75 per cent ☐
(B) Industrial sector was insignificant option ☐
(C) There were growing regional variation ☐
(D) Tertiary sector engaged the high proportion of workforce ☐

22. Match the following

	Column I		Column II
A.	VKRV Rao	(i)	Production from food crops to cash crops
B.	Commercialisation of agriculture	(ii)	1921
C.	Year of great divide	(iii)	1869
D.	Suez canal	(iv)	Most significant estimates of India's national and per capita income

Codes

	A	B	C	D	
(A)	(iv)	(ii)	(i)	(iii)	☐
(B)	(iv)	(i)	(iii)	(ii)	☐
(C)	(iv)	(iii)	(ii)	(i)	☐
(D)	(iv)	(i)	(ii)	(iii)	☐

23. Which of the following highlights worsening demographic profile of India's population on the eve of independence?

(A) High birth rate, High life expectancy rate, High infant mortality rate, Low literacy rate ☐
(B) High birth rate, Low life expectancy rate, High infant mortality rate, Low literacy rate ☐
(C) High birth rate, Low life expectancy rate, Low infant mortality rate, Low literacy rate ☐
(D) High birth rate, Low life expectancy rate, High infant mortality rate, High literacy rate ☐

24. Match the Column I with Column II in the following information

	Column I		Column II
A.	Agricultural sector	(i)	India was exporter of primary products and importer of finished consumer goods.

	Column I		Column II
B.	Industrial sector	(ii)	Development of postal services.
C.	Foreign trade	(iii)	Incorporation of TISCO.
D.	Infrastructure	(iv)	Main source of livelihood for about 75% of population.

Codes

	A	B	C	D
(A)	(iv)	(iii)	(i)	(ii)
(B)	(i)	(iii)	(iv)	(ii)
(C)	(ii)	(i)	(iv)	(iii)
(D)	(iii)	(i)	(iv)	(ii)

25. Match the correct pair

	Column I		Column II
A.	Introduction of railways	(i)	Created markets for Indian products.
B.	Land revenue settlement system	(ii)	Main reason for stagnation in agriculture sector.
C.	India became an exporter of	(iii)	Cotton clothes, woollen clothes and capital goods.
D.	Industrial sector	(iv)	Largest share of workforce

Codes

(A) A-(i) (B) B-(ii)
(C) C-(iii) (D) D-(iv)

Assertion-Reason Questions

No. of Questions : **8** Suggested Time : **15 Minutes**

Direction Each of the question given below consist of the two statements; one labelled as **Assertion** (A) and other as **Reason** (R). List of common options applicable for each question is given below

(A) Both Assertion (A) and Reason (R) are true and Reason (R) is the correct explanation of Assertion (A)
(B) Both Assertion (A) and Reason (R) are true, but Reason (R) is not the correct explanation of Assertion (A)
(C) Assertion (A) is true, but Reason (R) is false
(D) Assertion (A) is false, but Reason (R) is true

You have to select the codes as *A, B, C* or *D* as your answer to the question by marking (✓) in the response box given against each option.

1. Assertion (A) Agricultural productivity became low though, in absolute terms, the sector experienced some growth due to the expansion of the aggregate area under cultivation.

Reason (R) Low levels of technology, lack of irrigation facilities and negligible use of fertilisers, all added up to aggravate the plight of the farmers and contributed to the dismal level of agricultural productivity.

(A) (B) (C) (D)

2. Assertion (A) Commercialisation of agriculture helped farmers in improving their economic conditions.

Reason (R) As now farmers were producing cash crops instead of food crops.

(A) (B)
(C) (D)

3. Assertion (A) India's agriculture was starved for investment in terracing, flood control, drainage and desalinisation of soil.

Reason (R) In absolute terms, the sector experienced some growth due to the expansion of the aggregate area under cultivation.

(A) ☐ (B) ☐ (C) ☐ (D) ☐

4. **Assertion (A)** India could not develop a sound industrial base under the colonial rule.

Reason (R) The country's world famous handicraft industries and modern industrial base was uplifted due to the policies brought by the Britishers.

(A) ☐ (B) ☐ (C) ☐ (D) ☐

5. **Assertion (A)** The growth rate of the new industrial sector and its contribution to the Gross Domestic Product (GDP) or gross value added remained very small.

Reason (R) There was hardly any capital goods industry to help with further industrialisation in India.

(A) ☐ (B) ☐ (C) ☐ (D) ☐

6. **Assertion (A)** The export surplus generated on the eve of independence led to the drain of Indian wealth.

Reason (R) This export surplus did not result in any flow of gold or silver into India. Rather, this was used to make payments for the expenses incurred by an office set up by the colonial government in Britain, expenses on war, etc.

(A) ☐ (B) ☐ (C) ☐ (D) ☐

7. **Assertion (A)** Public health facilities were either unavailable to large chunks of population or whenever available, they were highly inadequate.

Reason (R) Water and air-borne diseases were rampant and took a huge toll on life.

(A) ☐ (B) ☐
(C) ☐ (D) ☐

8. **Assertion (A)** Under the colonial regime, basic infrastructure such as railways, ports, water transport, posts and telegraphs were developed.

Reason (R) The real motive behind this development was to provide basic amenities to the people and not to subserve various colonial interests.

(A) ☐ (B) ☐ (C) ☐ (D) ☐

Correct/Incorrect Statements

No. of Questions : **10** Suggested Time : **15 Minutes**

Direction Each of the question given below consist of the two statements. List of common options applicable for each question is given below.

(A) Both statements are correct
(B) Both statements are incorrect
(C) Statement I is correct and Statement II is incorrect
(D) Statement I is incorrect and Statement II is correct

You have to select the codes as *A, B, C* or *D* as your answer to the question by marking (✓) in the response box given against each option.

1. **Statement I** The stagnation in the agricultural sector was caused mainly because of the various systems of land settlement that were introduced by the colonial government.

Statement II The main interest of the zamindars was only to collect rent regardless of the economic condition of the cultivators.

(A) ☐ (B) ☐
(C) ☐ (D) ☐

2. **Statement I** Muslin is a type of cotton textile which had its origin in Bengal.

Statement II 'Daccai Muslin' had gained worldwide fame as an exquisite type of cotton textile.

(A) ☐ (B) ☐
(C) ☐ (D) ☐

3. **Statement I** Commercialisation of agriculture under the British rule was responsible for frequent famines between 1875 and 1900.

Statement II During British rule, India began to export foodgrains. *[CBSE 2024]*

(A) ☐ (B) ☐ (C) ☐ (D) ☐

4. **Statement I** The cotton textile mills dominated by foreigners, were located in the Western parts of the country, namely, Maharashtra and Gujarat.

Statement II The jute mills dominated by the Indians were mainly concentrated in Bengal.

(A) ☐ (B) ☐ (C) ☐ (D) ☐

5. **Statement I** The Tata Iron and Steel Company (TISCO) was incorporated in 1917.

Statement II The British introduced the railways in India in 1850.

(A) ☐ (B) ☐ (C) ☐ (D) ☐

6. **Statement I** The colonial government took sincere attempt to estimate India's national and per capita income.

Statement II Among the notable estimators – Dadabhai Naoroji, William Digby, Findlay Shirras, VKRV Rao and RC Desai – it was Rao, whose estimates during the colonial period was considered very significant.

(A) ☐ (B) ☐ (C) ☐ (D) ☐

7. **Statement I** Striking aspect of occupational structure on the eve of independence was the growing regional variation.

Statement II There had been a decrease in the share of workforce in agriculture during the same time in states such as Orissa, Rajasthan and Punjab.

(A) ☐ (B) ☐ (C) ☐ (D) ☐

8. **Statement I** On the eve of independence, water and air-borne diseases were rampant and took a huge toll on life.

Statement II Extensive poverty prevailed in India during the colonial period which contributed to the worsening profile of India's population of the time.

(A) ☐ (B) ☐ (C) ☐ (D) ☐

9. **Statement I** Britain maintained no control over India's exports and imports.

Statement II India's foreign trade throughout the colonial period resulted into trade deficit.

(A) ☐ (B) ☐ (C) ☐ (D) ☐

10. **Statement I** Introduction of railways fostered commercialisation of Indian agriculture which positively affected the village economies in India.

Statement II The volume of India's exports undoubtedly expanded but its benefits rarely accrued to the Indian people.

(A) ☐ (B) ☐ (C) ☐ (D) ☐

Case Based Questions

No. of Questions : 2 Suggested Time : **10 Minutes**

Direction This section contains 2 cases having 4 questions of 1 mark each. You have to write the answer of each question based on the context of the related case.

Case 1 Before the advent of colonial rule, India was a self-sufficient and flourishing economy. Evidently, our country was popularly known as the golden eagle. India had already established itself on the world map with a decent amount of exports. Although primarily it was an agrarian economy, many manufacturing activities were budding in the pre-colonial India.

Indian craftsmanship was widely popular around the world and garnered huge demands. The economy was well-known for its handicraft industries in the fields of cotton and silk textiles, metal and precious stone works, etc. Such developments lured the British to paralyse our State and use it for their home country's benefits.

Questions

(i) Which industries were set off back due to the advent of Britishers?

(A) Cotton textile industries ☐

(B) Jute textile industries ☐

(C) Handicraft industries ☐

(D) None of the above ☐

(ii) What was the primary characteristic of the Indian economy before colonial rule?

(A) Self-sufficiency and flourishing ☐

(B) Dependency on foreign imports ☐

(C) Limited exports ☐

(D) Weak manufacturing sector ☐

(iii) Before colonial rule, India was popularly known as the .... eagle.

(iv) Indian craftsmanship was widely popular around the world, especially in the fields of cotton and silk textiles, metal and .... works.

Case 2 If we start noting the pros and cons of British rule over India, the negatives column would definitely outgrow the positives. However, the infrastructure development, especially the railways, will certainly be one positive if not all. Ironically, as was with all colonial moves, the idea of railways again gained momentum to strengthen the British monopoly which was already on a high. Evidently, between 1860 and 1940, total railways route miles increased from 838 to 41,852.

The state of infrastructure during the pre-British India was very poor. The transportation and communication lines were below average. In fact, most of the villages had lack of connectivity by pucca roads. Water transport was not very popular except in some parts of North India where rivers were navigable.

In a nutshell, the pre-colonial state of infrastructure in India was far below satisfactory and the Britishers were responsible for most of our infrastructure development. In their long history of two centuries of exploitation, Britishers did everything to drain Indian wealth and support their home country.

The poor state of infrastructure was a major hurdle to this process. Transportation of materials from the countryside to ports was inefficient and time consuming. In fact, various routes became inaccessible due to an absence of permanent roads.

Development of infrastructure was thus a necessity to empower colonial motives. Hence, the development of telegraphs, roads, railways, ports and water transport was aimed at British empowerment rather than providing basic amenities to people.

Questions

(i) What was the primary purpose of developing railways in colonial India?

(A) To improve transportation for local communities ☐

(B) To facilitate British trade and administration ☐

(C) To promote tourism ☐

(D) To enhance cultural exchange ☐

(ii) What was the state of infrastructure in pre-British India?

(A) Well developed with efficient transportation ☐

(B) Poor, lacking permanent roads and connectivity ☐

(C) Focused on water transport ☐

(D) Highly advanced telegraph network ☐

(iii) In their long history of two centuries of ...., Britishers did everything to drain Indian wealth.

(iv) The development of railways in India between 1860 and 1940 resulted in an increase in total railways route miles from .... to ....

Subjective Questions

Free Response Questions, Open-ended Questions etc.

No. of Questions : **5** Suggested Time : **40 Minutes**

1. "The pre-independent India's occupational structure experienced growing regional variation." Justify the above statement with valid explanation.

2. Observe the picture given below and describe the state of Indian industries on the eve of independence.

3. One of the reasons of high death rate and low life expectancy at the time of independence was the frequent outbreak of famines. What were the causes of outbreak of famines? Do you think that the Britishers were sensitive towards the plight of the starving Indians?

4. "The railways affected the structure of the Indian economy positively, as well as negatively." Do you agree?

5. In pre-independence India, the British administration implemented policies that systematically de-industrialised the nation. This approach had far reaching consequences for India's economy, leading to a decline in indigenous manufacturing, loss of livelihoods and economic dependency on British imports. This de-industrialisation was done for two reasons.

(i) Identify and explain the two reasons.

(ii) Mention any four benefits of this approach.

Answers

If your answer matches with the answer given here then put (✓) in the box otherwise put (✗). In case you did not attempt the question leave the box blank.

Multiple Choice Questions

1. B ☐	2. B ☐	3. D ☐
4. B ☐	5. A ☐	6. D ☐
7. B ☐	8. C ☐	9. B ☐
10. B ☐	11. C ☐	12. C ☐
13. A ☐	14. D ☐	15. B ☐
16. C ☐	17. D ☐	18. B ☐
19. B ☐	20. C ☐	21. B ☐
22. D ☐	23. A ☐	24. A ☐
25. B ☐		

Your Score________ *(No. of Correct Answers)*

Assertion-Reason Questions

1. B ☐	2. D ☐
3. B ☐	4. C ☐
5. A ☐	6. A ☐
7. B ☐	8. C ☐

Your Score________ *(No. of Correct Answers)*

Correct/Incorrect Statements

1. A ☐	2. A ☐
3. A ☐	4. B ☐
5. D ☐	6. D ☐
7. C ☐	8. B ☐
9. D ☐	10. D ☐

Your Score________ *(No. of Correct Answers)*

Case Based Questions

1. (i) C ☐	(ii) A ☐
2. (i) B ☐	(ii) B ☐

Your Score________ *(No. of Correct Answers)*

Explanations

Multiple Choice Questions

1. (B) less than 2%, 0.5%
2. (B) protection and promotion of the economic interests of the Britain
3. (D) Land settlement system
4. (B) The headline highlights the challenges faced by Indian agriculture under British colonial rule, including low productivity and inadequate investment in infrastructure and technology.
5. (A) India suffered from large trade deficit
6. (D) (i) and (iii)
7. (B) Indians, foreigners
8. (C) food, cash
9. (B) Despite some growth, the industrial sector's contribution to India's GDP on the eve of independence remained relatively small compared to agriculture, which continued to be the primary source of livelihood for the majority of the population.
10. (B) drain of Indian wealth
11. (C) 1921
12. (C) Under British colonial rule, India's economy was structured to supply raw materials and agricultural products to Britain while serving as a market for British manufactured goods.

    This made India an exporter of primary products like cotton, jute, tea and spices, which were essential for British industries.
13. (A) transforming India into supplier of raw materials and consumer of finished industrial products from Britain
14. (D) The restrictive policies of commodity production, trade and tariff pursued by the colonial government adversely affected the structure, composition and volume of India's foreign trade
15. (B) Change in composition of India's foreign trade

16. (C) The introduction of railways in India primarily facilitated the transportation of raw materials and goods for the British colonial economy, often at the expense of Indian interests.
17. (D) During the colonial period, there was an increasing regional variation in the occupational structure due to the concentration of modern industries in certain regions, leading to disparities in economic development across different parts of India.
18. (B) (iii), (ii), (iv), (i)
19. (B) The colonial period roads were not fit for modern transport. There was an acute shortage of all weather roads. The roads that were built primarily served the purposes of mobilising army within the country and to facilitate the transportation of raw material to the port cities.
20. (C) Both (i) and (ii)
21. (B) During the colonial period in India, the tertiary sector, which includes services such as banking, education, healthcare and administration, typically did not engage a high proportion of the workforce.
22. (D) (iv) (i) (ii) (iii)
23. (A) A high birth rate coupled with high life expectancy and high infant mortality rates indicate poor healthcare and living conditions, while a low literacy rate reflects inadequate educational opportunities and development.
24. (A) (iv) (iii) (i) (ii)
25. (B) B-(ii)

Assertion-Reason Questions

1. (B) Both Assertion (A) and Reason (R) are true, but Reason (R) is not the correct explanation of Assertion (A)
2. (D) Commercialisation of agriculture did not universally benefit farmers; rather, it often exacerbated their economic conditions by pushing them into debt traps and dependency on cash crops.
3. (B) Both Assertion (A) and Reason (R) are true, but Reason (R) is not the correct explanation of Assertion (A)
4. (C) Assertion (A) is true, but Reason (R) is false
5. (A) Both Assertion (A) and Reason (R) are true and Reason (R) is the correct explanation of Assertion (A)
6. (A) Both Assertion (A) and Reason (R) are true and Reason (R) is the correct explanation of Assertion (A)
7. (B) Both Assertion (A) and Reason (R) are true, but Reason (R) is not the correct explanation of Assertion (A)
8. (C) The primary motive behind this development was to serve various colonial interests, such as facilitating trade and administration, rather than solely providing basic amenities to the people.

Correct/Incorrect Statements

1. (A) Both statements are correct
2. (A) Both statements are correct
3. (A) Both statements are correct
4. (B) The cotton textile mills dominated by foreigners were mainly located in the Eastern parts of India, particularly in regions like Bombay (now Mumbai) in Maharashtra and Ahmedabad in Gujarat.

   The jute mills dominated by Indians were primarily concentrated in regions like West Bengal, not in Bengal as a whole.
5. (D) TISCO was incorporated in 1907.
6. (D) The colonial government's attempts to estimate India's national and per capita income were not sincere.
7. (C) There was not a decrease but rather a shift in the share of the workforce in agriculture in certain states.
8. (B) The water and air-borne diseases were not rampant in India on the eve of independence.

   While poverty was extensive in colonial India, it's not the main reason for the worsening demographic profile, which was primarily influenced by factors like high infant mortality rates and low life expectancy.
9. (D) Britain exercised significant control over India's exports and imports during the colonial period.
10. (D) The commercialisation of Indian agriculture, driven by railway development, had adverse effects on village economies, as it often led to exploitation of farmers and increased indebtedness.

Case Based Questions

1. (i) (C) Handicraft industries
   (ii) (A) Self-sufficiency and flourishing
   (iii) golden
   (iv) precious stones
2. (i) (B) To facilitate British trade and administration
   (ii) (B) Poor, lacking permanent roads and connectivity
   (iii) exploitation
   (iv) 838 to 41,852

Subjective Questions

1. The pre-independent India's occupational structure experienced growing regional variation as
   (i) Parts of Madras Presidency, Bombay and Bengal witnessed a decline in the dependence of the workforce on the agricultural sector with a commensurate increase in the manufacturing and the services sectors.
   (ii) There had been an increase in the share of workforce in agriculture in states such as Orissa, Rajasthan and Punjab.
2. The industrial development pattern on the eve of independence was characterised by the following elements
   (i) The public sector enterprises such as railways, power, post and telegraph were confined to areas which would enlarge the size of market for British products in India.
   (ii) The industrial growth was lopsided, in the sense that consumer goods industry was not adequately supported by the capital goods industry.
   (iii) No priority was given for the development of basic and heavy industries. Tata Iron and Steel Corporation (TISCO) established in 1907, was the only basic industry in India.
   (iv) The pattern of development in the industrial sector was lopsided and was dominated by the presence of small industries and large industries, but very few medium industries.
3. Famines were a recurrent feature of the Indian economy in the pre-independence period. Famines in India resulted in many deaths over the course of the 18th, 19th and early 20th centuries. The last major famine was the Bengal famine of 1943.
   Some of the causes of outbreaks of famine were
   (i) In the pre-independent period, Indian agriculture was heavily dependent on monsoon. A bad monsoon led to the outbreak of famine.
   (ii) Amartya Sen found that the famines during British rule were not due to lack of food but due to inequalities in the distribution of food.
   (iii) Tirthankar Roy suggests that the famines in the British era were due to environmental factors inherent in Indian ecology.
   No, I do not think that the Britishers were sensitive to the plight of the starving Indians. No policies or programmes were initiated by the government to reduce prices of food products or to provide relief of any kind.
4. Yes, I agree. The railways affected the structure of the Indian economy positively in the following ways
   (i) It enabled people to undertake long distance travel and thereby break geographical and cultural barriers.
   (ii) It fostered commercialisation of Indian agriculture as agricultural produce could be sent to distant places. Farmers started viewing agriculture as a business rather than a way of subsistence.
   (iii) Railways enabled the government to supply foodgrains fastly to famine affected areas.
   The railways affected the Indian economy negatively in the following ways
   (i) It enabled the goods from British factories to be transported to various parts of the country, thereby expanding their market.
   (ii) It facilitated the transport of raw materials to the port cities and ensured their easy exportability.
   (iii) Commercialisation of agriculture affected the self-sufficiency of the rural areas.

5. (i) The following are the two-fold motive behind the systematic de-industrialisation affected by the British

(a) **Making India a Supplier of Raw Materials** The main motive of the British government was to make India a mere supplier of cheap raw materials to feed its own rapidly expanding industrial base.

(b) **Making India a Market for Finished Goods** Another important objective of the British government in de-industrialising Indian economy was to use India as a large and growing market to sell the finished goods produced by the British industries, so that their industries never face a demand shortage and could keep on flourishing.

(ii) The benefits are as follows

(a) **Increased Profitability** By sourcing raw materials from India at lower costs, British industries enjoyed higher profit margins, contributing to their economic growth.

(b) **Market Domination** With Indian industries weakened, British manufacturers monopolised the Indian market, expanding their sales and market share.

(c) **Economic Growth** The demand for British goods in India fueled industrial expansion in Britain, driving economic prosperity and development.

(d) **Colonial Control** Deindustrialisation reinforced British colonial dominance over India, enabling them to dictate economic policies and extract resources for their own benefit.

CHAPTER -2

Indian Economy (1950-1990)

PC Mahalanobis

Types & Nos. of Questions

Multiple Choice Questions - 30
Assertion-Reason Questions - 10
Correct/Incorrect Statements - 10
Case Based Questions - 2 Cases, *each with four Questions*
Subjective Questions - 7

Trend Analysis

On the basis of analysis of last 2 years' papers, it is found that on an average 2 Multiple Choice Questions and 1 Short Answer Type Question (Statement Based) are asked from this chapter. No case based question is asked but may be asked in coming exams.

Focus Topics of the Chapter

- Economic Planning in Independent India
- Effect of FYPs on Different Sectors between 1950-1990

Multiple Choice Questions

No. of Questions : **30** Suggested Time : **45 Minutes**

Direction Each of the question given below is Multiple Choice Question (MCQ) i.e. there are Four Options/ Choices for answer, out of which ONLY ONE is correct. You have to select the correct option.
A response box is given with each option, mark (✓) in the box of the correct option. For each correct answer you will get 1 mark, while there is no penalty for incorrect answer or missed out questions.

1. A good indicator of ...., in the language of economics, is steady increase in the Gross Domestic Product (GDP).

(A) agricultural development ☐
(B) industrial development ☐
(C) economic growth ☐
(D) modernisation ☐

2. Choose the incorrect statement.

(A) A plan spells out how the resources of nation should be put to use ☐
(B) The long-term plan which specifies the objectives to be achieved over a period of 20 years is called a perspective plan ☐
(C) All the goals of a plan are to be given equal importance in all the plans ☐
(D) A plan should have some general goals as well as specific objectives ☐

3. Which one of the following statements is incorrect in context of PC Mahalanobis?

(A) He was born in 1985 in Calcutta ☐
(B) He established the Indian Statistical Institute (ISI) in Calcutta and started a journal, Sankhya ☐
(C) He can be regarded as the architect of Indian planning ☐
(D) He can be regarded as the father of the second five year plan in India ☐

4. After independence, the rationale behind choosing modernisation as a planning objectives for the Indian economy were ....

(i) to brig positive changes in the social outlook
(ii) equitable distribution of income
(iii) technological upgradation
(iv) increase in economic divide *[CBSE 2024]*

Codes

(A) (i) and (ii) ☐
(B) (ii) and (iii) ☐
(C) (i) and (iii) ☐
(D) (i) and (iv) ☐

5. One of the goals of the five year plan is growth. Here, 'growth' signifies

(i) increase in the country's capacity to produce the goods and services with in the country.
(ii) a larger stock of productive capital.
(iii) increase in the efficiency of productive capital and services.

Codes

(A) Only (i) ☐
(B) Both (i) and (ii) ☐
(C) (i), (ii) and (iii) ☐
(D) None of the above ☐

6. The first seven five year plans gave importance to .... which means avoiding imports of those goods which could be produced in India itself.

(A) growth ☐ (B) modernisation ☐
(C) equity ☐ (D) self-reliance ☐

7. "It is important to ensure that the benefits of economic prosperity reach the poor sections as well instead of being enjoyed only by the rich." This is the objective of .... goal of five year plan.

(A) growth ☐ (B) modernisation ☐
(C) self-reliance ☐ (D) equity ☐

8. Identify the correct combination of the 'goals of Indian five year plans'.

(A) Growth, Equality, Modernisation, Self-reliance ☐
(B) Development, Equality, Modernisation, Sustainability ☐
(C) Good Health, Education, Modernisation, Sustainability ☐
(D) Growth, Equity, Modernisation, Self-reliance ☐

9. New Delhi : The NITI Aayog, which will replace the Planning Commission, will be responsible for formulating what the government described as 'a Bharatiya approach to development'. The new organisation – NITI stands for National Institution for Transforming India – is being seen as a think tank that will foster 'cooperative federalism.'

– The Economic Times

When was the planning commission abolished and replaced by the NITI Aayog?

(A) January 2015 ☐ (B) March 2015 ☐
(C) January 2014 ☐ (D) March 2014 ☐

10. Which of the following statements is incorrect?

(A) The land tenure system was characterised by intermediaries who merely collected rent from the actual tillers of the soil without contributing towards improvements on the farm ☐
(B) Equity in agriculture called for land reforms which primarily refer to change in the ownership of landholdings ☐
(C) The ownership conferred on tenants gave them the incentive to increase output and this contributed to growth in agriculture ☐
(D) The goal of equity was fully served by abolition of intermediaries ☐

11. The shackles of agriculture during the colonial rule were permanently broken by the green revolution that resulted from the application of ....

(i) High Yielding Varieties (HYV)
(ii) mechanisation of agriculture
(iii) chemical fertilisers and pesticides
(iv) organic fertilisers and pesticides

Codes

(A) (i), (ii) and (iv) ☐
(B) (i), (ii) and (iii) ☐
(C) (ii), (iii) and (iv) ☐
(D) (i), (iii) and (iv) ☐

12. The portion of agricultural produce which is sold in the market by the farmers is called ....

(A) import surplus ☐
(B) export surplus ☐
(C) trade surplus ☐
(D) marketable surplus ☐

13. Which of the following highlights the feature of the given image?

(A) A substantial amount of agricultural produce is sold in the market by the farmers, the higher output can make a difference to the economy ☐
(B) The farmers were still selling their produce to Britishers ☐
(C) No increase in agricultural production ☐
(D) Farmers were not able to use HYV seeds ☐

14. This policy aimed at replacing or substituting imports with domestic production. Identify the policy.

(A) Land ceiling policy ☐
(B) Import substitution policy ☐
(C) Survival for the fittest policy ☐
(D) Industrial policy ☐

15. Which of the following was not the benefit accruing from 'golden revolution'? *[CBSE 2023]*

(A) Increase in the income of the farmers ☐
(B) Increase in production of milk and related products ☐
(C) Increase in production and exports of fruits and vegetables ☐
(D) Employment for women in rural areas ☐

16. In a rural village, Rajesh, a struggling farmer, faced years of poor crop yields and food shortages. However, with the introduction of the green revolution, Rajesh saw hope. Embracing High Yielding Variety (HYV) seeds and modern farming techniques, he witnessed a remarkable increase in both crop production and productivity. This transformation not only improved Rajesh's livelihood but also brought prosperity to his village. What two major effects of the green revolution were as highlighted in the case study?

(A) Decrease in foodgrain production and decrease in productivity ☐
(B) Substantial rise in foodgrain production and decrease in productivity ☐
(C) Substantial rise in foodgrain production and rise in productivity ☐
(D) Decrease in foodgrain production and rise in productivity ☐

17. "As the green revolution spread across India, farmers across the nation began employing better irrigation methods, cross breeding in wheat crops and using higher quality of fertilisers, making India self-sufficient and ending its dependency on grain imports." - The Hindu.

What was the primary purpose of the revolution discussed in above lines?

(A) To decrease foodgrain production and increase productivity ☐
(B) To substantially reduce foodgrain production and maintain productivity ☐
(C) To achieve a substantial rise in foodgrain production and productivity ☐
(D) To maintain foodgrain production at current levels without impacting productivity ☐

18. The following image highlights, ... goal of five year plans.

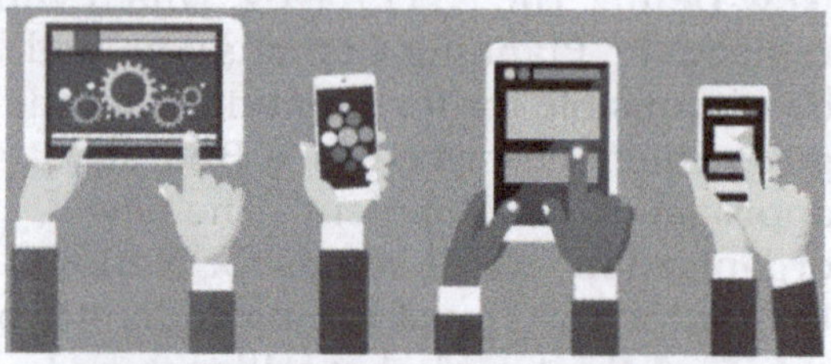

(A) growth ☐
(B) modernisation ☐
(C) equity ☐
(D) self-reliance ☐

19. Which statement is correct in context of green revolution?

(i) The green revolution enabled the government to procure sufficient amount of foodgrains to build a stock which could be used in times of food shortage.

(ii) One risk of green revolution was the possibility that it would increase the disparities between small and big farmers.

(iii) The green revolution benefitted the small as well as rich farmers.

Codes

(A) Only (i) ☐
(B) (i) and (ii) ☐
(C) (i), (ii) and (iii) ☐
(D) (ii) and (iii) ☐

20. "India commemorates National Small Industry Day on 30th August as a tribute to the invaluable role played by small-scale industries in the country's progress."
– The Financial Express

The given lines highlights about the role of small-scale industries.
What is the maximum investment allowed on the assets of a small scale industry?

(A) ₹ 5 lakh ☐ (B) ₹ 5 crore ☐
(C) ₹ 10 lakh ☐ (D) ₹ 10 crore ☐

21. "Economists have found that poor nations can progress only if they have a good industrial sector."

This is due to the reasons

(A) industry provides employment which is more stable than the employment in agriculture ☐
(B) it promotes modernisation and overall prosperity ☐
(C) Both (A) and (B) ☐
(D) Neither (A) nor (B) ☐

22. Identify the reasons which made the role of public sector extensive in industrial development.

(i) Indian industrialists did not have the capital to undertake investment in industrial ventures required for the development of Indian economy.

(ii) The market was also not big enough to encourage industrialists to undertake major projects even if they had the capital to do so.

Codes

(A) Only (i) ☐
(B) Only (ii) ☐
(C) Both (i) and (ii) ☐
(D) Neither (i) nor (ii) ☐

23. The purpose of giving tax concessions and subsidised electricity to the industries which were set-up in backward areas was to

(A) promote electricity ☐
(B) promote economic equality ☐
(C) promote social inequality ☐
(D) promote regional equality ☐

24. Identify the correct statement in context of small-scale industries.

(A) In 1945, the Village and Small-Scale Industries Committee, also called the Karve Committee, noted the possibility of using small-scale industries for promoting rural development ☐
(B) Small-scale industries are less 'labour intensive' ☐
(C) Production of a number of products was reserved for the large-scale industry ☐
(D) Development of small-scale industry requires them to be shielded from the large firms ☐

25. The protection from foreign competition was criticised

(A) as it continued even after it proved to do more good ☐
(B) as the Indian consumers had to purchase the goods of Indian and foreign producers both ☐
(C) as the producers were aware that they had a captive market ☐
(D) as competition from imports forces our producers to be more efficient ☐

26. The following picture indicates that SSIs are

(A) locational friendly ☐
(B) equity oriented ☐
(C) labour intensive ☐
(D) promoting regional equality ☐

27. "India's foreign trade policy during the first seven Five Year Plans (FYPs) was characterised by an inward-looking strategy. This approach focused on two main components; export promotion and import substitution."

Which of the following best describes the inward-looking trade strategy adopted by India during the first seven Five Year Plans?

(A) Promoting exports to earn foreign exchange and encouraging domestic production to replace imports ☐
(B) Increasing imports to meet domestic demand and reducing exports to maintain local supply ☐
(C) Promoting imports to foster international trade relations and reducing domestic production to focus on services ☐
(D) Focusing on foreign investment and reducing both imports and exports to stabilise the economy ☐

28. Match the following

	Column I		Column II
A.	Reduce foreign interference	(i)	Growth
B.	Increase in GDP	(ii)	Modernisation
C.	Reduce inequalities	(iii)	Equity
D.	Adoption of better technology	(iv)	Self-reliance

Codes

	A	B	C	D	
(A)	(iv)	(i)	(ii)	(iii)	☐
(B)	(i)	(iv)	(iii)	(ii)	☐
(C)	(iv)	(iii)	(i)	(ii)	☐
(D)	(iv)	(i)	(iii)	(ii)	☐

29. Match the following

	Column I		Column II
A.	Green revolution	(i)	Categorisation of industries
B.	Protection from foreign competition	(ii)	HYV seeds
C.	IPR 1956	(iii)	1950
D.	Planning commission	(iv)	Quotas and tariffs

Codes

	A	B	C	D	
(A)	(iv)	(ii)	(i)	(iii)	☐
(B)	(ii)	(iv)	(i)	(iii)	☐
(C)	(ii)	(i)	(iv)	(iii)	☐
(D)	(ii)	(iv)	(iii)	(i)	☐

30. Match the following

	Column I		Column II
A.	Planning commission	(i)	1948
B.	First industrial policy	(ii)	1951
C.	Karve committee	(iii)	1950
D.	First five year plan	(iv)	1955

Codes

	A	B	C	D	
(A)	(i)	(iii)	(iv)	(ii)	☐
(B)	(iii)	(iv)	(i)	(ii)	☐
(C)	(iii)	(i)	(iv)	(ii)	☐
(D)	(iii)	(i)	(ii)	(iv)	☐

Assertion-Reason Questions

No. of Questions : **10** Suggested Time : **15 Minutes**

Direction Each of the question given below consist of the two statements; one labelled as **Assertion** (A) and other as **Reason** (R). List of common options applicable for each question is given below

(A) Both Assertion (A) and Reason (R) are true and Reason (R) is the correct explanation of Assertion (A)

(B) Both Assertion (A) and Reason (R) are true, but Reason (R) is not the correct explanation of Assertion (A)

(C) Assertion (A) is true, but Reason (R) is false

(D) Assertion (A) is false, but Reason (R) is true

You have to select the codes as *A, B, C* or *D* as your answer to the question by marking (✓) in the response box given against each option.

1. **Assertion** (A) Growth refers to increase in the country's capacity to produce the output of goods and services within the country.

   Reason (R) A good indicator of economic growth in the language of economics, is steady increase in the Gross Domestic Product (GDP).

   (A) ☐ (B) ☐ (C) ☐ (D) ☐

2. **Assertion** (A) It was feared that dependence on imported food supplies, foreign technology and foreign capital may make India's sovereignty vulnerable to foreign interference in our policies.

   Reason (R) The first seven five year plans gave importance to self-reliance which means avoiding imports of those goods that could be produced in India itself.

   (A) ☐ (B) ☐ (C) ☐ (D) ☐

3. **Assertion** (A) Every Indian should be able to meet his or her basic needs such as food, a decent house, education and healthcare.

   Reason (R) It is important to ensure that the benefits of economic prosperity reach the rich sections.

   (A) ☐ (B) ☐ (C) ☐ (D) ☐

4. **Assertion** (A) The low productivity of the agricultural sector forced India to import food from the United States of America (USA).

   Reason (R) Land reforms means fixing the maximum size of land which could be owned by an individual.

   (A) ☐ (B) ☐ (C) ☐ (D) ☐

5. **Assertion** (A) The abolition of intermediaries meant that some where around 3 crore tenants came into direct contact with the zamindars.

   Reason (R) The ownership conferred on tenants gave them the incentive to increase output and this contributed to growth in agriculture.

   (A) ☐ (B) ☐ (C) ☐ (D) ☐

6. **Assertion** (A) The goal of equity was not just fully served by abolition of intermediaries.

   Reason (R) In some areas the former zamindars continued to own large areas of land by making use of some loopholes in the legislation.

   (A) ☐ (B) ☐
   (C) ☐ (D) ☐

7. **Assertion (A)** License Permit Raj was a major obstacle for growth of private sector.

Reason (R) Private sector wasted huge amount in obtaining licences, rather than on improving the product, quality and international competitiveness. *[CBSE 2024]*

(A) ☐ (B) ☐ (C) ☐ (D) ☐

8. **Assertion (A)** A good proportion of the rice and wheat produced during the green revolution period (available as marketed surplus) was sold by the farmers in the market.

Reason (R) The price of foodgrains declined relative to other items of consumption.

(A) ☐ (B) ☐
(C) ☐ (D) ☐

9. **Assertion (A)** Even an existing industry had to obtain a license for expanding output or for diversifying production.

Reason (R) This was meant to ensure that the quantity of goods produced was not more than what the economy required.

(A) ☐ (B) ☐ (C) ☐ (D) ☐

10. **Assertion (A)** The government protected the domestic industries from the foreign competition.

Reason (R) The policy of protection was based on the notion that industries of developing countries were not in a position to compete against the goods produced by the developed countries.

(A) ☐ (B) ☐
(C) ☐ (D) ☐

Correct/Incorrect Statements

No. of Questions : **10** Suggested Time : **15 Minutes**

Direction Each of the question given below consist of the two statements. List of common options applicable for each question is given below

(A) Both statements are correct
(B) Both statements are incorrect
(C) Statement I is correct and Statement II is incorrect
(D) Statement I is incorrect and Statement II is correct

You have to select the codes as *A, B, C* or *D* as your answer to the question by marking (✓) in the response box given against each option.

1. **Statement I** The socialist type of economic system appealed to Jawaharlal Nehru the most.

Statement II India would be a socialist society with a strong public sector but also with private property and democracy.

(A) ☐ (B) ☐
(C) ☐ (D) ☐

2. **Statement I** The first industrial policy was announced in 1956.

Statement II The first five year plan was announced in 1951.

(A) ☐
(B) ☐
(C) ☐
(D) ☐

3. **Statement I** In a socialist society the government decides what goods are to be produced in accordance with the needs of society.

Statement II In mixed economy, the government and the market together decides about what to produce, how to produce and how to distribute what is produced.

(A) ☐ (B) ☐ (C) ☐ (D) ☐

4. **Statement I** PC Mahalanobis established the Indian Statistical Institute (ISI) in Calcutta and started a journal, Sankhya.

Statement II PC Mahalanobis was the chairperson of the planning commission.

(A) ☐ (B) ☐ (C) ☐ (D) ☐

5. **Statement I** Modernisation refer only to the use of new technology.

Statement II The first seven five year plans gave importance to self-reliance.

(A) ☐ (B) ☐ (C) ☐ (D) ☐

6. **Statement I** Land ceiling was another policy to promote equity in the agricultural sector.

Statement II The purpose of land ceiling was to increase the concentration of land ownership in few hands.

(A) ☐ (B) ☐
(C) ☐ (D) ☐

7. **Statement I** The stagnation in agriculture during the colonial rule was permanently broken by the green revolution.

Statement II The spread of green revolution technology not helped India to achieve self-sufficiency in foodgrains.

(A) ☐ (B) ☐ (C) ☐ (D) ☐

8. **Statement I** Subsidies are meant to benefit the farmers but a substantial amount of fertiliser subsidy also benefits the fertiliser industry.

Statement II Subsidies had not benefit the target group and it is a huge burden on the government's finances.

(A) ☐ (B) ☐ (C) ☐ (D) ☐

9. **Statement I** Protection of domestic industries from imports took two forms: tariffs and quotas.

Statement II It was assumed that if the domestic industries were protected, they would learn to compete in the course of time.

(A) ☐ (B) ☐ (C) ☐ (D) ☐

10. **Statement I** It is easy to close a public sector firm if it incurs huge losses.

Statement II However it is difficult to close a private sector firm even if it is incurring huge losses.

(A) ☐ (B) ☐ (C) ☐ (D) ☐

Case Based Questions

No. of Questions : 2 Suggested Time : **10 Minutes**

Direction This section contains 2 cases each having 4 questions of 1 mark each. You have to write the answer of each question based on the context of the related case.

Case 1 The performance of Indian economy during the period of first seven five year plans (1950-1990) was satisfactory if not very impressive. On the eve of independence, India was an industrially backward country, but during this period of first seven plans our industries became far more diversified, with the stress being laid on the public investments in the industrial sector. The policy of import substitution led to protection of the domestic industries against the foreign producers but we failed to promote a strong export surplus.

Although public sector expanded to a large extent but it could not bring desired level of improvement in the secondary sector. Excessive government regulations prevented the natural trajectory of growth of entrepreneurship as there was no competition, no innovation and no modernisation on the front of the industrial sector. Many Public Sector Undertakings (PSU's) incurred huge losses due to operational inefficiencies, red-tapism, poor technology and other similar reasons.

These PSU's continued to function because it was difficult to close a government undertaking even it is a drain on country's limited resources. On the agricultural front, due to the measures taken under the green revolution, India more or less became self-sufficient in the production of foodgrains. So the needs for reform of economic policy was widely felt in the context of changing global economic scenario to achieve desired growth in the country. [CBSE QB]

Questions

(i) Which of the following was not a reason for the public sector to play a major role in the initial phase of Indian economic planning?

(A) Private entrepreneurs lacked sufficient capital for investment ☐

(B) Government aimed at social welfare ☐

(C) The market was big enough to encourage private industrialists for investment ☐

(D) The government wanted to protect the indigenous producers from the foreign competition ☐

(ii) Inward-looking trade strategy aimed at ....

(iii) State whether the given statement is true or false.

Mechanisation of the Indian agriculture was one of the cause of green revolution in India.

(iv) **Assertion** (A) Many public sector undertakings incurred huge losses due to operational inefficiencies.

Reason (R) Red-tapism was one of the reasons for continuation of such enterprises.

Alternatives

(A) Both Assertion (A) and Reason (R) are true

(B) Both Assertion (A) and Reason (R) are false

Case 2 The green revolution in India, initiated in the 1960s, aimed to increase agricultural productivity through the adoption of high yielding varieties of seeds, modern irrigation techniques and chemical fertilisers and pesticides. One of the key figures in this revolution was Dr. MS Swaminathan, an Indian geneticist known as the 'Father of the Green Revolution in India.'

Questions

(i) .... is often referred to as the 'Father of the Green Revolution in India.'

(ii) What was the primary objective of the green revolution in India?

(A) Reduce agricultural output to maintain environmental balance ☐

(B) Enhance agricultural productivity and food security ☐

(C) Promote traditional farming methods over modern techniques ☐

(D) Preserve indigenous crop varieties from extinction ☐

(iii) Which of the following was not a key component of the green revolution in India?

(A) Adoption of high yielding varieties of seeds ☐

(B) Expansion of traditional farming practices ☐

(C) Introduction of modern irrigation techniques ☐

(D) Increased use of chemical fertilisers and pesticides ☐

(iv) .... decade saw the initiation of the green revolution in India.

Subjective Questions

Free Response Questions, Open-ended Questions etc.

No. of Questions : 7 Suggested Time : **50 Minutes**

1. "Green revolution transformed India from a subsistent foodgrain economy to a food surplus economy." Justify the statement, giving reasons in support of your answer.

2. 'Atamnirbhar Bharat' had been at the roots of the Indian planning process in the form of 'self-reliance' as an objective of the planning process. Do you agree with the given statement? Justify the rationale of the given statement.

3. Goals of equity was fully served by 'abolition of the intermediaries' in agriculture in the post-independence period of India.

   Do you agree with given statement? Support your answer with valid arguments. *[CBSE 2024]*

4. During the initial phase of Indian economic planning, the government accorded a dominant role to Public Sector Undertakings (PSUs) to propel industrial development.

   This decision stemmed from several factors i.e. the inadequacy of private investment due to capital constraints, the government's focus on social welfare objectives, the imperative to build essential infrastructure and the strategic goal of ensuring economic sovereignty.

   These factors collectively drove the government to entrust PSUs with the task of driving industrial growth and fostering national self-reliance.

   Considering the role of Public Sector Undertakings (PSUs) in industrial development, why did the government assign a dominant role to these industries during the initial phase of Indian economic planning?

5. The Industrial Policy Resolution of 1956 laid out the framework for industrial development in India, delineating ownership categories for industries and introducing licensing requirements. Additionally, it aimed to stimulate industrial growth by providing incentives to private entrepreneurs, particularly for establishing units in underdeveloped regions.

   Why did the Industrial Policy Resolution of 1956 introduce classification of industries based on ownership and licensing requirements?

6. Which goal of the five year plan is violated in the given image? Identify the goal and explain it briefly.

7. The role of Small-Scale Industries (SSIs) in India's industrial development has been significant. Initially defined in terms of maximum investment limits, SSIs have evolved over time, with the current threshold set at investments not exceeding ₹ 5 crore.

   Recognising their potential, the Karve Committee in 1955 advocated for the promotion of SSIs to drive both industrial and rural development. SSIs were granted special privileges like lower excise duty and preferential access to bank loans, aiming to foster growth with equity and leverage their labour intensive nature.

(i) What criteria define a Small-Scale Industry (SSI) and how has this definition evolved over time in India's industrial landscape?

(ii) How did the recommendations of the Karve Committee contribute to the promotion and development of Small-Scale Industries (SSIs) in India and what specific privileges were granted to SSIs to facilitate their growth and sustainability?

Answers

If your answer matches with the answer given here then put (✓) in the box otherwise put (✗). In case you did not attempt the question leave the box blank.

Multiple Choice Questions

1. C ☐	2. C ☐
3. A ☐	4. C ☐
5. C ☐	6. D ☐
7. D ☐	8. D ☐
9. A ☐	10. D ☐
11. B ☐	12. D ☐
13. A ☐	14. B ☐
15. D ☐	16. C ☐
17. C ☐	18. B ☐
19. B ☐	20. B ☐
21. C ☐	22. C ☐
23. D ☐	24. D ☐
25. C ☐	26. C ☐
27. A ☐	28. D ☐
29. B ☐	30. C ☐

Your Score__________ *(No. of Correct Answers)*

Assertion-Reason Questions

1. B ☐	2. A ☐	3. C ☐
4. C ☐	5. D ☐	6. A ☐
7. A ☐	8. A ☐	9. A ☐
10. A ☐		

Your Score__________ *(No. of Correct Answers)*

Correct/Incorrect Statements

1. A ☐	2. D ☐	3. A ☐
4. C ☐	5. D ☐	6. C ☐
7. C ☐	8. A ☐	9. A ☐
10. B ☐		

Your Score__________ *(No. of Correct Answers)*

Case Based Questions

1. (i) C ☐	(iv) A ☐
2. (ii) B ☐	(iii) B ☐

Your Score__________ *(No. of Correct Answers)*

Explanations

Multiple Choice Questions

1. (C) Economic growth is typically measured by a steady increase in the Gross Domestic Product (GDP), which reflects the overall expansion of an economy's output of goods and services over time.

2. (C) In planning, not all goals are necessarily given equal importance. Prioritisation is essential and different goals may have varying levels of significance depending on the context and objectives of the plan.

3. (A) PC Mahalanobis was born on 29th June, 1893, in Calcutta, British India.

4. (C) (i) and (iii)

5. (C) (i), (ii) and (iii)

6. (D) The first seven five year plans in India emphasised self-reliance, which means avoiding imports of goods that could be produced domestically.

7. (D) equity
8. (D) Growth, Equity, Modernisation, Self-reliance
9. (A) January 2015
10. (D) While the abolition of intermediaries was a step towards achieving equity in agriculture, it did not fully serve the goal of equity, as other measures such as land reforms were also necessary to address inequities in land ownership.
11. (B) (i), (ii) and (iii)
12. (D) marketable surplus
13. (A) After the green revolution, there was a substantial increase in agricultural production, leading to a significant portion of farmers' produce being sold in the market, thereby positively impacting the economy.
14. (B) Import substitution policy was implemented to reduce dependency on foreign goods and promote self-sufficiency by encouraging the domestic production of goods that were previously imported.
15. (D) Employment for women in rural areas
16. (C) Substantial rise in foodgrain production and rise in productivity
17. (C) To achieve a substantial rise in foodgrain production and productivity
18. (B) modernisation
19. (B) (i) and (ii)
20. (B) ₹ 5 crore
21. (C) Both (A) and (B)
22. (C) Both (i) and (ii)
23. (D) promote regional equality
24. (D) Development of small-scale industry requires them to be shielded from the large firms
25. (C) as the producers were aware that they had a captive market
26. (C) labour intensive
27. (A) Promoting exports to earn foreign exchange and encouraging domestic production to replace imports
28. (D) (iv) (i) (iii) (ii)
29. (B) (ii) (iv) (i) (iii)
30. (C) (iii) (i) (iv) (ii)

Assertion-Reason Questions

1. (B) Both Assertion (A) and Reason (R) are true, but Reason (R) is not the correct explanation of Assertion (A)
2. (A) Both Assertion (A) and Reason (R) are true and Reason (R) is the correct explanation of Assertion (A)
3. (C) Assertion (A) is true, but Reason (R) is false
4. (C) Assertion (A) is true, but Reason (R) is false
5. (D) Assertion (A) is false, but Reason (R) is true
6. (A) Both Assertion (A) and Reason (R) are true and Reason (R) is the correct explanation of Assertion (A)
7. (A) Both Assertion (A) and Reason (R) are true and Reason (R) is the correct explanation of Assertion (A)
8. (A) Both Assertion (A) and Reason (R) are true and Reason (R) is the correct explanation of Assertion (A)
9. (A) Both Assertion (A) and Reason (R) are true and Reason (R) is the correct explanation of Assertion (A)
10. (A) Both Assertion (A) and Reason (R) are true and Reason (R) is the correct explanation of Assertion (A)

Correct/Incorrect Statements

1. (A) Both statements are correct
2. (D) The first industrial policy was announced in 1948.
3. (A) Both statements are correct
4. (C) PC Mahalanobis did establish the Indian Statistical Institute in Calcutta and initiated the journal Sankhya. However, he was not the chairperson of the planning commission.
5. (D) Modernisation extends beyond just adopting new technology; it also encompasses social and economic transformations.
6. (C) The purpose of land ceiling was not to concentrate land ownership but rather to decentralise it.
7. (C) The green revolution significantly increased agricultural productivity, breaking the stagnation during colonial rule. Additionally, the spread of green revolution technology did contribute to India's self-sufficiency in food grains.

8. (A) Both statements are correct
9. (A) Both statements are correct
10. (B) It is often more challenging to close a public sector firm due to political and social considerations, while private sector firms can be shut down more easily if they incur significant losses.

Case Based Questions

1. (i) (C) The market was big enough to encourage private industrialists for investment
   (ii) generating employment
   (iii) True
   (iv) (A) Both Assertion (A) and Reason (R) are true
2. (i) Dr. MS Swaminathan
   (ii) (B) Enhance agricultural productivity and food security
   (iii) (B) Expansion of traditional farming practices
   (iv) 1960s

Subjective Questions

1. Before the advent of green revolution, a large proportion of agricultural produce was consumed by the farmers themselves instead of being sold in the market. Green revolution led to an increase in the growth of agricultural output.

   After the green revolution, a greater proportion of the agro-produce (wheat and rice) was sold by the farmers in the market.

   That led to the attainment of marketed surplus and converted India into a food surplus economy from the food scarce one.

2. The given statement is correct, in the early post-independence period the aim of the government's policy was to reduce the dependence on the foreign countries for goods, services, technology and capital.

   It stressed on the use of domestic resources to avoid foreign interference, as it was feared that the dependence on the imported food supplies, foreign technology and foreign capital may increase foreign interference in the policies of our country.

   Similarly, the main thrust of the 'Atmanirbhar Bharat' is also to make India an economy that is self-reliant and self-sufficient.

3. The given statement is refuted as the objective of equity was not fully achieved in the post-independence period owing to the following reasons
   (i) In some areas, the former zamindars continued to own large areas of land while making use of some loopholes in the legislation.
   (ii) In some cases, tenants were evicted and zamindars claimed to be self-cultivators.
   (iii) Even after getting the ownership of land, the poorest of the agricultural labourers did not benefit from land reforms.

4. The government assigned a dominant role to Public Sector Undertakings (PSUs) during the initial phase of Indian economic planning due to various reasons
   (i) **Lack of Capital** Private entrepreneurs often lacked sufficient capital for investment, especially in heavy and basic industries. PSUs provided a means for the government to invest in these sectors where private capital was insufficient.
   (ii) **Low Inducement to Invest** Private investment was often driven by profit motives, which meant that industries vital for national development but less profitable were neglected.

   PSUs were established to invest in these sectors, prioritising national development goals over profit maximisation.
   (iii) **Social Justice and Growth** PSUs were seen as instruments for promoting social justice along with economic growth. By controlling key industries, the government aimed to ensure equitable distribution of resources and opportunities, thus addressing socio-economic disparities within the society.

5. The Industrial Policy Resolution of 1956 introduces classification of industries based on ownership and licensing requirements because
   (i) The Industrial Policy Resolution of 1956 classified industries based on ownership into three categories i.e. those exclusively under public sector, those open to both private and public sectors with a secondary role for private ownership and all other industries left to the private sector.

(ii) Industrial licensing was mandated for private sector industries, requiring government approval before establishment, aimed at regulating industrial expansion and ensuring orderly growth.

(iii) The policy offered various industrial incentives or concessions to private entrepreneurs to establish industrial units in backward regions, fostering development in economically disadvantaged areas.

(iv) These measures were designed to streamline industrial development, promote balanced growth across sectors and encourage investment in regions with limited industrial infrastructure.

(v) The Industrial Policy Resolution of 1956 laid the foundation for India's industrial development strategy, aiming to achieve self-sufficiency, promote equitable growth and foster industrial progress in the country.

6. The goal of equity is violated in the given image. This goal in the five year plans aimed at ensuring that the benefits of economic development were fairly distributed across society, particularly among marginalised and disadvantaged groups. It sought to reduce disparities in income, wealth and access to basic services such as healthcare, education and employment opportunities.

By prioritising equity, the plans aimed to create a more inclusive and socially just society where all individuals had the opportunity to improve their living standards and participate meaningfully in the nation's progress.

7. (i) The criteria defining a Small-Scale Industry (SSI) have undergone changes over time. Initially, in 1951, an SSI was defined as one with investments not exceeding ₹ 5 lakh. Presently, an SSI is characterised by investments not exceeding ₹ 5 crore, reflecting the growth and expansion of these enterprises over the years.

(ii) The recommendations of the Karve Committee played a crucial role in promoting and developing Small-Scale Industries (SSIs) in India.

By advocating for the promotion of SSIs to drive both industrial and rural development, the committee highlighted their potential for fostering growth with equity.

Additionally, SSIs were granted special privileges such as lower excise duty and preferential access to bank loans, which aimed to facilitate their growth and sustainability by providing them with a competitive edge in the market.

CHAPTER -3

Liberalisation, Privatisation and Globalisation: An Appraisal

Types & Nos. of Questions

Multiple Choice Questions	–	30
Assertion-Reason Questions	–	10
Correct/Incorrect Statements	–	10
Case Based Questions	–	2 Cases, *each with four Questions*
Subjective Questions	–	7

Trend Analysis

On the basis of analysis of last 2 years' papers, it is found that on an average 1 Short Answer Type Question (Statement Based) and 1 Long Answer Type Question (Case Based) are asked from this chapter.

Focus Topics of the Chapter

- Economic Crisis of 1991
- Liberalisation, Privatisation and Globalisation
- Demonetisation and GST

Multiple Choice Questions

No. of Questions : **30** Suggested Time : **45 Minutes**

Direction Each of the question given below is Multiple Choice Question (MCQ) i.e. there are Four Options/ Choices for answer, out of which ONLY ONE is correct. You have to select the correct option. A response box is given with each option, mark (✓) in the box of the correct option. For each correct answer you will get 1 mark, while there is no penalty for incorrect answer or missed out questions.

1. As the government was not able to generate the revenue, so it has become difficult to

(A) control the prices of essential goods ☐
(B) import the essential items like petrol ☐
(C) Both (A) and (B) ☐
(D) Neither (A) nor (B) ☐

2. The government was spending a large share of its income on areas like ...... and ...... which do not provide immediate returns.

(A) electronics, defence ☐
(B) social sector, defence ☐
(C) social sector, electronics ☐
(D) defence, banking ☐

3. In 1991, India met with an economic crisis due to

(i) the government not being able to make repayments on its borrowings from abroad.
(ii) foreign exchange reserves, which we generally maintain to import petrol and other important items, dropped to levels that were not sufficient for even a fortnight.
(iii) fall in prices due to excess supply.

Codes

(A) Both (i) and (ii) ☐
(B) (i), (ii) and (iii) ☐
(C) Only (i) ☐ (D) Only (ii) ☐

4. The sources for the government to meet its deficit are

(i) banks
(ii) people within the country
(iii) international financial institutions

Codes

(A) (ii) and (iii) ☐
(B) Both (i) and (ii) ☐
(C) Both (i) and (iii) ☐
(D) (i), (ii) and (iii) ☐

5. The policy which opened the door of the Indian economy for the global exposure for the first time was brought under the leadership of ...... and he appointed ...... as the finance minister.

(A) PV Narasimha Rao, Morarji Desai ☐
(B) Indira Gandhi, Manmohan Singh ☐
(C) Rajiv Gandhi, Manmohan Singh ☐
(D) PV Narasimha Rao, Manmohan Singh ☐

6. In the late 1980s, government expenditure began to exceed its revenue by such large margins that meeting the expenditure through .... became unsustainable.

(A) taxes ☐ (B) non-taxes ☐
(C) borrowings ☐ (D) disinvestments ☐

7. The New Economic Policy was broadly be classified into two groups i.e., the stabilisation measures and the structural reform measures. Stabilisation measures are

(A) measures which brought vitality to the economy and enhanced competitiveness ☐
(B) long-term measures, aimed at improving the efficiency of the economy and increasing its international competitiveness by removing the rigidities in various segments of the Indian economy ☐
(C) measures which addressed sector adaptation and supply side issues ☐

(D) short-term measures, intended to correct some of the weaknesses that have developed in the balance of payments and to bring inflation under control ☐

8. The policy which aimed at ending various rules and laws that were major hindrances in growth and development was ....

(A) globalisation ☐ (B) privatisation ☐

(C) liberalisation ☐ (D) disinvestment ☐

9. Few liberalisation measures were introduced in 1980s in the areas of

(A) industrial licensing and export-import policy ☐

(B) technology upgradation, fiscal policy and foreign investment ☐

(C) Both (A) and (B) ☐

(D) Neither (A) nor (B) ☐

10. Identify the correct statement in context of liberalisation policy.

(A) Regulation of industrial licensing under which every entrepreneur had to get permission from government officials to start a firm, close a firm or to decide the amount of goods that could be produced ☐

(B) Private sector was not allowed in many industries ☐

(C) Goods which could be produced only in small-scale industries were de-reserved ☐

(D) Controls on price fixation and distribution of selected industrial products ☐

11. Liberalisation of trade and investment regime was initiated to

(A) decrease international competitiveness of industrial production ☐

(B) decrease foreign investments ☐

(C) decrease the level of technology into the economy ☐

(D) promote the efficiency of local industries and adoption of modern technologies ☐

12. During the reform period

(A) the growth of agriculture has been remarkably shown ☐

(B) the industrial sector reported growth ☐

(C) the growth of the service sector has gone up ☐

(D) the secondary sector had shown the growth ☐

13. "Reforms have not been able to benefit agriculture, where the growth rate has been decelerating." In relation to the above statement, identify the incorrect reason.

(A) Since 1991, public investment in agriculture sector especially in infrastructure, which includes irrigation, power, etc. has fallen ☐

(B) The partial removal of fertiliser subsidy has led to increase in the cost of production, which has severely affected the small and marginal farmers ☐

(C) This sector has been experiencing a number of policy changes such as reduction in import duties on agricultural products, low minimum support price, etc ☐

(D) Due to lack of export oriented policy strategies in agriculture, there has been a shift from production for the export market towards production for the domestic market ☐

14. Identify the two renowned leaders who marked 1991 as a historical year in India.

(A) Rajiv Gandhi and Manmohan Singh ☐

(B) Morarji Desai and Manmohan Singh ☐

(C) PV Narsimha Rao and Manmohan Singh ☐

(D) Pranab Mukherjee and Manmohan Singh ☐

15. One of the major aims of financial sector reforms is to reduce the role of RBI from regulator to facilitator of financial sector. This has not led to

(A) establishment of private sector banks, Indian as well as foreign ☐

(B) foreign investment limit in banks was raised to around 74 per cent ☐

(C) Foreign Institutional Investors (FII) such as merchant bankers, mutual funds and pension funds are now allowed to invest in Indian financial markets ☐

(D) restrictions to set-up new branches without the approval of the RBI and rationalise their existing branch networks. ☐

16. According to the following chart given below, which sector has shown improvement in contribution to GDP?

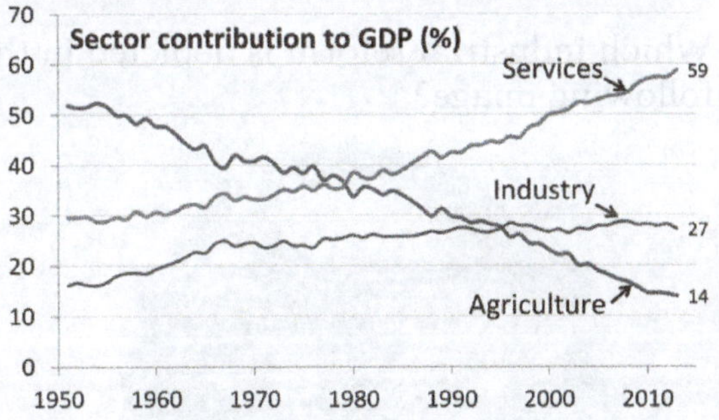

(A) Agriculture ☐ (B) Industrial ☐

(C) Services ☐ (D) None of these ☐

17. The tax reduction in the economic reform period was aimed at

(i) additional tax revenues

(ii) additional tax evasion

(iii) create 'one nation, one tax and one market'.

Codes

(A) (i), (ii) and (iii) ☐

(B) Both (i) and (ii) ☐

(C) Both (i) and (iii) ☐

(D) Only (i) ☐

18. .... is an outcome of the set of various policies that are aimed at transforming the world towards greater interdependence and integration.

(A) Liberalisation ☐

(B) Privatisation ☐

(C) Globalisation ☐ (D) Disinvestment ☐

19. Which one of the following statements is not correct in context of outsourcing?

(A) India is considered to be hub for outsourcing destination ☐

(B) Developed countries outsource to India due to presence of cheap and skilled labour ☐

(C) Developing countries are benefitted from outsourcing ☐

(D) Governments of developed countries also feel benefitted from outsourcing ☐

20. A developing country like India still does not have the access to developed countries' markets because of

(A) high non-tariff barriers ☐

(B) low quotas ☐

(C) high borrowings ☐

(D) high export duties ☐

21. Globalisation should be seen as an opportunity in terms of

(i) greater access to global markets, high technology.

(ii) increased possibility of large industries of developing countries to become important players in the international arena.

Codes

(A) Only (i) ☐

(B) Only (ii) ☐

(C) Both (i) and (ii) ☐

(D) Neither (i) nor (ii) ☐

22. Identify the incorrect statement.

(A) It has been pointed out that market driven globalisation has widened the economic disparities among nations and people ☐

(B) Globalisation has increased the income and quality of consumption of only high income groups and the growth has been concentrated only in some select areas in the services sector such as telecommunication, information technology, etc. ☐

(C) Due to reforms, agriculture and industry had also been upgraded which provide livelihoods to millions of people in the country ☐

(D) The critics argue that globalisation is a strategy of the developed countries to expand their markets in other countries ☐

23. "New Delhi: The government said demonetisation of high value currency notes in November, 2016 achieved the objectives 'quite substantially' even as the Reserve Bank of India reported most of the demonetised currency was back with the banks." – The Economic Times

According to the government, which of the following is an objective of demonetisation related to illegal activities?

(A) Increase foreign trade ☐

(B) Stop funds flow to illegal activities ☐

(C) Boost industrial growth ☐

(D) Promote agricultural development ☐

24. "Finance Minister Nirmala Sitharaman highlighted the significant impact of GST on the economy, praising its role in benefitting the poor by lowering taxes on essential items and improving tax buoyancy across states." – The Economic Times

What is one of the benefits of GST for the poor?

(A) Increasing prices of essential items ☐

(B) Lowering taxes on essential items ☐

(C) Decreasing the availability of essential items ☐

(D) Increasing import duties on essential items ☐

25. Identify the message not perceived from the image.

(A) Indian took a loan from IMF to manage the economic crisis ☐

(B) It was a conditioned loan ☐

(C) India was ready to bring economic reforms ☐

(D) India was not ready to pay the loan amount ☐

26. Which industrial reform is depicted in the following image?

(A) Goods and services tax ☐

(B) Privatisation ☐

(C) Globalisation ☐ (D) Demonetisation ☐

27. Match the following

	Column I		Column II
A.	Fall in foreign exchange reserves	(i)	1980s
B.	Traces of inefficient management of Indian economy	(ii)	Stabilisation and structural measures

Column I	Column II
C. International Bank for Reconstruction and Development (IBRD)	(iii) Need for economic policy
D. New economic policy	(iv) World bank

Codes

	A	B	C	D	
(A)	(iii)	(iv)	(i)	(ii)	☐
(B)	(iii)	(i)	(ii)	(iv)	☐
(C)	(ii)	(i)	(iv)	(iii)	☐
(D)	(iii)	(i)	(iv)	(ii)	☐

28. Match the Column I with Column II in the following information

Column I	Column II
A. World bank	(i) Established in 1948
B. RBI	(ii) Solve international trade disputes
C. WTO	(iii) Conditioned loan
D. GATT	(iv) Regulator to facilitator

Codes

	A	B	C	D	
(A)	(iii)	(iv)	(i)	(ii)	☐
(B)	(iv)	(iii)	(i)	(ii)	☐
(C)	(iii)	(iv)	(ii)	(i)	☐
(D)	(iii)	(ii)	(iv)	(i)	☐

29. Match the Column I with Column II in the following information

Column I	Column II
A. Industrial sector reforms	(i) Tax rates were moderated
B. Financial sector reforms	(ii) Devaluation of currency
C. Taxation reforms	(iii) Foreign investment limit increased
D. Foreign exchange reforms	(iv) Industrial licensing was abolished except few products.

Codes

	A	B	C	D	
(A)	(iv)	(i)	(iii)	(ii)	☐
(B)	(iv)	(iii)	(i)	(ii)	☐
(C)	(iii)	(iv)	(ii)	(i)	☐
(D)	(iii)	(ii)	(iv)	(i)	☐

30. Match the following

Column I	Column II
A. LPG	(i) 1948
B. GATT	(ii) 1991
C. WTO	(iii) 2001
D. Export duties removed	(iv) 1995

Codes

	A	B	C	D	
(A)	(ii)	(iv)	(i)	(iii)	☐
(B)	(iv)	(iii)	(i)	(ii)	☐
(C)	(iii)	(iv)	(ii)	(i)	☐
(D)	(ii)	(i)	(iv)	(iii)	☐

Assertion-Reason Questions

No. of Questions : **10** Suggested Time : **15 Minutes**

Direction Each of the question given below consist of the two statements; one labelled as **Assertion** (A) and other as **Reason** (R). List of common options applicable for each question is given below

(A) Both Assertion (A) and Reason (R) are true and Reason is the correct explanation of Assertion (A)
(B) Both Assertion (A) and Reason (R) are true, but Reason is not the correct explanation of Assertion (A)
(C) Assertion (A) is true, but Reason (R) is false
(D) Assertion (A) is false, but Reason (R) is true

You have to select the codes as *A, B, C* or *D* as your answer to the question by marking (✓) in the response box given against each option.

1. **Assertion (A)** Few liberalisation measures were introduced in 1980s.
Reason (R) There was no need to comprehend the policy of liberalisation in 1991.
(A) ☐ (B) ☐
(C) ☐ (D) ☐

2. **Assertion (A)** Since 1991, there has been a continuous reduction in the taxes on individual incomes.
Reason (R) High rates of income tax were an important reason for tax evasion.
(A) ☐ (B) ☐
(C) ☐ (D) ☐

3. **Assertion (A)** Various liberalisation of trade and investment regime were initiated in the Indian economy in 1991.
Reason (R) International competitiveness of industrial production, foreign investments and technology into the economy could be increased.
(A) ☐ (B) ☐
(C) ☐ (D) ☐

4. **Assertion (A)** It was the need of 1991 to go with privatisation.
Reason (R) There was no modernised industrial sector even after 40 years of active participation of public sector in industrial sector.
(A) ☐ (B) ☐
(C) ☐ (D) ☐

5. **Assertion (A)** In 1991, as an immediate measure to resolve the balance of payments crisis the rupee was devalued against foreign currencies.
Reason (R) Devaluation of currency was eminent, to replenish the deteriorated foreign exchange reserves.
(A) ☐ (B) ☐ (C) ☐ (D) ☐

6. **Assertion (A)** Our foreign exchange, borrowed from other countries and international financial institutions, was spent on meeting consumption needs.
Reason (R) Many attempts were made to reduce such profligate spending and sufficient attention was given to boost exports to pay for the growing imports.
(A) ☐ (B) ☐ (C) ☐ (D) ☐

7. **Assertion (A)** India agreed to the conditionalities of world bank and IMF and announced the New Economic Policy (NEP).
Reason (R) India met with an economic crisis relating to its external debt, declining foreign exchange rerserves, adverse BoP and inflation.
(A) ☐ (B) ☐ (C) ☐ (D) ☐

8. **Assertion (A)** The Indian economy was going through shortage of forex reserves.
Reason (R) The Indian government took the decision to revalue the currency.
(A) ☐ (B) ☐ (C) ☐ (D) ☐

9. **Assertion (A)** Globalisation can't turn the world into one whole or a borderless world.
Reason (R) It works in creation of networks and activities transcending economic, social and geographical boundaries.
(A) ☐ (B) ☐
(C) ☐ (D) ☐

10. **Assertion (A)** As an important member of WTO, India has been in the forefront of framing fair global rules, regulations and safeguards and advocating the interests of the developing world.
Reason (R) India has got the same benefits of being member of WTO as all developed countries has got.
(A) ☐ (B) ☐
(C) ☐ (D) ☐

Correct/Incorrect Statements

No. of Questions : **10** Suggested Time : **15 Minutes**

Direction Each of the question given below consist of the two statements; one labelled. List of common options applicable for each question is given below

(A) Both statements are correct
(B) Both statements are incorrect
(C) Statement I is correct and Statement II is incorrect
(D) Statement I is incorrect and Statement II is correct

You have to select the codes as *A, B, C* or *D* as your answer to the question by marking (✓) in the response box given against each option.

1. **Statement I** The origin of the financial crisis can be traced from the inefficient management of the Indian economy in the 1980s.

   Statement II The continued spending on development programmes of the government helped in generating additional revenue.

   (A) ☐ (B) ☐ (C) ☐ (D) ☐

2. **Statement I** Structural measures are short-term measures, intended to correct some of the weaknesses that have developed in the balance of payments and to bring inflation under control.

   Statement II Stabilisation reform policies are long-term measures, aimed at improving the efficiency of the economy and increasing its international competitiveness by removing the rigidities in various segments of the Indian economy.

   (A) ☐ (B) ☐ (C) ☐ (D) ☐

3. **Statement I** The de-regualtion of industrial sector under liberalisation measures helped Indian economy to strengthen its industrial sector.

   Statement II The competition among private sector enhanced due to less number of industries being reserved for the public sector.

   (A) ☐ (B) ☐
   (C) ☐ (D) ☐

4. **Statement I** No efforts have been made to reform the indirect taxes, taxes levied on commodities, in order to facilitate the establishment of a common national market for goods and commodities.

   Statement II In order to encourage better compliance on the part of taxpayers, many procedures have been simplified and the rates also substantially lowered.

   (A) ☐ (B) ☐ (C) ☐ (D) ☐

5. **Statement I** To protect domestic industries, India was following a regime of quantitative restrictions on imports.

   Statement II High tariffs reduced efficiency and competitiveness which led to slow growth of the manufacturing sector.

   (A) ☐ (B) ☐ (C) ☐ (D) ☐

6. **Statement I** Import licensing was abolished except in case of hazardous and environmentally sensitive industries.

   Statement II Quantitative restrictions on imports of manufactured consumer goods and agricultural products were also fully removed from April 2010.

   (A) ☐ (B) ☐ (C) ☐ (D) ☐

7. **Statement I** Privatisation of the public sector enterprises by selling off part of the equity of PSEs to the public is known as globalisation.

Statement II It was also envisaged that private capital and managerial capabilities could be effectively utilised to improve the performance of the PSUs.

(A) ☐ (B) ☐
(C) ☐ (D) ☐

8. **Statement I** All the three sectors of the economy were grown tremendously good under the policy of 1991.

Statement II The post 1991 India witnessed a rapid growth in GDP on a continual basis for two decades.

(A) ☐ (B) ☐
(C) ☐ (D) ☐

9. **Statement I** India is one of the largest foreign exchange reserve holders in the world.

Statement II Since 1991, India is seen as a successful exporter of auto parts, pharmaceutical goods, engineering goods, IT software and textiles.

(A) ☐ (B) ☐ (C) ☐ (D) ☐

10. **Statement I** WTO is expected to establish a rule-based trading regime in which nations cannot place arbitrary restrictions on trade.

Statement II WTO also ensures optimum utilisation of world resources and protect the environment.

(A) ☐ (B) ☐ (C) ☐ (D) ☐

Case Based Questions

No. of Questions : **2** Suggested Time : **10 Minutes**

Direction This section contains 2 cases each having 4 questions of 1 mark each. You have to write the answer of each question based on the context of the related case.

Case 1 In 1991, India was facing a severe economic crisis characterised by a balance of payments crisis, high inflation, low foreign exchange reserves and a burgeoning fiscal deficit.

The government, under Prime Minister Narasimha Rao and Finance Minister Dr. Manmohan Singh, implemented a series of significant economic reforms to address these challenges and liberalise the Indian economy.

The reforms included

- **Liberalisation** Abolition of the license raj, which had imposed stringent controls and regulations on industries and opening up various sectors to foreign investment and competition.
- **Privatisation** Disinvestment of State Owned Enterprises (SOEs) to reduce the government's fiscal burden and improve efficiency in sectors previously dominated by public enterprises.
- **Globalisation** Integration of the Indian economy with the global economy through trade liberalisation, removal of trade barriers and encouragement of Foreign Direct Investment (FDI).
- **Stabilisation Measures** Adoption of fiscal and monetary policies to stabilise the economy, control inflation and restore confidence in the financial markets.
- **Structural Reforms** Overhauling of the tax system, financial sector reforms and modernisation of infrastructure to foster sustainable economic growth.

These reforms marked a paradigm shift in India's economic policies, transforming it from a largely closed and regulated economy to one that embraced globalisation and market-oriented principles.

Questions

(i) Which one of the following is the key component of economic reforms in India in 1991?

(A) Reinforcement of the license raj ☐

(B) Expansion of State Owned Enterprises (SOEs) ☐

(C) Liberalisation and abolition of the license raj ☐

(D) Increase in trade barriers and restrictions on foreign investment ☐

(ii) What was the aim of privatisation as part of the economic reforms in India in 1991?

(A) Increase government control over the economy ☐

(B) Reduce efficiency in sectors dominated by public enterprises ☐

(C) Improve fiscal burden and efficiency by disinvesting state owned enterprises ☐

(D) Encourage foreign investment in public enterprises ☐

(iii) .... policies aimed to integrate the Indian economy with the global economy.

(iv) The primary goal of the structural reforms implemented in India in 1991 was ....

Case 2 India's post-1990 economic strategy entailed three important breaks with the past

- To dismantle the vast network of controls and permits that dominated the economic system.
- To re-define the role of the state as a facilitator of economic transactions and as a neutral regulator rather than the primary provider of goods and services. To move away from a regime of import substitution and to integrate fully with the global trading system.

The 1991 reforms unleashed the energies of Indian entrepreneurs and gave untold choice to the consumers and changed the face of the Indian economy. The reform agenda constituted a paradigm shift and has defined the broad contours of economic policy-making for three decades.

Liberalisation was adopted as the guiding principle of governance and all governments since 1991 have broadly stuck to that path. Today we don't need a paradigm shift. We need to look at individual sectors and see which one of these, need reforms to create a competitive environment and improve efficiency. The power sector, the financial system, governance structures and even agricultural marketing need reforms.

Today's reforms also require much more discussion and consensus building. The central government needs to work in tandem with state governments and consult different stakeholders impacted by reform decisions. Timing and sequencing are critically important in the new reforms' of agenda.

Questions

(i) What was one of the key breaks with the past in India's post-1990 economic strategy?

(A) Increase in import substitution policies ☐

(B) Reinforcement of controls and permits ☐

(C) Re-definition of the state's role as a primary provider of goods and services ☐

(D) Integration with the global trading system ☐

(ii) Which guiding principle of governance has been adopted since 1991 according to the passage?

(A) Protectionism ☐ (B) Liberalisation ☐

(C) Centralisation ☐ (D) Subsidisation ☐

(iii) The 1991 reforms in India .... the energies of Indian entrepreneurs and gave untold choice to the consumers.

(iv) Today's reforms require much more .... and consensus building, with the central government needing to work in tandem with state governments and consult different stakeholders.

Subjective Questions

Free Response Questions, Open-ended Questions etc.

No. of Questions : 7 | Suggested Time : **50 Minutes**

1. Imagine you are tasked with presenting a compelling case relating to the need for economic reforms in India to a diverse audience, including policy-makers, business leaders and the general public.

How would you structure your argument, considering the challenges faced by the Indian economy?

2. "The opening up of the Indian economy has led to a rapid increase in foreign direct investments and foreign exchange reserves of the country." Defend or refute the given statement.

3. "New Economic Policy 1991 altered the role of Reserve Bank of India (RBI) in the economy." Justify the given statement with valid explanation. *[CBSE 2024]*

4. Agriculture sector has been adversely affected by the economic reform process. Comment. *[CBSE 2023]*

5. Which concept of economics is depicted in the below image? Identify and explain.

6. India has experienced demonetisation three times in its history: the first in 1946, the second in 1978 and the most recent on 8th November, 2016. The primary reason behind these measures was to combat the circulation of black money.

The 2016 demonetisation, announced by Prime Minister Narendra Modi, banned ₹ 500 and ₹ 1,000 currency notes with immediate effect. This move aimed to address several issues, including corruption, black money, inflation, illegal funding and tax evasion.

The ban on ₹ 500 and ₹ 1,000 notes also pushed the country towards digitalisation. With the widespread use of mobile phones, online wallets became increasingly popular, facilitating electronic transactions.

However, the sudden announcement led to significant inconvenience for the public, causing a severe cash crunch due to the unavailability of smaller currency denominations.

(i) What were the primary objectives behind the 2016 demonetisation policy in India?

(ii) How did demonetisation in 2016 impact the movement towards digital transactions and online wallets?

7. The stabilisation and structural adjustment measures, initiated under the 1991 'economic reforms' mark a watershed moment in India's economic policies.

For almost three decades since independence, India's development strategy and economic policies were guided by the objectives of accelerating the growth of output and employment with social justice and equity.

Ever since the 1970's, it was realised that many of the regulations on economic activities have outlived their usefulness and were in fact hampering economic growth and development.

In response to this, the government initiated some milder liberalisa- tion reforms for almost a decade since the early 1980's.

However, the Indian economy soon had to face the Gulf crisis and consequently

- The uncertainties about the oil prices
- The external payment problems
- The serious inflationary pressures
- The scarcities of essential commodities
- The deterioration of fiscal discipline, etc.

These led to the Indian economy on the verge of economic crisis.

In response to this emerging crisis, the government initiated a set of stabilisation and structural reforms like

- Reduction in fiscal deficit
- Containment of growth in money supply
- An exchange rate adjustment system, etc.

The key objective of stabilisation policy was to bring the growth of aggregate demand in line with long-term growth path of the economy.

In conjunction the strucutral adjustment measures like

- industrial delicensing
- liberalisation of policy regime governing international trade
- de-regulation of financial sector

Were taken to improve the supply side of the economy. This shifted the long-term growth part of the economy itself completely

(Adapted and modified)

Source *https:\\niti.gov.in\planningcommission.gov.in\docs\reports\generep\arep9099\ at94-95.htm* **[CBSE 2023]**

(i) Discuss any two reasons behind the introduction of economic reforms in 1991.

(ii) "In response to the emerging crisis in 1991, the government initiated a set of stabilisation and structural reforms."

Briefly discuss any three of such measures.

Answers

If your answer matches with the answer given here then put (✓) in the box otherwise put (✗). In case you did not attempt the question leave the box blank.

Multiple Choice Questions

1. C ☐	2. B ☐
3. A ☐	4. D ☐
5. D ☐	6. C ☐
7. D ☐	8. C ☐
9. C ☐	10. C ☐
11. D ☐	12. C ☐
13. D ☐	14. C ☐
15. D ☐	16. C ☐
17. C ☐	18. C ☐
19. D ☐	20. A ☐
21. C ☐	22. C ☐
23. B ☐	24. B ☐
25. D ☐	26. D ☐
27. D ☐	28. C ☐
29. B ☐	
30. D ☐	

Your Score__________ (*No. of Correct Answers*)

Assertion-Reason Questions

1. C ☐	2. A ☐
3. A ☐	4. A ☐
5. A ☐	6. C ☐
7. A ☐	8. C ☐
9. D ☐	10. C ☐

Your Score__________ (*No. of Correct Answers*)

Correct/Incorrect Statements

1. C ☐	2. B ☐
3. A ☐	4. D ☐
5. A ☐	6. C ☐
7. D ☐	8. D ☐
9. A ☐	10. A ☐

Your Score__________ (*No. of Correct Answers*)

Case Based Questions

1. (i) C ☐	(ii) C ☐
2. (i) D ☐	(ii) B ☐

Your Score__________ (*No. of Correct Answers*)

Explanations

Multiple Choice Questions

1. (C) Both (A) and (B)
2. (B) social sector, defence
3. (A) Both (i) and (ii)
4. (D) (i), (ii) and (iii)
5. (D) PV Narasimha Rao, Manmohan Singh
6. (C) borrowings
7. (D) short-term measures, intended to correct some of the weaknesses that have developed in the balance of payments and to bring inflation under control
8. (C) liberalisation
9. (C) Both (A) and (B)
10. (C) Goods which could be produced only in small-scale industries were de-reserved
11. (D) promote the efficiency of local industries and adoption of modern technologies
12. (C) During the reform period in India, the service sector experienced significant growth compared to agriculture and industry. This includes IT, telecommunications, finance and other service oriented industries that saw substantial expansion.
13. (D) One of the issues faced by the agricultural sector was actually the lack of adequate domestic support rather than a shift away from export oriented strategies.
14. (C) PV Narsimha Rao and Manmohan Singh
15. (D) Financial sector reforms aimed to reduce the RBI's regulatory role and establish private banks, increase foreign investment and allow foreign institutional investors, but did not eliminate the need for RBI approval to set-up new branches.
16. (C) Services
17. (C) Tax reductions during economic reforms aimed to increase tax revenues by broadening the tax base and to create a unified tax system, fostering a more integrated national market.
18. (C) Globalisation
19. (D) While outsourcing can reduce costs for companies in developed countries, it often leads to concerns among their governments and citizens about job losses and the negative impact on the domestic labour market.
20. (A) high non-tariff barriers
21. (C) Both (i) and (ii)
22. (C) Despite reforms, the agricultural sector in particular has not seen significant upgrades and continues to face numerous challenges.
23. (B) Stop funds flow to illegal activities
24. (B) Finance Minister Nirmala Sitharaman praised GST for its role in benefitting the poor by lowering taxes on essential items. This means that essential goods have become more affordable due to reduced tax rates under GST, which helps lower income individuals by reducing their cost of living.
25. (D) India was not ready to pay the loan amount
26. (D) Demonetisation
27. (D) (iii) (i) (iv) (ii)
28. (C) (iii) (iv) (ii) (i)
29. (B) (iv) (iii) (i) (ii)
30. (D) (ii) (i) (iv) (iii)

Assertion-Reason Questions

1. (C) Liberalisation measures were introduced in the 1980s. Understanding of liberalisation was crucial in 1991 to address economic challenges.
2. (A) Both Assertion (A) and Reason (R) are true and Reason (R) is the correct explanation of Assertion (A)
3. (A) Both Assertion (A) and Reason (R) are true and Reason (R) is the correct explanation of Assertion (A)
4. (A) Both Assertion (A) and Reason (R) are true and Reason (R) is the correct explanation of Assertion (A)
5. (A) Both Assertion (A) and Reason (R) are true and Reason (R) is the correct explanation of Assertion (A)
6. (C) Assertion (A) is true, but Reason (R) is false
7. (A) Both Assertion (A) and Reason (R) are true and Reason (R) is the correct explanation of Assertion (A)
8. (C) Assertion (A) is true, but Reason (R) is false

9. (D) Assertion (A) is false, but Reason (R) is true
10. (C) Assertion (A) is true, but Reason (R) is false

Correct/Incorrect Statements

1. (C) Statement I is correct and Statement II is incorrect
2. (B) Structural measures are long-term policies aimed at improving efficiency and competitiveness, not short-term measures like stabilisation policies. Stabilisation reform policies are typically short-term measures aimed at stabilising the economy, not long-term measures focused on improving efficiency and competitiveness.
3. (A) Both statements are correct
4. (D) Efforts were made to reform indirect taxes as part of the GST (Goods and Services Tax) implementation, aiming to establish a common national market for goods and commodities.
5. (A) Both statements are correct
6. (C) Quantitative restrictions on imports of manufactured consumer goods and agricultural products were, fully removed from April 2000, not April 2010.
7. (D) Selling off part of public sector enterprises' equity to the public is known as privatisation.
8. (D) While all sectors of the economy experienced growth post-1991 reforms, it's not accurate to say that all grew tremendously well.
9. (A) Both statements are correct
10. (A) Both statements are correct

Case Based Questions

1. (i) (C) Liberalisation and abolition of the license raj
   (ii) (C) Improve fiscal burden and efficiency by disinvesting state owned enterprises
   (iii) Trade liberalisation
   (iv) reform of the tax system, financial sector and infrastructure
2. (i) (D) Integration with the global trading system
   (ii) (B) Liberalisation
   (iii) unleashed (iv) discussion

Subjective Questions

1. Considering the challenges faced by Indian economy, need for economic reforms has arisen due to the following reasons
   (i) The government was not able to make repayments on its borrowings from abroad.
   (ii) Foreign exchange reserves, which we generally maintain to import petroleum and other important items, dropped to levels that were not sufficient for even a fortnight.
   (iii) The crisis was further compounded by rising prices of essential goods.
2. The given statement is true to its character. The foreign investments, both Foreign Direct Investment (FDI) and Foreign Institutional Investment (FII), have increased from about US $100 million in 1990-91 to US $ 74 billion recently. This has changed the status of India from a 'begging bowl' in 1990's to a 'self-dependent' economy in the present ages.

   Due to the opening up of the Indian economy, she has become one of the largest foreign exchange reserve holders in the world. India been able to register an increase in the foreign exchange reserves from about US $ 6 billion in 1990-91 to about US $ 321 billion in 2014-15.
3. I agree with the given statement. Prior to liberalisation, RBI used to regulate and control the financial sector including financial institutions like commercial banks, investment banks, stock exchange operations and foreign exchange market. With the economic liberalisation and financial sector reforms, RBI needed to shift its role from a controller to a facilitator of the financial sector.

   This implies that the financial organisations were free to make their own decisions on many matters without consulting the RBI. This opened up the gates of financial sectors for the private players.
4. Agriculture sector has been adversely affected by the economic reform process due to following reasons
   (i) Reduction of public investment in providing sufficient irrigation facilities, electricity, information system and roads.
   (ii) Removal of subsidies on fertilisers made farming more expensive.
   (iii) Shift of agricultural production form food grains to the production of cash crops that led to reduced availability of foodgrains.
   (iv) Liberalisation and reduction in import duties on agricultural products forced the poor and marginal farmers to compete with their foreign counterparts in the international markets.

5. The concept highlighted is globalisation. Globalisation in economics refers to the integration of national and regional economies, societies and cultures through global trade, communication, immigration and transportation networks. This process has significantly impacted the global economy by facilitating the free flow of goods, services, information and capital across borders.

Key aspects of economic globalisation include trade liberalisation, capital flow, technology and information exchange, labour mobility, multinational corporations and global supply chains. These elements collectively contribute to increased economic efficiency, productivity and growth by allowing countries to specialise in areas where they have a comparative advantage, providing consumers with a wider variety of goods and services at competitive prices and accelerating technological advancement through the transfer of innovation and practices.

6. (i) The primary objectives behind the 2016 demonetisation policy were

(a) **Combat Corruption** To make India corruption free by eliminating counterfeit currency and illegal cash holdings.

(b) **Curb Black Money** To reduce the amount of black money circulating in the economy.

(c) **Control Inflation** To control escalating price rise by reducing excess money in circulation.

(d) **Halt Illegal Funding** To stop the flow of funds to illegal activities, such as terrorism and smuggling.

(e) **Ensure Accountability** To make people accountable for every rupee they possess and ensure proper tax compliance.

(f) **Promote Cashless Society** To promote a cashless society and advance the digital India initiative by encouraging the use of digital transactions.

(ii) Demonetisation in 2016 significantly accelerated the movement towards digital transactions and the use of online wallets. With the sudden unavailability of ₹ 500 and ₹ 1,000 notes, people were compelled to explore alternative payment methods.

The widespread use of mobile phones facilitated the adoption of online wallets, which allowed individuals to make electronic transactions easily.

This shift towards digital payments was a step towards creating a cashless society and advancing the digital India initiative.

Online wallets became a popular and convenient option for many, reducing dependency on cash and enhancing the digital economy.

7. (i) The reasons behind the introduction of economic reforms in 1991 are as follows

(a) **The adverse Balance of Payments** One of the biggest factors that played a major role behind the introduction of economic reforms in 1991 was the fact that India's balance of payments were unsustainable.

(b) **The Serious Inflationary Pressures** In 1991, inflation was on rise and could not be curbed. The centre did not have any funds in its hands. Consequently, the Government of India took a decision that would lead to the implementation of NEP. This was done to bring about the Indian economic reforms.

(ii) In response to the emerging crisis in 1991, the government initiated a set of stabilisation and structural reforms which are as follows

(a) **Reduction in Fiscal Deficit** In response to the emerging crisis in 1991, the government reduced the fiscal deficit. The budget for 1991-92 took a bold step in the direction of correcting fiscal imbalance.

In envisaged a reduction in fiscal deficit by nearly 2% points of GDP form 8.4% in 1991-91 to 6.5% in 1991-92

(b) **Containment of Growth in Money Supply** After emerging crisis in 1991, the government had containment of growth in money supply.

As per reports, money supply M_2 in India averaged 15,457.60 INR billion from 1991 until 2023, reaching an all time high of 57,876.21 INR billion in February of 2023 and a record low of 1,127.49 INR billion in November, 1991.

(c) **Globalisation** In response to the emerging crises in 1991, government undertook steps to promote globalisation like increase in equity limit of foreign investment, partial convertibility, reduction in tariff, etc.

CHAPTER -4

Human Capital Formation in India

Types & Nos. of Questions

Multiple Choice Questions	-	25
Assertion-Reason Questions	-	7
Correct/Incorrect Statements	-	9
Case Based Questions	-	2 Cases, *each with four Questions*
Subjective Questions	-	6

Trend Analysis

On the basis of analysis of last 2 years' papers, it is found that on an average 2 Multiple Choice Questions and 2 Short Answer Type Questions (Statement Based) are asked from this chapter. No case based question is asked but may be asked in coming exams.

Focus Topics of the Chapter

- Concept of Human Capital Formation
- Human Capital and Human Development
- Education Sector in India

Multiple Choice Questions

No. of Questions : **25** Suggested Time : **40 Minutes**

Direction Each of the question given below is Multiple Choice Question (MCQ) i.e. there are Four Options/Choices for answer, out of which ONLY ONE is correct. You have to select the correct option. A response box is given with each option, mark (✓) in the box of the correct option. For each correct answer you will get 1 mark, while there is no penalty for incorrect answer or missed out questions.

1. Which of the following statement is not true in context of human capital?

(A) We need good human capital to produce other human capital ☐

(B) We need sufficient human capital to further produce better human capital ☐

(C) It includes skilled, expert and trained people in an economy who contributes to the GDP ☐

(D) Human capital is a flow concept ☐

2. Identify, which of the following are associated with the problem of human capital formation in India. *[CBSE 2023]*

(i) Brain drain

(ii) Low academic standards

(iii) Rising population

(iv) Changes in social outlook

Codes

(A) (i) and (ii) ☐

(B) (ii) and (iii) ☐

(C) (i), (ii) and (iii) ☐

(D) (i) and (iv) ☐

3. Which of the following fits best in relation to the difference between human capital and physical capital?

(A) Physical capital is tangible whereas human capital is intangible ☐

(B) The physical capital is separable from its owner, whereas human capital is inseparable from its owner ☐

(C) Physical capital is completely mobile whereas human capital is not perfectly mobile ☐

(D) Physical capital creates both private and social benefits, whereas human capital creates only private benefit ☐

4. Economy is concerned about creating human capital as it leads to economic growth. Human capital contributes to economic growth

(A) by increasing the physical capital of a nation ☐

(B) by reducing the labour force participation rate ☐

(C) by improving the skills, knowledge and productivity of the workforce ☐

(D) by decreasing investment in education and training programmes ☐

5. An analysis of improvement in education and health sectors and growth in real per capita income in both developing and developed countries shows that there is convergence in the measures of human capital but no sign of convergence of ....

(A) human capital formation ☐

(B) per capita real income ☐

(C) economic growth ☐

(D) physical capital formation ☐

6. Trained and educated on sound lines, a large population can itself become .... in accelerating economic growth and in ensuring .... in desired directions.

(A) liability, social change ☐

(B) an asset, physical change ☐

(C) liability, technical change ☐

(D) an asset, social change ☐

7. The two terms human capital and human development sound similar but there is a clear distinction between them. Which of the following highlights is the correct distinction?

(i) Human development considers education and health as a means to increase labour productivity whereas human capital is based on the idea that education and health are integral to human well-being.

(ii) Human development treats human beings as a means to an end whereas human capital treats human beings as ends in themselves.

Codes

(A) Both (i) and (ii) ☐
(B) Only (i) ☐
(C) Only (ii) ☐
(D) Neither (i) nor (ii) ☐

8. In India there are many organisations which play important role in developing education and health sector. Which of the following best suits as a function of ICMR?

(A) Developing academic course content for classes 1 to 12 ☐
(B) Ensures the maintenance of ethical standards in higher education institutions ☐
(C) Advancing scientific knowledge related to health and medicine ☐
(D) Shaping technical education in India ☐

9. "The contribution to GDP of an educated labour is higher than the uneducated labour."

It is due to the reason that

(A) educated is more labour intensive based than capital intensive based ☐
(B) labour skills and training of an educated person is more than that of an uneducated person ☐
(C) educated labour struggles with specialised knowledge skills ☐
(D) educated labour produces products of low quality ☐

10. Identify the type of capital depicted in the following picture.

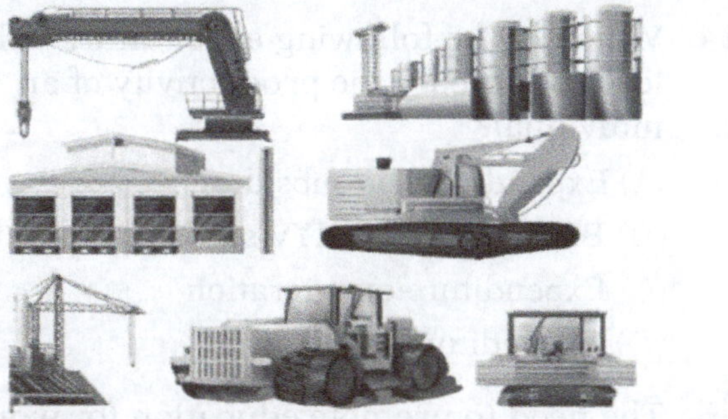

(A) Human capital ☐
(B) Physical capital ☐
(C) Financial capital ☐
(D) Technical capital ☐

11. How does the National Education Policy (NEP) 2020 aim to enhance human capital development in India?

(A) By emphasing traditional role learning methods ☐
(B) By reducing the accessibility of education for marginalised communities ☐
(C) By promoting holistic and multi-disciplinary education approaches ☐
(D) By limiting the use of technology in the learning process ☐

12. .... education takes a major share of total education expenditure and the share of the .... education (institutions of higher learning like colleges, polytechnics and universities) is the least.

(A) Primary, elementary ☐
(B) Elementary, secondary ☐
(C) Elementary, tertiary ☐
(D) Tertiary, secondary ☐

13. The government takes various efforts time-to-time to improve the status of education in the economy. In the light of this, identify the act which made free education a fundamental right of all children.

(A) Beti Bachao Beti Padao Act ☐
(B) Right of Children to Free and Compulsory Education Act ☐

(C) Sakshar Bharat ☐
(D) Mid Day Meal Scheme ☐

14. Which of the following expenditure will lead to increase the productivity of an individual?
(A) Expenditure on subsidies ☐
(B) Expenditure on HYV seeds ☐
(C) Expenditure on migration ☐
(D) Expenditure on defense ☐

15. The need to promote education for women in India is imminent for various reasons such as
(A) improving economic dependence ☐
(B) improving social status of men ☐
(C) unfavourable impact on fertility rate ☐
(D) favourable impact on healthcare of women and children ☐

16. 'Skill India' programme launched by the government is not an attempt to increase .... in India. *[CBSE 2023]*
(A) human capital formation ☐
(B) efficient utilisation of inputs ☐
(C) increase in GDP growth ☐
(D) inadequate spread of vocational education ☐

17. The expenditure on preventive medicines include
(A) expenditure on medical intervention ☐
(B) expenditure on vaccination ☐
(C) expenditure on health literacy ☐
(D) expenditure on clean drinking water and good sanitation ☐

18. Ms. Ramanpreet has started a new business venture, she intends to spend a huge amount towards 'on-the-job training' of her workers before putting them to work. It exhibits the right step in the direction of human capital formation.
Spot which of the following does not directly contributes to the process of human capital formation by Ms. Ramanpreet?
(A) Adds skills and expertise ☐
(B) Improves efficiency ☐
(C) Ensures gender equity ☐
(D) Increases output productivity ☐

19. A firm can increase the output scale by incurring expenditure on 'on-the-job' training programmes, which may be done in the following form(s)
(i) The workers may be trained in the firm itself under the supervision of a skilled worker.
(ii) The workers may be sent for off-campus training.

Codes
(A) Only (i) ☐
(B) Only (ii) ☐
(C) Both (i) and (ii) ☐
(D) Neither (i) nor (ii) ☐

20. Why a firm incurs expenditure on 'on-the-job' training programmes when it adds to the cost of production to the firm?
(A) The expenditure provides a narrow skill set to the employees ☐
(B) The benefits of on-the-job training programme are constrained to theoretical knowledge only ☐
(C) It offers limited time period benefits to employees ☐
(D) The benefits of on-the-job training programmes are far more than the benefits derived from it ☐

21. The following picture depicts the expenditure on the .... to form human capital.

(A) education ☐
(B) health ☐
(C) on-the-job-training programme ☐
(D) migration ☐

22. Rahul is a young entrepreneur who is starting his own business in the field of online education. He believes that providing accurate and timely information to students about various job opportunities and educational institutes is crucial for their personal and professional development.

As part of his business plan, Rahul intends to invest a significant amount in developing a platform that offers comprehensive information on job opportunities, career paths and educational programmes.

How does Rahul's investment in developing a platform for job opportunities and educational institutes contribute to human capital formation?

(A) It facilitates access to relevant information, enabling individuals to make informed decisions about their education and career paths ☐
(B) It reduces the need for educational institutions to improve their academic standards ☐
(C) It limits individuals' options, thereby hindering human capital formation ☐
(D) It increases the cost of accessing information, making it difficult for individuals to enhance their skills and knowledge ☐

23. Match the Column I with Column II in the following information

Column I	Column II
A. Expenditure on education	(i) Increases the supply of healthy labour force
B. Expenditure on health	(ii) Psychic costs of living
C. Expenditure on migration	(iii) Increasing future income
D. Expenditure on information	(iv) Right type of employable skills

Codes

	A	B	C	D	
(A)	(iv)	(i)	(ii)	(iii)	☐
(B)	(i)	(iii)	(ii)	(iv)	☐
(C)	(iii)	(i)	(ii)	(iv)	☐
(D)	(iii)	(ii)	(i)	(iv)	☐

24. Match the Column I with Column II in the following information

Column I	Column II
A. Physical capital	(i) Human beings are ends in themselves
B. Human capital	(ii) Flow concept
C. Human capital formation	(iii) Not sold in the market
D. Human development	(iv) Perfectly mobile

Codes

	A	B	C	D	
(A)	(iii)	(iv)	(ii)	(i)	☐
(B)	(i)	(iii)	(ii)	(iv)	☐
(C)	(iv)	(ii)	(iii)	(i)	☐
(D)	(iv)	(iii)	(ii)	(i)	☐

25. Match the situations given in Column I with their respective implications given in Column II

Column I	Column II
A. Migration	(i) Reduced in per capita economic growth
B. Low level of academic standards	(ii) Imbalance between demand and supply of human resource
C. Population high growth rate	(iii) Brain drain
D. Lack of proper manpower planning	(iv) Mismatch between required skill and academic standards

Codes

	A	B	C	D	
(A)	(ii)	(iii)	(iv)	(i)	☐
(B)	(iii)	(iv)	(i)	(ii)	☐
(C)	(i)	(ii)	(iii)	(iv)	☐
(D)	(ii)	(iv)	(i)	(iii)	☐

Assertion-Reason Questions

No. of Questions : 7 Suggested Time : **15 Minutes**

Direction Each of the question given below consist of the two statements; one labelled as **Assertion** (A) and other as **Reason** (R). List of common options applicable for each question is given below

(A) Both Assertion (A) and Reason (R) are true, but Reason (R) is the correct explanation of Assertion (A)

(B) Both Assertion (A) and Reason (R) are true, but Reason (R) is not the correct explanation of Assertion (A)

(C) Assertion (A) is true, but Reason (R) is false

(D) Assertion (A) is false, but Reason (R) is true

You have to select the codes as *A, B, C or D* as your answer to the question by marking (✓) in the response box given against each option.

1. **Assertion (A)** The enhanced productivity of human beings or human capital contributes substantially towards increasing labour productivity.

   Reason (R) It neither stimulate innovations nor creates ability to absorb new technologies.

   (A) ☐ (B) ☐ (C) ☐ (D) ☐

2. **Assertion (A)** Empirical evidence to prove that increase in human capital causes economic growth is rather nebulous.

   Reason (R) Education measured in terms of years of schooling, teacher-pupil ratio and enrollment rates may not reflect the quality of education.

   (A) ☐ (B) ☐ (C) ☐ (D) ☐

3. **Assertion (A)** The economy is in the need for expanding educational opportunities as it accelerates the development process.

   Reason (R) Labour skill of an educated person is more than that of an uneducated person and hence the former is able to generate more income than the latter and his or her contribution to economic growth is, consequently, more.

   (A) ☐ (B) ☐ (C) ☐ (D) ☐

4. **Assertion (A)** Health expenditure indirectly increases the supply of healthy labour force.

   Reason (R) A sick labourer without access to medical facilities is compelled to abstain from work and there is loss of productivity.

   (A) ☐ (B) ☐ (C) ☐ (D) ☐

5. **Assertion (A)** Human capital is not traded in the market, however its services are traded.

   Reason (R) Human capital is intangible in nature. *[CBSE 2023]*

   (A) ☐ (B) ☐ (C) ☐ (D) ☐

6. **Assertion (A)** Basic education and basic health are important in themselves, irrespective of their contribution to labour productivity.

   Reason (R) Human welfare should be increased through investments in education and health.

   (A) ☐ (B) ☐ (C) ☐ (D) ☐

7. **Assertion (A)** The level of unemployment among educated youth is the least.

   Reason (R) The government should increase allocation for higher education and also improve the standard of higher education institutions.

   (A) ☐ (B) ☐ (C) ☐ (D) ☐

Correct/Incorrect Statements

No. of Questions : **9** Suggested Time : **15 Minutes**

Direction Each of the question given below consist of the two statements. List of common options applicable for each question is given below

(A) Both statements are correct
(B) Both statements are incorrect
(C) Statement I is correct and Statement II is incorrect
(D) Statement I is incorrect and Statement II is correct

You have to select the codes as *A, B, C* or *D* as your answer to the question by marking (✓) in the response box given against each option.

1. **Statement I** We need investment in human capital to produce more human capital out of human resources.

Statement II Education is an important input for development of an individual as well as nation while health is an important input only for development of an individual and not for the development of nation.

(A) ☐ (B) ☐ (C) ☐ (D) ☐

2. **Statement I** The human capital formation is mainly an economic and technical process.

Statement II Physical capital formation is partly a social process and partly a conscious decision of the possessor of the human capital.

(A) ☐ (B) ☐ (C) ☐ (D) ☐

3. **Statement I** Higher income causes building of high level of human capital.

Statement II It is difficult to establish a relation of cause-and-effect from the growth of human capital (education and health) to economic growth.

(A) ☐ (B) ☐ (C) ☐ (D) ☐

4. **Statement I** Education confers higher earning capacity.

Statement II The availability of educated labour force facilitates adaptation of new technologies.

(A) ☐ (B) ☐ (C) ☐ (D) ☐

5. **Statement I** The Education Commission (1964-66) had recommended that at least 6 per cent of GDP be spent on education so as to make a noticeable rate of growth in educational achievements.

Statement II Compared to this desired level of education expenditure of around 6 per cent of GDP, the current level of a little over 4 per cent has been quite inadequate.

(A) ☐ (B) ☐ (C) ☐ (D) ☐

6. **Statement I** The revenue from education cess has been earmarked for spending on primary education.

Statement II Government of India has also started levying a 2 per cent 'education cess' on all union taxes.

(A) ☐ (B) ☐ (C) ☐ (D) ☐

7. **Statement I** The Indian education pyramid is steep, indicating lesser and lesser number of people reaching the higher education level.

Statement II India has a less stock of scientific and technical manpower in the world.

(A) ☐ (B) ☐
(C) ☐ (D) ☐

8. **Statement I** Unemployment is the reason for the rural-urban migration in India.

Statement II Expenditure on migration involves cost of transport, higher cost of living in the migrated places and psychic costs of living in a strange socio-cultural set-up.

(A) ☐ (B) ☐
(C) ☐ (D) ☐

9. **Statement I** People do not spend to acquire information relating to the labour market and other markets like education and health.

Statement II This information is not necessary to make decisions regarding investments in human capital as well as for efficient utilisation of the acquired human capital stock.

(A) ☐ (B) ☐ (C) ☐ (D) ☐

Case Based Questions

No. of Questions : 2 Suggested Time : **10 Minutes**

Direction This section contains 2 cases each having 4 questions of 1 mark each. You have to write the answer of each question based on the context of the related case.

Case 1 In the rapidly evolving global economy, human capital plays a critical role in driving economic growth and development. Countries like India which is a developing nation, recognises the significance of investing in its human capital to achieve sustainable growth.

The government has implemented various policies to improve education, healthcare and skill development programmes across the country. As a result, there has been a noticeable increase in literacy rates, healthcare outcomes and skilled workforce participation.

Furthermore, foreign investors are increasingly attracted to these countries due to its growing pool of educated and skilled labour, leading to greater foreign direct investment and economic prosperity.

Questions

(i) How does investing in human capital contribute to economic growth in the countries?

(A) By neglecting education and healthcare initiatives ☐

(B) By decreasing workforce participation rates ☐

(C) By improving literacy rates, healthcare outcomes and skill development programmes ☐

(D) By solely relying on natural resources for economic development ☐

(ii) The government's investment in human capital has led to a remarkable improvement in .... across the country, contributing significantly to economic growth and development.

(iii) Foreign investors are increasingly drawn to countries like India due to its growing pool of ...., which has resulted from the government's focus on education, healthcare and skill development initiatives.

(iv) Which sector benefits the most from the government's investment in human capital?

(A) Agriculture ☐

(B) Healthcare ☐

(C) Defense ☐

(D) Entertainment ☐

Case 2 When we talk about economic growth, human capital is the main reason for accelerated growth and expansion for many countries which provide investment in human capital. This gives the best advantages to these countries for providing the best situation for work and life.

A significant advantage in generating a stable environment for growth is that the nation has the expanded high quality of human capital in fields like health, science, management, education and other fields.

Here the main components of human capital are definitely human beings but presently, the principal component is creative, an educated and enterprising person, with a high level of professionalism.

Questions

(i) ...... refers to the stock of skill, ability, expertise, education and knowledge in a nation at a point of time.

(A) Human capital ☐
(B) Physical capital ☐
(C) Natural capital ☐
(D) Owner's capital ☐

(ii) Human capital increases

(A) labour in market ☐
(B) labour in productivity ☐
(C) trained labour ☐
(D) None of the above ☐

(iii) Innovation leads to ....

(iv) The human capital in the economy manages the central portion of the ...... of the country.

Subjective Questions

Free Response Questions, Open-ended Questions etc.

No. of Questions : **6** Suggested Time : **30 Minutes**

1. "Investing in the growth and well-being of individuals within an organisation not only enhances their skills and knowledge but also boosts overall productivity and innovation." Defend/Refute the statement with reason.

2. State with valid reasons whether the following statements are true or false.

(i) Rising population is not the cause for quality of human capital formation.

(ii) Higher productivity and production are the outcome of investment in human resources. *[CBSE 2023]*

3. "Expenditure on on-the-job training is an important means of human capital formation in an economy." Give valid reasons to justify the given statement. *[CBSE 2023]*

4. Identify the source of human capital formation and explain it.

5. "National Education Policy, 2020 of India stresses a lot on in-service teachers' training." In the light of the given statement, state and explain any two advantages of such on-the- job trainings in upliftment of education sector of any nation. *[CBSE 2024]*

6. In a middle income nation, the government faces challenges in human capital formation due to inadequate investment in the education and health sectors.

Despite economic growth, significant portions of the population lack access to quality education and healthcare services, leading to low literacy rates, poor health outcomes and a skilled labour shortage.

Recognising the crucial role of human capital in driving sustainable development, the government decides to intervene by implementing comprehensive policies aimed at improving education and healthcare.

To address the education sector's shortcomings, the government launches initiatives such as building new schools, providing scholarships for underprivileged students and upgrading curriculum standards to meet modern workforce demands.

Additionally, efforts are made to enhance teacher training programmes and incentivise educators to improve teaching quality. In the healthcare sector, the government focuses on expanding access to primary healthcare services, especially in rural areas, through the establishment of clinics and mobile health units.

Furthermore, investments are made in medical infrastructure, equipment and workforce training to improve healthcare delivery and reduce mortality rates.

As a result of these interventions, significant progress is observed in human capital formation. The literacy rates increase, leading to a more educated workforce capable of contributing to economic growth and innovation.

Similarly, improved healthcare services lead to better health outcomes, reduced absenteeism due to illness and increased productivity among the workforce. Moreover, the government's interventions attract foreign investment and aid, as investors and international organisations recognise the potential for sustainable development in countries with a well-educated and healthy population.

With continued government support and effective implementation of policies, country is on track to achieve higher levels of human capital formation, driving long-term economic prosperity and social development.

(i) Discuss the importance of government intervention in the education and health sectors for human capital formation.

(ii) Examine the potential challenges faced by governments in implementing interventions in the education and health sectors to improve human capital formation.

Answers

If your answer matches with the answer given here then put (✓) in the box otherwise put (✗). In case you did not attempt the question leave the box blank.

Multiple Choice Questions

1. D ☐ 2. C ☐ 3. D ☐ 4. C ☐ 5. B ☐ 6. D ☐ 7. D ☐ 8. C ☐ 9. B ☐ 10. B ☐ 11. C ☐ 12. C ☐ 13. B ☐ 14. C ☐ 15. D ☐ 16. D ☐ 17. B ☐ 18. C ☐ 19. C ☐ 20. D ☐ 21. C ☐ 22. A ☐ 23. C ☐ 24. D ☐ 25. B ☐

Your Score_________ *(No. of Correct Answers)*

Assertion-Reason Questions

1. C ☐ 2. A ☐
3. A ☐ 4. D ☐
5. A ☐ 6. A ☐
7. D ☐

Your Score________ (No. of Correct Answers)

Correct/Incorrect Statements

1. C ☐ 2. B ☐

3. B ☐ 4. A ☐
5. A ☐ 6. D ☐
7. A ☐ 8. A ☐
9. B ☐

Your Score________ (No. of Correct Answers)

Case Based Questions

1. (i) C ☐ (iv) B ☐
2. (i) A ☐ (ii) B ☐

Your Score________ (No. of Correct Answers)

Explanations

Multiple Choice Questions

1. (D) Human capital is considered a stock concept, as it accumulates over time with education, experience and skills.
2. (C) (i), (ii) and (iii)
3. (D) Physical capital creates both private and social benefits, whereas human capital creates only private benefit
4. (C) by improving the skills, knowledge and productivity of the workforce
5. (B) per capita real income
6. (D) an asset, social change
7. (D) Neither (i) nor (ii)
8. (C) Advancing scientific knowledge related to health and medicine
9. (B) labour skills and training of an educated person is more than that of an uneducated person
10. (B) Physical capital
11. (C) By promoting holistic and multidisciplinary education approaches
12. (C) Elementary, tertiary
13. (B) Right of Children to Free and Compulsory Education Act
14. (C) Expenditure on migration can lead to increased productivity as individuals move to areas with better job opportunities, education and healthcare, enhancing their overall potential and contribution to the economy.
15. (D) favourable impact on healthcare of women and children
16. (D) The 'Skill India' programme was initiated to address the deficiency in the spread of vocational education across the country. By focusing on skill development and vocational training, the programme aims to bridge the gap between demand and supply of skilled workforce in various sectors.
17. (B) expenditure on vaccination
18. (C) Ms. Ramanpreet's 'on-the-job training' boosts human capital by adding skills, improving efficiency and increasing productivity. Ensuring gender equity, while important, does not directly contribute to human capital formation.
19. (C) Both (i) and (ii)
20. (D) On-the-job training improves employee skills and productivity significantly, which outweighs the initial costs of the training programmes.
21. (C) on-the-job-training programme
22. (A) It facilitates access to relevant information, enabling individuals to make informed decisions about their education and career paths
23. (C) (iii) (i) (ii) (iv)
24. (D) (iv) (iii) (ii) (i)
25. (B) (iii) (iv) (i) (ii)

Assertion-Reason Questions

1. (C) Investing in human capital does stimulate innovations and creates the ability to absorb new technologies.

2. (A) Both Assertion (A) and Reason (R) are true and Reason (R) is the correct explanation of Assertion (A)

3. (A) Both Assertion (A) and Reason (R) are true and Reason (R) is the correct explanation of Assertion (A)

4. (D) Health expenditure directly contributes to the health of the workforce rather than indirectly increasing the supply of healthy labour.

5. (A) Both Assertion (A) and Reason (R) are true and Reason (R) is the correct explanation of Assertion (A)

6. (A) Both Assertion (A) and Reason (R) are true and Reason (R) is the correct explanation of Assertion (A)

7. (D) Assertion (A) is false, but Reason (R) is true

Correct/Incorrect Statements

1. (C) Both education and health are critical inputs for the development of both individuals and nations.

2. (B) Human capital formation involves not only economic and technical processes but also social and personal development. Additionally, physical capital formation is not solely based on conscious decisions but also involves economic considerations.

3. (B) Higher income alone does not lead to the development of human capital; instead, investments in education and health contribute to its growth. While there's a correlation between human capital and economic growth, establishing a direct cause-and-effect relationship is challenging.

4. (A) Both statements are correct

5. (A) Both statements are correct

6. (D) The revenue from education cess isn't exclusively designated for primary education; it can be allocated to various educational initiatives.

7. (A) Both statements are correct

8. (A) Both statements are correct

9. (B) Acquiring information about labour markets and other areas is crucial for informed decision-making. Such information is essential for decisions regarding investments in human capital and its efficient utilisation.

Case Based Questions

1. (i) (C) By improving literacy rates, healthcare outcomes and skill development programmes
   (ii) healthcare outcomes and literacy rates
   (iii) educated and skilled labour
   (iv) (B) Healthcare

2. (i) (A) Human capital
   (ii) (B) labour in productivity
   (iii) growth, production and development
   (iv) national wealth

Subjective Questions

1. The given statement is defended. To boost the growth of individuals by enhancing their skills is beneficial for themselves as the organisation. So, the organisations or firms spend on giving on-the-job training to their workers. This may take different forms
   (i) The workers may be trained in the firm itself under the supervision of a skilled worker.
   (ii) The workers may be sent for off-campus training.

   In both these cases, firms incur some expenses. Firms will, thus, insist that the workers should work for a specific period of time, after their on-the-job training, during which it can recover the benefits of the enhanced productivity owing to the training.

   Expenditure regarding on-the-job training is a source of human capital formation as the return of such expenditure in the form of enhanced labour productivity is more than the cost of it.

2. (i) False. Rapidly rising population adversely affects the quality of human capital, as it reduces per head availability of the facilities. Accordingly, capacities to acquire knowledge and specialised skills are reduced.
   (ii) True. Investment in human capital helps in acquiring new skills and knowledge relating to management of resources, technology and production. Thus, human capital formation raises the productivity and production as skilled worker makes better use of the resources.

3. Firms provide on-the-job training to their workers to enhance their skills which helps in human capital formation.

On-the-job training is an important factor of human capital formation as it results in enhanced labour productivity. On-the-job training allows trainees and employees to get acquainted with their co-workers. Training allows the supervisors or managers to assess progress of a person over a short period of time enabling them to determine any flaws or problems and rectifying the problem on the spot. This leads to higher efficiency of not only the person under training but also the organisation as a whole.

4. The source of human capital formation highlighted is expenditure on healthcare.

It is a crucial component of human capital formation as it plays a fundamental role in enhancing the productivity and well-being of individuals.

When a nation invests in healthcare infrastructure, services and programmes, it ensures that its population has access to essential medical facilities, preventive care and treatments.

A healthy workforce is more productive, as individuals are less likely to suffer from illnesses that could hinder their ability to work effectively. Moreover, by investing in health, a country can reduce absenteeism due to sickness and promote higher levels of labour force participation.

5. On-the-job trainings offer several advantages in uplifting the education sector (any two)

(i) **Practical Application of Knowledge** These trainings allow candidates to apply theoretical knowledge gained in classrooms to real world scenarios. This hands on experience enhances their understanding of concepts and helps to bridge the gap between theory and practice.

(ii) **Skill Development** These trainings help candidates to develop practical skills that are essential for success in their chosen field. By working alongside experienced professionals, candidates learn valuable skills such as problem-solving, communication, teamwork and time management, which are critical for their professional development.

(iii) **Cost Effective Learning** It can be a cost effective learning approach for educational institutions and students alike. By partnering with industry organisations to provide training opportunities, educational institutions can leverage existing resources and facilities, reducing the cost of delivering practical training.

6. (i) Importance of government intervention can be understood with the help of following points

(a) Education and healthcare services create both private and social benefits and this is the reason for the existence of public institutions in the education and health service markets.

(b) Expenditures on education and health make substantial long-term impact and they cannot be easily reversed; hence, government intervention is essential.

(c) The role of government in this situation is to ensure that the private providers of these services adhere to the standards stipulated by the government and charge the correct price.

(ii) Implementing interventions in the education and health sectors poses several challenges for governments, including inadequate funding, resource constraints, bureaucratic inefficiencies and resistance to change.

Additionally, socio-cultural factors, such as gender disparities in education and healthcare access and geographic disparities in rural areas, can complicate intervention efforts.

Furthermore, political instability, corruption and competing priorities may divert attention and resources away from human capital development initiatives.

Overcoming these challenges requires comprehensive policy frameworks, effective governance structures, stakeholder collaboration and sustainable funding mechanisms.

CHAPTER -5

Rural Development

Types & Nos. of Questions

Multiple Choice Questions – 30
Assertion-Reason Questions – 8
Correct/Incorrect Statements – 10
Case Based Questions – 2 Cases, *each with four Questions*
Subjective Questions – 7

Trend Analysis

On the basis of analysis of last 2 years' papers, it is found that on an average 2 Multiple Choice Questions and 2 Short Answer Type Questions (Statement Based) are asked from this chapter. No case based question is asked but may be asked in coming exams.

Focus Topics of the Chapter

- Rural Credit
- Agricultural Marketing
- Diversification of Agricultural Activities
- Sustainable Development and Organic Farming

Multiple Choice Questions

No. of Questions : **30** Suggested Time : **45 Minutes**

Direction Each of the question given below is Multiple Choice Question (MCQ) i.e. there are Four Options/ Choices for answer, out of which ONLY ONE is correct. You have to select the correct option. A response box is given with each option, mark (✓) in the box of the correct option. For each correct answer you will get 1 mark, while there is no penalty for incorrect answer or missed out questions.

1. The green revolution was a harbinger of major changes in the credit system. This system was not required to

(A) free small and marginal farmers and landless labourers from being exploited by landlords, etc. by lending to them on high interest rates and by manipulating the accounts to keep them in a debt-trap ☐

(B) fill the gap in the formal credit system ☐

(C) meet the needs of rural credit ☐

(D) encourage farmers to take more loans from non-institutional sources of credit ☐

2. Identify, which of the following alternative indicates towards incorrect components combination of agricultural marketing system? *[CBSE 2024]*

(A) Assembling, storage, processing, packaging ☐

(B) Production, assembling, processing, grading ☐

(C) Assembling, processing, packaging, transportation ☐

(D) Processing, packaging, grading, distribution ☐

3. Government is taking so many efforts to improve the status of rural areas from so many years. But some fresh initiatives for development in rural India are needed. These include

(i) development of human resources and productive resources

(ii) land reforms, infrastructure development

(iii) special measures for alleviation of poverty

Codes

(A) Only (i) ☐

(B) Only (ii) ☐

(C) Only (iii) ☐

(D) (i), (ii) and (iii) ☐

4. Government intervention in agricultural marketing became necessary to regulate the activities of the private traders as

(i) farmers, while selling their produce to traders, suffered from faulty weighing and manipulation of accounts.

(ii) farmers who did not have the required information on prices prevailing in markets were often forced to sell at low prices.

Codes

(A) Only (i) ☐

(B) Only (ii) ☐

(C) Both (i) and (ii) ☐

(D) Neither (i) nor (ii) ☐

5. There were many measures that were initiated by government to improve the agricultural marketing aspect.

These measures didn't include

(A) regulation of markets ☐

(B) provision of physical infrastructure ☐

(C) cooperative marketing ☐

(D) micro credit programmes ☐

6. Government is taking continuous efforts to empower farmers and enhance their economic prospects. In this regard, in 2020, the Indian Parliament introduced some significant agricultural reforms. How many reforms have been introduced?

(A) 2 ☐ (B) 3 ☐

(C) 4 ☐ (D) 5 ☐

7. .... towards new areas is necessary to reduce the risk from agriculture sector but also to provide productive sustainable livelihood options to rural people.

(A) Upgradation ☐

(B) Modernisation ☐

(C) Diversification ☐

(D) Realisation ☐

8. Which of the following best defines the concept of diversification of crops in agriculture?

(A) Planting a single type of crop across multiple fields to increase yield ☐

(B) Rotating crops seasonally to maintain soil fertility and reduce pest infestation ☐

(C) Introducing a variety of crops within a single field to minimise risks associated with market fluctuations and environmental factors ☐

(D) Using genetically modified organisms to enhance crop resilience and adaptability to different climates ☐

9. .... is a system whereby all the farmers can pool their milk produced according to different grading (based on quality), processed and marketed to urban centres through cooperatives.

(A) Operation pink ☐

(B) Operation flood ☐

(C) Operation Vijay ☐

(D) Operation crop ☐

10. India has adopted growing of diverse horticultural crops like ....

(i) fruits and vegetables

(ii) tuber crops, flowers, medicinal and aromatic plants

(iii) spices and plantation crops

Codes

(A) Both (i) and (ii) ☐

(B) Both (ii) and (iii) ☐

(C) (i), (ii) and (iii) ☐

(D) None of the above ☐

11. Which of the following statement does not relate to horticulture?

(A) Horticulture sector contributes nearly one-third of the value of agriculture output and six per cent of gross domestic product of India ☐

(B) India has emerged as a world leader in producing a variety of fruits like mangoes, bananas, coconuts, cashewnuts and a number of spices and is the second largest producer of fruits and vegetables ☐

(C) Economic condition of many farmers engaged in horticulture has not improved and it has become a means of improving livelihood for very few unprivileged classes ☐

(D) Horticulture has emerged as a successful sustainable livelihood option and needs to be encouraged significantly ☐

12. .... agriculture relies heavily on chemical fertilisers and toxic pesticides, etc. whereas .... agriculture is a whole system of farming that restores, maintains and enhances the ecological balance.

(A) Organic, conventional ☐

(B) Conventional, organic ☐

(C) Mechanical, traditional ☐

(D) Traditional, mechanical ☐

13. One of the farmers in a village is considering transitioning to organic farming methods. Which of the following will be in the support of their decision?

(A) Inadequate infrastructure and the problem of marketing ☐

(B) Yields from organic farming are less than modern agricultural farming in the initial years ☐

(C) Organic produce may also have more blemishes and a shorter shelf life than sprayed produce ☐

(D) Organic agriculture also generates income through exports as the demand for organically grown crops is on a rise ☐

14. .... is a process, which include the activities from sowing till sale of the final produce in the market. *[CBSE 2023]*

(A) Rural development ☐

(B) Agricultural diversification ☐

(C) Organic farming ☐

(D) Agricultural marketing ☐

15. How does the adoption of organic farming contribute to the goals of rural development in India?

(A) By increasing the dependency on chemical inputs ☐

(B) By encouraging mono-culture and reducing crop diversity ☐

(C) By enhancing soil fertility and promoting eco-friendly practices ☐

(D) By prioritising high yielding crops over traditional varieties ☐

16. Which type of farming is depicted in the below image?

(A) Organic farming ☐

(B) Sustainable farming ☐

(C) Developmental farming ☐

(D) Inorganic farming ☐

17. In 1995, a thrift and credit society was started as a small savings bank for poor women with the objective to encourage savings. Identify the society.

(A) Kudumbashree ☐

(B) Tamil Nadu Women in Agriculture (TANWA) ☐

(C) National Bank for Agriculture and Rural Development (NABARD) ☐

(D) Community Investment Support Fund (CISF) ☐

18. Ramu is a farmer having a small land for farming in a small village located in Tamil Nadu. He was talking to his friend Shamu about his need of credit. He would not be requiring credit for

(A) buying land or tractor ☐

(B) buying the inputs like seeds, fertilisers, tools, etc ☐

(C) beyond agricultural needs, he might face problems in meeting his personal expenses like marriage, death, religious ceremonies, etc ☐

(D) performing small business activities like carpentary, handicrafts, etc ☐

19. .... are expected to dispense adequate credit at cheaper rates.

(A) Landlords ☐ (B) Moneylenders ☐

(C) Big traders ☐

(D) Regional rural banks ☐

20. In a rural village named Sundarpur, a group of women came together to form a group with the aim of improving their economic status. Each member contributed a small amount regularly to create a fund that could be used for lending among themselves.

Over time, they utilised this collective savings to start small businesses, such as tailoring and vegetable vending. As their businesses grew, they were able to generate additional income and uplift their families economically.

Which institutional source for rural credit is the group created by the village women?

(A) Commercial banks ☐

(B) Regional rural banks ☐

(C) Self-help groups ☐

(D) Credit societies ☐

21. In the context of importance of rural credit, which option suits the best?

(A) Growth of rural economy does not depend primarily on infusion of capital, from time-to-time, to realise higher productivity in agriculture and non-agriculture sectors ☐

(B) As the time gestation between crop sowing and realisation of income after production is short, farmers do not require to borrow from various sources to meet their initial investment on seeds, fertilisers, etc ☐

(C) India adopted social banking and multi-agency approach to adequately meet the needs of farmers since independence ☐

(D) The SHGs promote thrift in small proportions by a minimum contribution from each member ☐

22. In recent years, all the adults are encouraged to open bank accounts as a part of a scheme known as Jan Dhan Yojana. The primary objective of this yojana is

(A) Inclusivity : Ensuring access to basic banking facilities for excluded sections, weaker sections and low-income groups. ☐

(B) Profitability : Maximising returns for financial institutions through increased account openings. ☐

(C) Urbanisation : Focusing on urban areas for rapid economic growth. ☐

(D) Exclusivity : Limiting access to financial services to a select group of individuals. ☐

23. ...... is the apex institution which plans and evaluates policies related rural credit needs. *[CBSE 2023]*

(A) Cooperative credit societies ☐

(B) Regional rural banks ☐

(C) Self-help groups ☐

(D) NABARD ☐

24. The scheme of 'micro finance' is extended through ...... credit provision. *[CBSE 2024]*

(A) self-help groups ☐

(B) land development banks ☐

(C) regional rural banks ☐

(D) commercial banks ☐

25. The situation given in picture can be considered under which activity?

(A) Animal husbandry ☐

(B) Horticulture ☐

(C) Fisheries ☐

(D) Organic farming ☐

26. "The state government is all set to crack a whip against the Primary Land Development Bank (PLDB) of the cooperatives department, especially those who are struggling with losses." – Times of India

Which of the following best describes the function of land development banks in rural areas?

(A) Providing short-term loans for agricultural inputs like seeds and fertilisers ☐

(B) Offering financial support for constructing rural infrastructure such as roads and bridges ☐

(C) Providing long-term loans secured against land for activities like purchasing tractors and digging tube wells ☐

(D) Facilitating micro credit programmes for women's self-help groups in rural communities ☐

27. Which institution's logo is depicted in the image below?

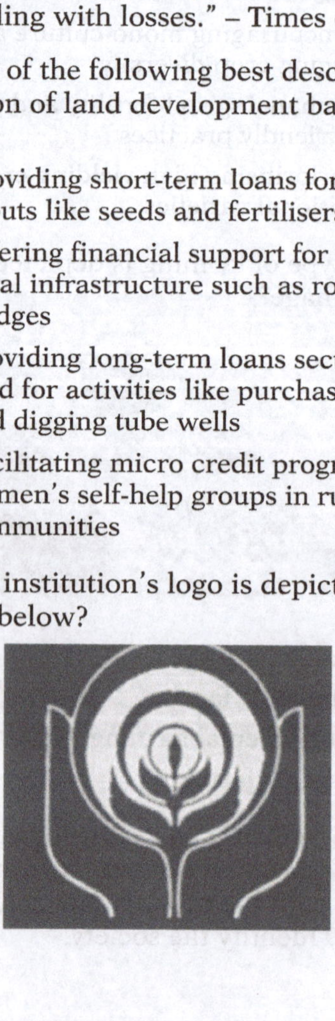

(A) National Bank for Agriculture and Rural Development (NABARD) ☐
(B) Commercial bank ☐
(C) Regional Rural Bank (RRB) ☐
(D) Land development bank ☐

28. Match the Column I with Column II

Column I		Column II
A. Credit societies	(i)	Alternative to traditional commercial banks.
B. Self-help groups	(ii)	Offer long-term loans secured by land to support agricultural activities.
C. Land development banks	(iii)	Provide credit facilities and other financial services to their members.
D. Regional rural banks	(iv)	Community based organisations where members pool their resources to save money.

Codes

	A	B	C	D	
(A)	(iv)	(i)	(ii)	(iii)	☐
(B)	(i)	(ii)	(iii)	(iv)	☐
(C)	(ii)	(iii)	(i)	(iv)	☐
(D)	(iii)	(iv)	(ii)	(i)	☐

29. Match the following

Column I		Column II
A. NABARD	(i)	Ecological balance
B. Saansad Adarsh Gram Yojana	(ii)	1982
C. Organic farming	(iii)	Horticulture
D. Golden revolution	(iv)	2014

Codes

	A	B	C	D	
(A)	(iv)	(ii)	(i)	(iii)	☐
(B)	(ii)	(iv)	(iii)	(i)	☐
(C)	(ii)	(i)	(iv)	(iii)	☐
(D)	(ii)	(iv)	(i)	(iii)	☐

30. Match the following

Column I		Column II
A. The poor's women bank	(i)	Pune
B. Hadaspar mandi	(ii)	Tamil Nadu
C. Operation flood	(iii)	Kudumbashree
D. Uzhavar sandies	(iv)	Milk cooperatives

Codes

	A	B	C	D	
(A)	(i)	(iii)	(iv)	(ii)	☐
(B)	(iii)	(i)	(iv)	(ii)	☐
(C)	(iii)	(iv)	(i)	(ii)	☐
(D)	(i)	(iii)	(ii)	(iv)	☐

Assertion-Reason Questions

No. of Questions : **8** Suggested Time : **15 Minutes**

Direction Each of the question given below consist of the two statements; one labelled as **Assertion** (A) and other as **Reason** (R). List of common options applicable for each question is given below

(A) Both Assertion (A) and Reason (R) are true and Reason (R) is the correct explanation of Assertion (A)
(B) Both Assertion (A) and Reason (R) are true, but Reason (R) is not the correct explanation of Assertion (A)
(C) Assertion (A) is true, but Reason (R) is false
(D) Assertion (A) is false, but Reason (R) is true

You have to select the codes as *A, B, C* or *D* as your answer to the question by marking (✓) in the response box given against each option.

1. **Assertion (A)** During 2014-15, the GVA growth rate of agriculture and its allied sectors was less than five per cent.

Reason (R) Fall in public investment, inadequate infrastructure, lack of alternate employment opportunities in the industry or service sector, increasing casualisation of employment, etc. impede rural development.

(A) ☐ (B) ☐ (C) ☐ (D) ☐

2. **Assertion (A)** Growth of rural economy depends primarily on infusion of capital, from time-to-time, to realise higher productivity in agriculture and non-agriculture sectors.

Reason (R) A major change occurred after 1979 when India adopted social banking and multiagency approach to adequately meet the needs of rural credit.

(A) ☐ (B) ☐ (C) ☐ (D) ☐

3. **Assertion (A)** Several national and multinational fast food chains are increasingly entering into contracts/ alliances with farmers to encourage them to cultivate farm products of the desired quality.

Reason (R) Such arrangements will help in reducing the price risks of the farmers and would also expand the markets for farm products.

(A) ☐ (B) ☐ (C) ☐ (D) ☐

4. **Assertion (A)** Government intervention became necessary to regulate the activities of the private traders.

Reason (R) The success of milk cooperatives in transforming the social and economic landscape of Gujarat and some other parts of the country is testimony to the role of cooperatives.

(A) ☐ (B) ☐ (C) ☐ (D) ☐

5. **Assertion (A)** Livestock production provides increased stability in income, food security, transport, fuel and nutrition for the family without disrupting other food producing activities.

Reason (R) Livestock sector alone provides alternate livelihood options to over 700 million small and marginal farmers including landless labourers.

(A) ☐ (B) ☐ (C) ☐ (D) ☐

6. **Assertion (A)** Diversification of productive activities means growing more than one crop at a time.

Reason (R) There is a need to focus on allied activities, non-farm employment and other emerging alternatives of livelihood, though there are many other options available for providing sustainable livelihoods in rural areas.

(A) ☐ (B) ☐ (C) ☐ (D) ☐

7. **Assertion (A)** The fishing community regards the water body as 'mother' or 'provider'.

Reason (R) The water bodies consisting of sea, oceans, rivers, lakes, natural aquatic ponds, streams, etc. are therefore, an integral and life giving source for the fishing community.

(A) ☐ (B) ☐
(C) ☐ (D) ☐

8. **Assertion (A)** Since the default rates of farm loans have become chronically high due to multiple reasons, the rural banks are facing a lot of cash crunch.

Reason (R) Due to lack of proper storage facilities a lot of farm produce is wasted.

(A) ☐ (B) ☐
(C) ☐ (D) ☐

Correct/Incorrect Statements

No. of Questions : **10** Suggested Time : **15 Minutes**

Direction Each of the question given below consist of the two statements. List of common options applicable for each question is given below

(A) Both statements are correct
(B) Both statements are incorrect
(C) Statement I is correct and Statement II is incorrect
(D) Statement I is incorrect and Statement II is correct

You have to select the codes as *A, B, C* or *D* as your answer to the question by marking (✓) in the response box given against each option.

1. Statement I Rural development is a comprehensive term. It essentially focuses on action for the development of areas that are lagging behind in the overall development of the village economy.

Statement II Decline in public investment since 1991 was the major reason for declining agricultural sector.

(A) ☐ (B) ☐ (C) ☐ (D) ☐

2. Statement I Agricultural marketing is a process that involves the production, assembling, storage, processing, transportation, packaging, grading and distribution of different agricultural commodities across the country.

Statement II Agricultural marketing has come a long way with the intervention of the government in various forms.

(A) ☐ (B) ☐ (C) ☐ (D) ☐

3. Statement I Much of the agricultural employment activities are concentrated in Rabi season.

Statement II But during the Kharif season, in areas where there are inadequate irrigation facilities, it becomes difficult to find gainful employment.

(A) ☐ (B) ☐ (C) ☐ (D) ☐

4. Statement I Poultry accounts for the least share in livestock farming.

Statement II Gujarat state is held as a success story in the efficient implementation of milk cooperatives which has been emulated by many states.

(A) ☐ (B) ☐ (C) ☐ (D) ☐

5. Statement I India has emerged as a world leader in producing a variety of fruits like mangoes, bananas, coconuts, cashewnuts and a number of spices and is the second largest producer of fruits and vegetables.

Statement II Improved veterinary care and credit facilities to small and marginal farmers and landless labourers would enhance sustainable livelihood options through livestock production.

(A) ☐ (B) ☐ (C) ☐ (D) ☐

6. Statement I There is broad consensus that IT can play a critical role in achieving sustainable development and food security in the twenty-first century.

Statement II Experiments with IT and its application to rural development are still not carried out in different parts of India.

(A) ☐ (B) ☐
(C) ☐ (D) ☐

7. Statement I Popularising conventional farming requires awareness and willingness on the part of farmers to adapt to new technology.

Statement II There is need to invent or procure alternate sets of eco-friendly technologies that lead to sustainable development in different circumstances.

(A) ☐ (B) ☐ (C) ☐ (D) ☐

8. Statement I The emergence of Self-Help Groups (SHGs) ensured the reduction in the fissures of the formal credit system.

Statement II The borrowings from SHGs mainly confined to consumption purposes by its members.

(A) ☐ (B) ☐ (C) ☐ (D) ☐

9. Statement I Self-Help Groups (SHGs) have emerged to fill the gap in the informal credit system.

Statement II SHGs have helped in the empowerment of women.

(A) ☐ (B) ☐ (C) ☐ (D) ☐

10. Statement I With the possible exception of the commercial banks, other formal institutions have failed to develop a culture of deposit mobilisation.

Statement II Agriculture loan default rates have been chronically high. It is alleged that farmers are deliberately refusing to pay back loans.

(A) ☐ (B) ☐
(C) ☐ (D) ☐

Case Based Questions

No. of Questions : **2** Suggested Time : **10 Minutes**

Direction This section contain 2 cases each having 4 questions of 1 mark each. You have to write the answer of each question based on the context of the related case.

Case 1 Adoption of Village by Parliamentarians

In October, 2014, The Government of India introduced a new scheme called Saansad Adarsh Gram Yojana (SAGY). Under this scheme, members of India's Parliament need to identify and develop one village from their constituencies. To begin with, MPs can develop one village as a model village by 2016 and two more by 2019, covering over 2,500 villages in India.

According to the scheme, the village can have a population of 3,000-5,000 in the plains and 1,000-3,000 in the hills and should not be MPs' own or their spouse's village. MPs are expected to facilitate a village development plan, motivate villagers to take up activities and built infrastructure in the areas of health, nutrition and education.

Questions

(i) What was the purpose of SAGY?

I. Contribution in rural development.

II. Built infrastructure in the areas of health, nutrition and education.

Codes

(A) Only I ☐
(B) Only II ☐
(C) Both I and II ☐
(D) Neither I nor II ☐

(ii) How much will be the gap in taking one village as model and then taking the other?

(A) 1 year ☐ (B) 2 years ☐
(C) 3 years ☐ (D) 4 years ☐

(iii) According to the scheme, the village can have a population of .... in the plains and 1,000-3,000 in the hills and should not be MPs' own or their spouse's village.

(iv) The Saansad Adarsh Gram Yojana (SAGY) scheme, introduced by the Government of India, requires members of Parliament to identify and develop .... village from their constituencies.

Case 2 Since ages, farmers in India have taken recourse to debt. In the earlier times the same was from informal sources. Since independence with the efforts of the government, formal sector has actively come into picture. Farmers borrow not only to meet their investment needs but also to satisfy their personal needs.

Uncertainty of income caused by factors likes crop failure caused by irregular rainfall, reduction in ground water table, locust/other pest attack etc. These reasons push them into the clutches of the private money lenders, who charge exorbitant rates of interest which add to their miseries.

Various governments in India, at different times for different reasons, introduced debt relief/ waiver schemes. These schemes are used by governments as a quick means to extricate farmers from their indebtedness, helping to restore their capacity to invest and produce, in short to lessen the miseries of the farmers across India. The costs and benefits of such debt relief schemes are, however, a widely debated topic among economists.

Some economists argue that such schemes are extremely beneficial to the poor and marginalised farmers while others argue that these schemes add to the fiscal burden of the government, others believe that these schemes may develop the expectation of repeated bailouts among farmers which may spoil the credit culture among farmers.

Questions

(i) Uncertainty of income for farmers in India is majorly caused by ....

(A) irregular rainfall ☐

(B) unavailability of loans ☐

(C) Both (A) and (B) ☐

(D) None of the above ☐

(ii) Some economists argue that debt waiver schemes are extremely beneficial to the poor and marginalised farmers, as these schemes reduce the burden of ....

(A) indebtedness ☐

(B) personal expenditures ☐

(C) Both (A) and (B) ☐

(D) None of the above ☐

(iii) The rural banking structure in India consists of a set of multi-agency institutions .... is expected to dispense credit at cheaper rates for agricultural purposes to farmers.

(iv) .... is the most prominent body responsible for providing loans for long-term land development.

Subjective Questions

Free Response Questions, Open-ended Questions etc.

No. of Questions : 7 | Suggested Time : **50 Minutes**

1. What role do the group highlighted in the image plays in promoting economic empowerment and social cohesion among rural communities?

2. "Recently the Government of India has taken numerous steps towards increasing the farmer's income through agricultural diversification." In light of the above statement, explain any two advantages of diversification in agriculture. *[CBSE 2023]*

3. Though, in terms of numbers, our livestock population is quite impressive but its productivity is quite low as compared to other countries. Considering the multifaceted challenges in animal husbandry, suggest the various ways to improve the area.

4. "Farm subsidies put a huge burden on the government finances, but are necessary for the poor and marginal farmers." Justify the given statement. *[CBSE 2024, 23]*

5. "India can transform itself knowledge based economy by using information technology." Justify the given statement. *[CBSE 2024]*

6. When conventional agriculture relies heavily on chemical fertilisers and toxic pesticides, etc. which is not good for heath and organic farming is so eco-friendly and essential for sustainable development, then why government cannot take up the organic farming completely?

7. Transforming Agricultural Marketing in a Rural District

In a rural district characterised by diverse agricultural production, farmers face challenges in accessing markets, obtaining fair prices for their produce and adding value to their products.

Limited infrastructure, lack of market information and middlemen exploitation exacerbate these challenges, impacting farmers' incomes and livelihoods.

To address these issues, the district administration, in collaboration with local NGOs and farmer cooperatives, initiated a comprehensive agricultural marketing programme.

The programme aimed to enhance market access, improve price transparency, promote value addition and empower farmers to actively participate in the marketing process.

Key interventions included the establishment of rural market hubs equipped with storage facilities, the development of a mobile application for real time market information dissemination, capacity building workshops on value addition techniques and the formation of Farmer Producer Organisations (FPOs) to facilitate collective marketing and negotiation with buyers.

(i) How do you evaluate the effectiveness of the agricultural marketing programme in addressing the challenges faced by farmers in the rural district?

(ii) What strategies can be implemented to sustain and scale-up the successes of the agricultural marketing programme beyond the pilot phase?

Answers

If your answer matches with the answer given here then put (✓) in the box otherwise put (✗). In case you did not attempt the question leave the box blank.

Multiple Choice Questions

1. D ☐ 2. B ☐
3. D ☐ 4. C ☐
5. D ☐ 6. B ☐
7. C ☐ 8. C ☐
9. B ☐ 10. C ☐
11. C ☐ 12. B ☐
13. D ☐ 14. D ☐
15. C ☐ 16. A ☐
17. A ☐ 18. D ☐
19. D ☐ 20. C ☐
21. D ☐ 22. A ☐
23. D ☐ 24. A ☐
25. B ☐ 26. C ☐
27. A ☐ 28. D ☐
29. D ☐ 30. B ☐

Your Score__________ *(No. of Correct Answers)*

Assertion-Reason Questions

1. D ☐ 2. C ☐
3. A ☐ 4. B ☐
5. C ☐ 6. D ☐
7. A ☐ 8. B ☐

Your Score__________ *(No. of Correct Answers)*

Correct/Incorrect Statements

1. A ☐ 2. D ☐
3. B ☐ 4. D ☐
5. A ☐ 6. C ☐
7. D ☐ 8. A ☐
9. D ☐ 10. A ☐

Your Score__________ *(No. of Correct Answers)*

Case Based Questions

1. (i) C ☐ (ii) B ☐
2. (i) A ☐ (ii) A ☐

Your Score__________ *(No. of Correct Answers)*

Explanations

Multiple Choice Questions

1. (D) The green revolution aimed to reduce dependency on non-institutional sources of credit, such as moneylenders, who often charged high interest rates and trapped farmers in debt cycles.

2. (B) Production, assembling, processing, grading

3. (D) (i), (ii) and (iii) **4.** (C) Both (i) and (ii)

5. (D) While the government has implemented various measures to improve agricultural marketing, such as regulating markets, providing physical infrastructure and promoting cooperative marketing, micro credit programmes are typically aimed at providing small loans to individuals, especially those in rural areas, for various purposes other than agricultural marketing.

6. (B) In 2020, the Indian Parliament introduced three significant agricultural reforms aimed at bringing transformative changes to the agricultural sector and empowering farmers.

7. (C) Diversification

8. (C) Introducing a variety of crops within a single field to minimise risks associated with market fluctuations and environmental factors

9. (B) Operation flood

10. (C) India has adopted the cultivation of diverse horticultural crops, including fruits and vegetables, tuber crops, flowers, medicinal and aromatic plants, as well as spices and plantation crops.

11. (C) Economic condition of many farmers engaged in horticulture has not improved and it has become a means of improving livelihood for very few unprivileged classes
12. (B) Conventional, organic
13. (D) Organic agriculture also generates income through exports as the demand for organically grown crops is on a rise
14. (D) Agricultural marketing
15. (C) Organic farming methods prioritise the use of organic inputs such as compost, crop rotation and biological pest control, which improve soil fertility and reduce environmental pollution.
16. (A) Organic farming
17. (A) Kudumbashree
18. (D) Ramu, as a small farmer, may require credit for agricultural inputs like seeds and fertilisers, as well as for personal expenses like marriage or religious ceremonies. However, credit for small business activities like carpentry or handicrafts would be less relevant.
19. (D) Regional rural banks
20. (C) Self-help groups
21. (D) The SHGs promote thrift in small proportions by a minimum contribution from each member
22. (A) Inclusivity : Ensuring access to basic banking facilities for excluded sections, weaker sections and low-income groups.
23. (D) NABARD
24. (A) self-help groups
25. (B) Horticulture
26. (C) Providing long-term loans secured against land for activities like purchasing tractors and digging tube wells
27. (A) National Bank for Agriculture and Rural Development (NABARD)
28. (D) (iii) (iv) (ii) (i)
29. (D) (ii) (iv) (i) (iii)
30. (B) (iii) (i) (iv) (ii)

Assertion-Reason Questions

1. (D) Assertion (A) is false, but Reason (R) is true
2. (C) Assertion (A) is true, but Reason (R) is false
3. (A) Both Assertion (A) and Reason (R) are true and Reason (R) is the correct explanation of Assertion (A)
4. (B) Both Assertion (A) and Reason (R) are true, but Reason (R) is not the correct explanation of Assertion (A)
5. (C) Assertion (A) is true, but Reason (R) is false
6. (D) Diversification of productive activities refers to engaging in a variety of income-generating activities beyond just agriculture, such as livestock rearing, handicrafts or small-scale industries.
7. (A) Both Assertion (A) and Reason (R) are true and Reason (R) is the correct explanation of Assertion (A)
8. (B) Both Assertion (A) and Reason (R) are true, but Reason (R) is not the correct explanation of Assertion (A)

Correct/Incorrect Statements

1. (A) Both statements are correct
2. (D) Statement I is incorrect and Statement II is correct
3. (B) Agricultural employment activities are not solely concentrated in the Rabi season. While inadequate irrigation facilities during the Kharif season can limit employment opportunities, it doesn't necessarily mean employment is difficult to find.
4. (D) Poultry farming accounts for a significant share in livestock farming.
5. (A) Both statements are correct
6. (C) Statement I is correct and Statement II is incorrect
7. (D) Statement I is incorrect and Statement II is correct
8. (A) Both statements are correct
9. (D) While Self-Help Groups (SHGs) have indeed emerged to empower women and provide them with access to financial resources, they primarily aim to fill the gap in the formal credit system.
10. (A) Both statements are correct

Case Based Questions

1. (i) (C) Both I and II
   (ii) (B) MPs are required to develop one village as a model village by 2016 and two more by 2019, indicating a gap of 2 years between developing each village.
   (iii) 3,000 to 5,000
   (iv) one

2. (i) (A) irregular rainfall
(ii) (A) indebtedness
(iii) regional rural banks
(iv) Land development banks

Subjective Questions

1. The group highlighted in the picture is Self-Help Groups (SHGs). They play a crucial role in promoting economic empowerment and social cohesion among rural communities by providing a platform for members to pool resources, access credit facilities and engage in collective decision- making processes for mutual benefit.
Through regular savings, collective lending and skill development programmes, SHGs empower individuals, especially women, to become financially independent and contribute to their community's development.

2. Diversification in agriculture implies the provision of alternate employment opportunities for the labour force engaged in agriculture. The advantages of agricultural diversification are as follows
(i) To provide supplementary gainful employment and in realising higher level of income for rural people to overcome poverty.
(ii) To provide sustainable livelihood options to rural people.

3. It requires improved technology and promotion of good breeds of animals to enhance productivity.
Improved veterinary care and credit facilities to small and marginal farmers and landless labourers would enhance sustainable livelihood options through livestock production.

4. Farm subsidies impose an additional burden on government finances. However, in countries like India it is necessary for the farmers as there are large numbers of small and marginal farmers.
The following arguments are provided
(i) The economists who are in favour of subsidies believe that the government should continue to grant agricultural subsidies because, in India, farming is a risky business.
Also, the majority of farmers are so poor that without subsidies they will not be able to afford the input required for farming.
Therefore, if the government eliminates subsidies, it will increase the income inequality between the rich and poor farmers, which will ultimately violate the government's final goal of equity.
(ii) The economists who are against subsidies believe that since the government grants subsidies to poor farmers as an incentive for them to adopt new HYV technology, then it should phase out subsidies once the new technology is widely accepted and the purpose of granting subsidies has been fulfilled.
They also believe that the poor and small farmers are not getting benefits from subsidies as the benefits from the substantial amount of subsidy go to big farmers and the fertiliser industry.

5. India has the potential to transform itself into a knowledge based economy by leveraging Information Technology (IT) for several reason
(i) **Abundance of Skilled IT Workforce** India is known for its large pool of highly skilled IT professionals, including software engineers, developers and data scientists. The country's robust education system produces a significant number of graduates in STEM (Science, Technology, Engineering and Mathematics) fields, providing a strong foundation for building a knowledge based economy.
(ii) **Global Leader in IT Services** India has emerged as a global leader in IT services, particularly in software development, outsourcing and consulting.
Indian IT companies, such as Tata Consultancy Services (TCS), Infosys and Wipro, have established themselves as major players in the global market, providing innovative solutions and services to clients worldwide.
(iii) **Digital Infrastructure** India has made significant investments in digital infrastructure, including broadband connectivity, mobile networks and digital payment systems.
The widespread availability of internet connectivity and mobile technology has created opportunities for digital transformation across various sectors, including healthcare, education, finance and agriculture.

6. Organic farming can't be taken completely due to the following disadvantages
   (i) There is inadequate infrastructure and the problem of marketing the products are major concerns which need to be addressed apart from an appropriate agriculture policy to promote organic farming.
   (ii) It has been observed that the yields from organic farming are less than modern agricultural farming in the initial years.
   (iii) Organic produce may also have more blemishes and a shorter shelf life than sprayed produce.
   (iv) Moreover choice in production of off-season crops is quite limited in organic farming.
7. (i) The agricultural marketing programme has demonstrated significant positive impacts on farmers' livelihoods and market participation.
   Market hubs have improved market access by providing a centralised location for farmers to sell their produce, reducing transportation costs and time.
   The mobile application has empowered farmers with timely market information, enabling them to make informed decisions and negotiate better prices.
   Capacity building workshops on value addition have enhanced farmers' skills and diversified their product offerings, leading to higher profitability.
   The formation of FPOs has strengthened farmers' collective bargaining power, resulting in fairer transactions and reduced exploitation by middlemen. Overall, these interventions have contributed to a more inclusive, transparent and resilient agricultural marketing system in the rural district.
   (ii) To sustain and scale-up the successes of the agricultural marketing programme, several strategies can be considered.
   Firstly, continued investment in infrastructure, such as expanding market hubs and improving transportation networks, is essential to accommodate growing demand and reach more remote farming communities.
   Secondly, ongoing support for technology adoption and capacity-building initiatives, including regular training sessions on market analysis and value addition techniques, can ensure farmers remain competitive and adaptable to changing market dynamics.
   Additionally, fostering partnerships with private sector stakeholders, such as agribusinesses and retail chains, can create new market opportunities and facilitate value chain integration.
   Lastly, promoting policy reforms that prioritise farmer friendly regulations, fair trade practices and market access initiatives can create an enabling environment for sustainable agricultural marketing development in the district and beyond.

CHAPTER-6

Employment : Growth, Informalisation and Other Issues

Types & Nos. of Questions

Multiple Choice Questions - 30
Assertion-Reason Questions - 8
Correct/Incorrect Statements - 10
Case Based Questions - 2 Cases, *each with four Questions*
Subjective Questions - 8

Trend Analysis

On the basis of analysis of last 2 years' papers, it is found that on an average 2 Multiple Choice Questions and 2 Short Answer Type Questions (Statement Based and Graph Based) are asked from this chapter. No case based question is asked but may be asked in coming exams.

Focus Topics of the Chapter

- Meaning of Employment
- Growth and Changing Structure of Employment
- Meaning of Unemployment
- Government and Employment Generation

Multiple Choice Questions

No. of Questions : **30**

Suggested Time : **45 Minutes**

Direction Each of the question given below is Multiple Choice Question (MCQ) i.e. there are Four Options/ Choices for answer, out of which ONLY ONE is correct. You have to select the correct option. A response box is given with each option, mark (✓) in the box of the correct option. For each correct answer you will get 1 mark, while there is no penalty for incorrect answer or missed out questions.

1. Why does the rural workforce outnumber the urban workforce in many developing countries, including India?

(A) Limited access to education and skill development opportunities in rural areas ☐

(B) Majority of people reside in rural areas ☐

(C) Greater preference for rural lifestyles and cultural ties to agricultural communities ☐

(D) Lack of infrastructure and basic amenities in rural areas, leading to limited urban migration ☐

2. Identify, which of the following is the correct formula for calculating 'worker-population ratio'. *[CBSE 2023]*

(A) $\frac{\text{Total Labour Force}}{\text{Total Population}} \times 100$ ☐

(B) $\frac{\text{Total Workers}}{\text{Total Population}} \times 100$ ☐

(C) $\frac{\text{Total Population}}{\text{Total Labour Force}} \times 100$ ☐

(D) $\frac{\text{Total Population}}{\text{Total Workers}} \times 100$ ☐

3. Consider the concept of the worker population ratio in the context of assessing the labour market. Which of the following statements best reflects about this measure?

(A) Worker-population ratio is an indicator which is used for analysing the disguised unemployment situation in the country ☐

(B) This ratio is useful in knowing the proportion of population that is actively contributing to the production of goods and services of a country ☐

(C) If the ratio is higher, it means that the engagement of people is less; if the ratio for a country is medium or low, it means that a very high proportion of its population is involved directly in economic activities ☐

(D) Worker-population ratio is calculated as dividing the total population by total workforce and multiplying it by 100 ☐

4. Which of the following individuals would be classified as self-employed?

(A) An accountant working for a multinational corporation ☐

(B) A teacher employed by a private school ☐

(C) A freelance graphic designer who works from home ☐

(D) A factory worker employed by a manufacturing company ☐

5. There are various sources of data on unemployment. Identify them from the following.

(i) Reports of Census of India.

(ii) National Sample Survey Organisation's Reports of Employment and Unemployment Situation.

(iii) Directorate General of Employment and Training Data of Registration with Employment Exchanges.

Codes

(A) Only (i) ☐

(B) Only (ii) ☐

(C) Only (iii) ☐ (D) All of the above ☐

6. Sam, a skilled carpenter, decides to start his own wood working business. He sets-up a small workshop in his backyard and begins crafting furniture and home decor items. Despite the initial challenges, Sam's business gradually gains traction and he starts generating a steady income from his craftsmanship.

   Which type of employment does Sam, the carpenter, exemplify?

   (A) Self-employment ☐
   (B) Wage employment ☐
   (C) Unemployment ☐
   (D) Seasonal employment ☐

7. Jobless growth leads to unemployment because .... *[CBSE 2023]*

   (A) labour refuses to migrate ☐
   (B) labour is very expensive ☐
   (C) growth rate is low ☐
   (D) growth is due to technological development ☐

8. Which of the following statements is incorrect?

   (A) When there is jobless growth, the GDP rises and creates employment opportunities ☐
   (B) India has experienced the phenomenon of jobless growth ☐
   (C) Jobless growth refers to no growth in employment opportunities ☐
   (D) Indian economy has produced more goods and services but the employment opportunities have not increased ☐

9. Identify the formal sector organisation from the following.

   (A) A private sector undertaking employing 7 workers ☐
   (B) A showroom owner employing 2 hired workers ☐
   (C) A farmer farming in his own field ☐
   (D) Samsung electronics company limited ☐

10. When a big firm finds it profitable to close down some of its specialist departments (for example, legal or computer programming or customer service sections) and hand over a large number of small piecemeal jobs to very small enterprises or specialist individuals, sometimes situated even in other countries, it is called as

    (A) insourcing ☐
    (B) internationalisation ☐
    (C) on-shoring ☐
    (D) outsourcing ☐

11. In the fictional country of Arcadia, the government implemented several economic policies aimed at boosting industrial output and GDP growth.

    As a result, manufacturing sectors witnessed significant expansion, with factories ramping up production to meet growing demand both domestically and internationally. However, despite the apparent economic prosperity, concerns arose regarding the labour market.

    Despite the booming industrial sector, the unemployment rate in Arcadia continued to rise steadily. Many citizens, particularly those in rural areas, struggled to find stable employment opportunities matching their skill sets.

    Even though the GDP of the country soared, the job market remained stagnant, leading to widespread frustration and social unrest.

    Which term best describes the economic situation described in the case of Arcadia?

    (A) Jobless growth ☐
    (B) Full employment ☐
    (C) Structural unemployment ☐
    (D) Inflationary growth ☐

12. From the following pictures, identify the formal worker.

(A) ☐

(B) ☐

(C) ☐

(D) ☐

13. The informal sector includes enterprises and workers without regular income, government protection or regulation. Workers can be dismissed without compensation. The economic reforms of 1991 led to many workers being dismissed from the formal sector and moving to the informal sector, increasing the rate of informalisation.

What was a significant consequence of the economic reforms of 1991 on employment?

(A) Increase in government protection for informal sector workers ☐

(B) Rise in informalisation due to formal sector dismissals ☐

(C) Improvement in job security in the informal sector ☐

(D) Decrease in informal sector employment ☐

14. The primary importance of work in the context of economic development is

(A) Work provides individuals with a source of income to fulfill their basic needs and improve their standard of living ☐

(B) Work enhances social status and prestige, leading to greater recognition within the community ☐

(C) Work promotes physical and mental well-being by providing a sense of purpose and accomplishment ☐

(D) Work gives us a sense a sense of accomplishment when we work to meet the requirements of those who are dependent on us ☐

15. Identify the incorrect statement.

(A) Compared to females, more males are found to be working ☐

(B) The difference in participation rates between males and females is very large in urban areas ☐

(C) It is common to find that where men are able to earn high incomes, families discourage female members from taking up the jobs ☐

(D) The females who are actively engaged in household work are also categorised as workers ☐

16. As per 2017-18 analysis, arrange the following sectors of the economy in descending order based on their share of the workforce, from highest to lowest.

(A) Primary sector, Tertiary sector, Secondary sector ☐

(B) Tertiary sector, Primary sector, Secondary sector ☐

(C) Secondary sector, Tertiary sector, Primary sector ☐

(D) Primary sector, Secondary sector, Tertiary sector ☐

17. .... type of unemployment occurs when individuals are between jobs or entering the labour force for the first time.

(i) Frictional

(ii) Casual

(iii) Seasonal

(iv) Cyclic

Codes

(A) Both (i) and (ii) ☐

(B) Only (i) ☐

(C) Only (iv) ☐

(D) Both (ii) and (iv) ☐

18. Developmental planning envisaged that as the economy grows, more and more workers would become ....

(A) casual workers ☐
(B) informal workers ☐
(C) formal workers ☐
(D) seasonal workers ☐

19. The primary purpose of the International Labour Organisation (ILO) is

(A) to promote global trade agreements among member countries ☐
(B) to ensure the protection of workers' rights and improve working conditions worldwide ☐
(C) to facilitate international cooperation in the field of environmental conservation ☐
(D) to regulate the international exchange of goods and services to promote economic stability ☐

20. National Sample Survey Office (NSSO) define unemployment as

(A) individuals who are not willing to work so they are not employed ☐
(B) individuals who are not actively seeking employment so have not found a job ☐
(C) individuals who, owing to lack of work, are not working but either seeking work through employment exchanges, intermediaries, friends or relatives or by making applications to prospective employers ☐
(D) individuals who are employed part time but desire full time employment ☐

21. As per chart given below, the percentage of people involved in self-employment in urban areas is .... and the least percentage of people employed in rural areas is in ....

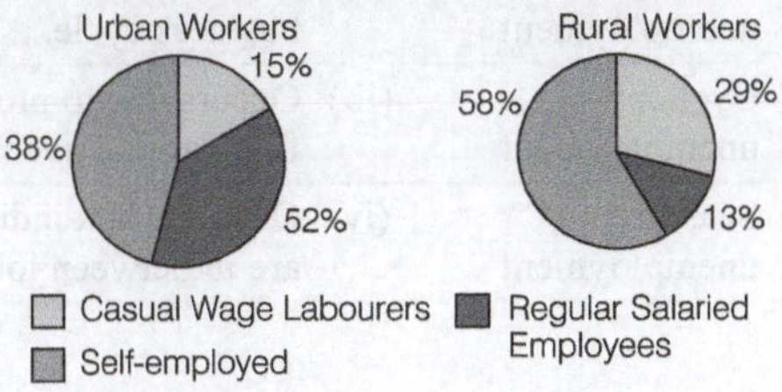

(A) 38%, casual wage labourers ☐
(B) 38%, self-employed ☐
(C) 38%, regular salaried employment ☐
(D) 15%, regular salaried employment ☐

22. In a rural village, there is a small agricultural farm where four family members work together to cultivate crops. The farm requires only two workers to efficiently manage all farming activities.

However, all four family members continue to work on the farm, even though their labour contribution is not necessary for its operation.

Which of the following best describes the situation described in the case?

(A) Seasonal unemployment ☐
(B) Disguised unemployment ☐
(C) Frictional unemployment ☐
(D) Structural unemployment ☐

23. Which of the following statements best illustrates a critical understanding of the features of seasonal unemployment?

(A) Seasonal unemployment, primarily affects individuals in urban areas who work in manufacturing industries ☐
(B) Seasonal unemployment occurs when workers are unable to find employment due to fluctuations in the business cycle ☐
(C) Seasonal unemployment is characterised by predictable patterns of joblessness that coincide with changes in weather, agricultural seasons or holiday demand ☐
(D) Seasonal unemployment is a temporary phenomenon that typically lasts for an extended period, leading to long-term economic instability ☐

24. Identify the incorrect statement from the following.

(A) Casualisation refers to the movement from regular salaried to causal wage workers ☐
(B) Over the last five decades, casualisation is picking up in India ☐

(C) The government exercises control over the informal sector ☐

(D) Workers do not get regular incomes in the informal sector ☐

25. Which of the following are the causes for unemployment?

(i) Technological advancements
(ii) Structural changes
(iii) Immigration
(iv) High wages

Codes

(A) Both (i) and (iii) ☐
(B) Both (iii) and (iv) ☐
(C) Both (i) and (ii) ☐
(D) All of the above ☐

26. In Metroville, the formal sector serves as a cornerstone of the city's economy, providing stability and security to thousands of workers. One such formal sector establishment is Metro Manufacturing Ltd. a leading automobile manufacturing company known for its adherence to labour laws and employee welfare policies.

Recently, a group of employees at Metro Manufacturing Ltd. filed a complaint with the labour department regarding alleged violations of labour laws by the company. They claimed that despite being classified as a formal sector establishment, Metro Manufacturing Ltd. was neglecting certain provisions mandated by labour laws, such as overtime pay, workplace safety standards and employee benefits.

Which of the following characteristics defines a formal sector establishment like Metro Manufacturing Ltd. in Metroville?

(A) Employing fewer than 10 hired workers ☐
(B) Adhering to labour laws and providing employee benefits ☐
(C) Operating without government oversight ☐
(D) Being exempt from labour regulations ☐

27. Matching the following

Column I		Column II
A. Workers	(i)	Marginal productivity of labour
B. Disguised unemployment	(ii)	Daily wage earners
C. Worker-population ratio	(iii)	Contributing to GDP
D. Casual workers	(iv)	Analyse the employment situation

Codes

	A	B	C	D	
(A)	(i)	(iii)	(iv)	(ii)	☐
(B)	(iii)	(i)	(ii)	(iv)	☐
(C)	(iii)	(iv)	(i)	(ii)	☐
(D)	(iii)	(i)	(iv)	(ii)	☐

28. Match the following

Column I		Column II
A. Formal workers	(i)	Earn wages and salaries
B. Informal workers	(ii)	Social security benefits
C. Self-employed workers	(iii)	Not protected by labour laws
D. Hired workers	(iv)	Earn profits

Codes

	A	B	C	D	
(A)	(ii)	(iii)	(iv)	(i)	☐
(B)	(iii)	(ii)	(iv)	(i)	☐
(C)	(ii)	(iii)	(i)	(iv)	☐
(D)	(ii)	(iv)	(iii)	(i)	☐

29. Match the following

Column I		Column II
A. Frictional unemployment	(i)	Arises from fundamental shifts in the economy.
B. Structural unemployment	(ii)	Tied to fluctuations in the business cycle.
C. Cyclical unemployment	(iii)	Occurs due to predictable fluctuations in demand.
D. Seasonal unemployment	(iv)	Occurs when individuals are in between jobs.

Codes

	A	B	C	D
(A)	(ii)	(iii)	(iv)	(i)
(B)	(iii)	(iv)	(i)	(ii)
(C)	(iv)	(i)	(ii)	(iii)
(D)	(i)	(iv)	(iii)	(ii)

30. Match the following

Column I	Column II
A. Casualisation	(i) No labour laws protection.
B. Jobless growth	(ii) Movement from regular salaried to causal wage.
C. Formal sector	(iii) GDP grows, but employment does not.
D. Informal sector	(iv) Control of government.

Codes

	A	B	C	D
(A)	(ii)	(iii)	(iv)	(i)
(B)	(iii)	(iv)	(i)	(ii)
(C)	(iv)	(i)	(ii)	(iii)
(D)	(i)	(iv)	(iii)	(ii)

Assertion-Reason Questions

No. of Questions : **8** Suggested Time : **15 Minutes**

Direction Each of the question given below consist of the two statements; one labelled as **Assertion** (A) and other as **Reason** (R). List of common options applicable for each question is given below

(A) Both Assertion (A) and Reason (R) are true and Reason (R) is the correct explanation of Assertion (A)

(B) Both Assertion (A) and Reason (R) are true, but Reason (R) is not the correct explanation of Assertion (A)

(C) Assertion is true, but Reason is false

(D) Assertion is false, but Reason is true

You have to select the codes as *A, B, C* or *D* as your answer to the question by marking (✓) in the response box given against each option.

1. **Assertion** (A) The nature of employment in India is multifaceted.

Reason (R) Some get employment throughout the year, some others get employed for only a few months in a year.

(A) ☐ (B) ☐ (C) ☐ (D) ☐

2. **Assertion** (A) Women carry out works like cooking, fetching water and fuel wood and participate in farm labour. They are not paid wages in cash.

Reason (R) The women working at home are not considered as workers.

(A) ☐ (B) ☐ (C) ☐ (D) ☐

3. **Assertion** (A) Since the late 1970s, many developing countries, including India, started paying attention to enterprises and workers in the informal sector as employment in the formal sector is not growing.

Reason (R) Workers are dismissed without any compensation. Technology used in the informal sector enterprises is outdated. Workers of this sector live in slums and are squatters.

(A) ☐

(B) ☐

(C) ☐

(D) ☐

4. **Assertion (A)** People are being forced to accept jobs that nobody else would do, unpleasant or even dangerous jobs in unclean or unhealthy surroundings.

Reason (R) People cannot remain completely unemployed for very long because their desperate economic condition would not allow them to be so.

(A) ☐ (B) ☐ (C) ☐ (D) ☐

5. **Assertion (A)** Informal sector provides better wages and salaries, job security and also protected by the labour laws.

Reason (R) Employment in formal sector should be increased.

(A) ☐ (B) ☐ (C) ☐ (D) ☐

6. **Assertion (A)** Labour laws are passed for formal sector to protect the interest of workers.

Reason (R) The government has a control on the workings of the formal sector.

(A) ☐ (B) ☐ (C) ☐ (D) ☐

7. **Assertion (A)** In the course of economic development of a country, labour flows from agriculture and other related activities to industry and services.

Reason (R) Eventually, at a much later stage, the industrial sector will begin to lose its share of total employment as the primary sector will enter a period of rapid expansion.

(A) ☐ (B) ☐ (C) ☐ (D) ☐

8. **Assertion (A)** In the last few decades, there has been rapid growth in the gross domestic product, but without simultaneous increase in employment opportunities.

Reason (R) Government is not taking up any initiatives in generating employment opportunities particularly in the rural areas.

(A) ☐ (B) ☐
(C) ☐ (D) ☐

Correct/Incorrect Statements

No. of Questions : **10** Suggested Time : **15 Minutes**

Direction Each of the question given below consist of the two statements. List of common options applicable for each question is given below

(A) Both statements are correct
(B) Both statements are incorrect
(C) Statement I is correct and Statement II is incorrect
(D) Statement I is incorrect and Statement II is correct

You have to select the codes as *A, B, C* or *D* as your answer to the question by marking (✓) in the response box given against each option.

1. **Statement I** The nature of unemployment problem in India is uni-faceted.

Statement II Worker-population ratio is an indicator used for analysing the employment situation in a country.

(A) ☐ (B) ☐
(C) ☐ (D) ☐

2. **Statement I** Workers who own and operate an enterprise to earn their livelihood are known as hired workers.

Statement II When a worker is engaged by someone or an enterprise and paid his or her wages on a regular basis, they are known as self-employed workers.

(A) ☐ (B) ☐ (C) ☐ (D) ☐

3. **Statement I** During the period 1950-2010, Gross Domestic Product (GDP) of India grew positively and was higher than the employment growth.

Statement II In the late 1990s, employment growth started declining and reached the level of growth that India had in the early stages of planning.

(A) ☐ (B) ☐
(C) ☐ (D) ☐

4. **Statement I** The distribution of workforce in different status indicates that over the last five decades (1972-2018), people have moved from casual wage work to self-employment and regular salaried employment.

Statement II Formal sector includes millions of farmers, agricultural labourers, owners of small enterprises and people working in those enterprises and also the self-employed who do not have any hired workers.

(A) ☐ (B) ☐
(C) ☐ (D) ☐

5. **Statement I** People in rural areas have infinite resources to earn a higher income and participate more in the employment market.

Statement II Urban people have a variety of employment opportunities. They look for the appropriate job to suit their qualifications and skills.

(A) ☐ (B) ☐
(C) ☐ (D) ☐

6. **Statement I** Those activities which contribute to the gross national product are called economic activities.

Statement II All those who are engaged in economic activities, in whatever capacity, high or low, are workers.

(A) ☐ (B) ☐ (C) ☐ (D) ☐

7. **Statement I** Though both men and women workers are concentrated in the primary sector, women workers' concentration is very high there.

Statement II It is not easy for men to get opportunities in secondary and service sectors.

(A) ☐ (B) ☐
(C) ☐ (D) ☐

8. **Statement I** Frictional unemployment occurs when workers are temporarily between jobs or are searching for new jobs.

Statement II Cyclical unemployment is the result of technological advancements that make certain job skills obsolete.

(A) ☐ (B) ☐
(C) ☐ (D) ☐

9. **Statement I** Structural unemployment occurs due to changes in the structure of an economy, such as technological advancements or shifts in consumer demand.

Statement II High wages mandated by the government can lead to an increase in structural unemployment.

(A) ☐ (B) ☐
(C) ☐ (D) ☐

10. **Statement I** As per National Sample Survey Organisation (NSSO), unemployment is a situation in which all those who, owing to lack of work, are not working, but seeking work from prospective employers, expressed their willingness to work under the prevailing condition of work and remuneration.

Statement II Disguised unemployment is generally a massive problem in the highly populated country like India. *[CBSE 2024]*

(A) ☐ (B) ☐ (C) ☐ (D) ☐

Case Based Questions

No. of Questions : 2 Suggested Time : **10 Minutes**

Direction This section contains 2 cases each having 4 questions of 1 mark each. You have to write the answer of each question based on the context of the related case.

Case 1 In a rural village named Sundarpur, located in the heart of India, traditional agricultural practices have been the primary source of livelihood for generations. However, in recent years, the younger population has been facing challenges in finding employment opportunities within the village due to limited land availability and declining agricultural productivity.

As a result, many young individuals have migrated to nearby urban areas in search of better job prospects. Upon observing this trend, the local government of Sundarpur decides to implement the Mahatma Gandhi National Rural Employment Guarantee Act (MGNREGA) to address unemployment and provide sustainable livelihoods within the village.

Under the MGNREGA scheme, various projects such as water conservation, road construction and afforestation are initiated, aiming to generate employment opportunities for the local population. Rajesh, a 25 years old resident of Sundarpur, who had previously migrated to the city in search of employment, decides to return to his village to participate in the MGNREGA projects.

He joins a team working on a road construction project and receives guaranteed wages for his labour.

Questions

(i) .... is the competency, which Rajesh demonstrate by participating in the MGNREGA project in Sundarpur.

(ii) The primary objective of the Mahatma Gandhi National Rural Employment Guarantee Act (MGNREGA) as illustrated in the case study is ....

(iii) Which factor contributed to the decision of many young individuals from Sundarpur to migrate to urban areas prior to the implementation of MGNREGA?

(A) Availability of better healthcare facilities in urban areas ☐

(B) Limited land availability and declining agricultural productivity in the village ☐

(C) Lack of educational institutions and quality schooling options in the village ☐

(D) Cultural and social attractions of urban lifestyle ☐

(iv) What role does the MGNREGA scheme play in addressing the unemployment challenges faced by rural communities like Sundarpur?

(A) It provides direct cash transfers to unemployed individuals ☐

(B) It facilitates skill development and vocational training programmes ☐

(C) It offers guaranteed wage employment opportunities through public works projects ☐

(D) It encourages entrepreneurship and small business development ☐

Case 2 Informalisation in Ahmedabad

Ahmedabad is a prosperous city with its wealth based on the produce of more than 60 textile mills with a labour force of 1,50,000 workers employed in them. These workers had, over the course of the century, acquired a certain degree of income security.

They had secure jobs with a living wage; they were covered by social security schemes protecting their health and old age. They had a strong trade union which not only represented them in disputes but also ran activities for the welfare of workers and their families.

In the early 1980s, textile mills all over the country began to close down. In some places, such as Mumbai, the mills closed rapidly. In Ahmedabad, the process of closure was long drawn out and spread over 10 years.

Over this period, approximately over 80,000 permanent workers and over 50,000 non-permanent workers lost their jobs and were driven to the informal sector. The city experienced an economic recession and public disturbances, especially communal riots. A whole class of workers was thrown back from the middle class into the informal sector, into poverty. There was widespread alcoholism and suicides, children were withdrawn from school and sent to work.

Questions

(i) Which of the following is not characterised by the formal sector workers?

(A) Job security ☐

(B) Social security benefits ☐

(C) Form a trade union ☐

(D) Not protected by labour laws ☐

(ii) The movement of labour from formal sector to informal sector is known as ....

(iii) Identify the incorrect statement in context of the above case study.

(A) In the early 1980s, textile mills all over the country began to close down. In some places, such as Mumbai, the mills closed rapidly ☐

(B) In Ahmedabad, the process of closure was long drawn out and spread over 10 years ☐

(C) There had been a shift of workforce from informal sector to formal sector ☐

(D) There was widespread alcoholism and suicides, children were withdrawn from school and sent to work ☐

(iv) Over this period, approximately over 80,000 permanent workers and over 50,000 non-permanent workers lost their jobs and were driven to the .... sector.

Subjective Questions

Free Response Questions, Open-ended Questions etc.

No. of Questions : **8** Suggested Time : **50 Minutes**

1. "In the late 1990's India experienced a widening gap between the growth of GDP and employment generation." Discuss. *[CBSE 2023]*

2. Yet literacy rate is better among females in urban areas, mention the reasons for low female workforce in urban areas in comparison to rural female workforce.

3. "It is necessary to generate employment in the formal sector rather than the informal sector." Justify the given statement with valid agruments. *[CBSE 2024]*

4. Identify the phenomenon indicated by the picture below. Also, explain the causes for it and its significance in the economy.

5. Why the workforce in self-employment is least in urban areas and highest in rural areas?

6. Study the following chart showing the growth of employment and gross domestic product and analyse the trend of the two variables from 1990-2012. *[CBSE 2024]*

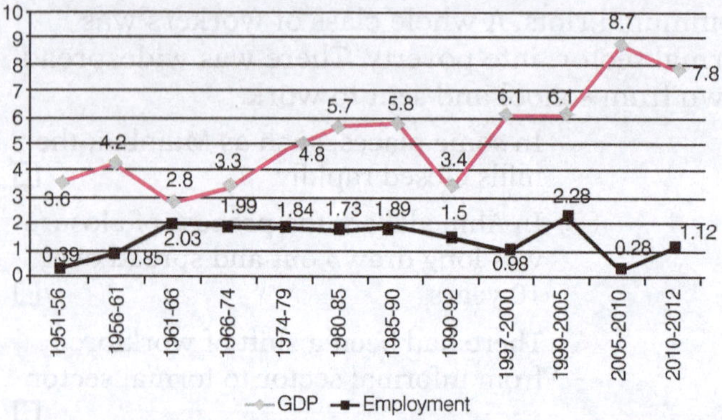

Growth of Employment and Gross Domestic Product, 1951–2012 (%)

7. "Mr. Rishi, after completing his education, has joined his family business but his marginal productivity is zero." Comment upon the employment status of Mr. Rishi. Give valid reasons in support of your answer. *[CBSE 2023]*

8. Avinash lived in a joint family. As he grew up, he started working with his father, uncles and cousins in their farm. They worked and earned well but Avinash thought that the people working on the farm were more that what were actually required.

He moved to the city soon after, he did not get job because he didn't have the required degree. He enrolled himself in a college where he studied hard and after that, he got a well paid job. He felt satisfied.

(i) In the first part, which type of unemployment is being reflected? Discuss.

(ii) What are the causes of unemployment in India? Explain any four.

Answers

If your answer matches with the answer given here then put (✓) in the box otherwise put (✗). In case you did not attempt the question leave the box blank.

Multiple Choice Questions

1. B ☐	2. B ☐
3. B ☐	4. C ☐
5. D ☐	6. A ☐
7. D ☐	8. A ☐
9. D ☐	10. D ☐
11. A ☐	12. D ☐
13. B ☐	14. A ☐
15. D ☐	16. A ☐
17. B ☐	18. C ☐
19. B ☐	20. C ☐
21. C ☐	22. B ☐
23. C ☐	24. C ☐
25. C ☐	26. B ☐
27. D ☐	28. A ☐
29. C ☐	30. A ☐

Your Score__________ *(No. of Correct Answers)*

Assertion-Reason Questions

1. A ☐	2. A ☐
3. B ☐	4. A ☐
5. D ☐	6. A ☐
7. C ☐	8. C ☐

Your Score__________ *(No. of Correct Answers)*

Correct/Incorrect Statements

1. D ☐	2. B ☐
3. A ☐	4. B ☐
5. D ☐	6. A ☐
7. C ☐	8. C ☐
9. A ☐	10. A ☐

Your Score__________ *(No. of Correct Answers)*

Case Based Questions

1. (iii) B ☐	(iv) C ☐
2. (i) D ☐	(iii) C ☐

Your Score__________ *(No. of Correct Answers)*

Explanations

Multiple Choice Questions

1. (B) Majority of people reside in rural areas
2. (B) $\frac{\text{Total Worker}}{\text{Total Population}} \times 100$
3. (B) This ratio is useful in knowing the proportion of population that is actively contributing to the production of goods and services of a country
4. (C) A freelance graphic designer who works from home
5. (D) All of the above
6. (A) Self-employment
7. (D) growth is due to technological development
8. (A) Jobless growth refers to a situation where economic growth occurs without a corresponding increase in employment opportunities. In such cases, although the Gross Domestic Product (GDP) may rise, it does not necessarily lead to the creation of sufficient jobs.
9. (D) Samsung electronics company limited
10. (D) outsourcing
11. (A) The case of Arcadia illustrates a scenario of jobless growth, where the economy experiences GDP growth without a corresponding increase in employment opportunities.
12. (D) Formal workers typically refer to individuals who are employed in jobs that are regulated by labour laws and are part of the formal economy.
13. (B) Rise in informalisation due to formal sector dismissals
14. (A) The primary importance of work in the context of economic development is to provide individuals with a source of income. This income enables people to meet their basic needs (such as food, shelter and clothing) and improves their standard of living.
15. (D) In official labour force surveys, females who are engaged in household work are generally not categorised as workers.
16. (A) Primary sector, Tertiary sector, Secondary sector
17. (B) Only (i)
18. (C) formal workers
19. (B) to ensure the protection of workers' rights and improve working conditions worldwide
20. (C) individuals who, owing to lack of work, are not working but either seeking work through employment exchanges, intermediaries, friends or relatives or by making applications to prospective employers
21. (C) 38%, regular salaried employment
22. (B) Disguised unemployment
23. (C) Seasonal unemployment is characterised by predictable patterns of joblessness that coincide with changes in weather, agricultural seasons or holiday demand
24. (C) The informal sector typically operates outside formal regulatory frameworks and often involves small-scale or unregistered enterprises.
25. (C) Technological advancements and structural changes disrupt traditional job markets, leading to unemployment by replacing human labour with automation and altering industry demands, respectively.
26. (B) Adhering to labour laws and providing employee benefits
27. (D) (iii) (i) (iv) (ii) 28. (A) (ii) (iii) (iv) (i)
29. (C) (iv) (i) (ii) (iii)
30. (A) (ii) (iii) (iv) (i)

Assertion-Reason Questions

1. (A) Both Assertion (A) and Reason (R) are true and Reason (R) is the correct explanation of Assertion (A)
2. (A) Both Assertion (A) and Reason (R) are true and Reason (R) is the correct explanation of Assertion (A)
3. (B) Both Assertion (A) and Reason (R) are true, but Reason (R) is not the correct explanation of Assertion (A)
4. (A) Both Assertion (A) and Reason (R) are true and Reason (R) is the correct explanation of Assertion (A)
5. (D) The informal sector often offers lower wages, limited job security and lacks adequate protection by labour laws compared to the formal sector.

6. (A) Both Assertion (A) and Reason (R) are true and Reason (R) is the correct explanation of Assertion (A)
7. (C) Assertion (A) is true, but Reason (R) is false
8. (C) Governments often implement various initiatives and policies aimed at boosting employment, including rural employment schemes, skill development programmes and investment in infrastructure.

Correct/Incorrect Statements

1. (D) The nature of unemployment in India is not uni-faceted; it is complex and multi-faceted.
2. (B) Workers who own and operate an enterprise to earn their livelihood are known as self-employed workers. Hired workers are those who work for someone else or an enterprise and receive regular wages or salary.
3. (A) Both statements are correct
4. (B) The casual wage work has increased, not decreased. The formal sector includes large enterprises and public sector units, not small farmers or self-employed without hired workers.
5. (D) People in rural areas generally do not have infinite resources to earn a higher income.
6. (A) Both statements are correct
7. (C) Men generally have more opportunities to transition to the secondary (industrial) and service sectors compared to women.
8. (C) Cyclical unemployment is caused by economic downturns and fluctuations in the business cycle.
9. (A) Both statements are correct
10. (A) Both statements are correct

Case Based Questions

1. (i) Adaptability and willingness to learn new skills
   (ii) to provide guaranteed employment and livelihood opportunities in rural areas
   (iii) (B) The primary reason for migration was the limited land availability and declining agricultural productivity, which made it difficult for young people to find employment in the village.
   (iv) (C) It offers guaranteed wage employment opportunities through public works projects
2. (i) (D) Formal sector workers typically have job security, receive social security benefits and have the right to form trade unions. They are protected by labour laws, unlike informal sector workers.
   (ii) informalisation of workforce
   (iii) (C) There had been a shift of workforce from informal sector to formal sector
   (iv) informal

Subjective Questions

1. During the period 1960-2000, GDP of India grew positively and was higher than the employment growth. However, there were always fluctuation in the growth of GDP. But in the late 1990s, employment growth started declining and reached the level of gowth that India had in the early stages of planning.
   During these years, India experienced a widening gap between the growth of GDP and employment generation. That means, India has been able to produce more goods and services without generating employment. The difference between the growth rate of employment generation and GDP is indicative of the phenomenon of 'jobless growth'.
2. As poverty ratio is high in rural areas, so, rural females are compelled to engage in any economic activity, whereas in urban areas, it is common to find that men are able to earn high incomes, so families discourage female members from taking up jobs.
   Secondly, in rural areas agriculture is the main occupation which is the part of self-employment, so all the members of the family become the part of the work whereas in urban areas, higher number of the people are engaged in regular salaried employment.
3. Generating employment in the formal sector is crucial for several reasons
   (i) **Job Security** Formal sector jobs typically offer greater job security as compared to informal sector employment. Workers in the formal sector are often covered by labour laws and regulations that protect their rights, including provisions for minimum wages, benefits and job stability. This stability provides employees with a sense of security and stability, allowing them to plan for their future and invest in their careers.

(ii) **Social Security Benefits** Formal sector jobs often come with social security benefits such as health insurance, pension plans and unemployment benefits. These benefits provide financial protection to employees and their families during times of illness, disability or unemployment, helping to alleviate poverty and improve overall well-being.

(iii) **Higher Wages and Better Working Conditions** Formal sector jobs tend to offer higher wages and better working conditions as compared to informal sector employment. Formal sector employers are more likely to comply with labour standards and regulations, providing employees with fair wages, safe working environments and opportunities for skills development and career advancement.

4. The picture indicates the concept of 'jobless growth'.

Causes of jobless growth are as follows

(i) **Shift in Production Techniques** The adoption of capital intensive techniques over labour intensive ones in various industries leads to reduced demand for labour.

(ii) **Technological Advancements** Rapid technological progress often results in automation and mechanisation, reducing the need for manual labour.

(iii) **Globalisation** Increased competition from global markets may force companies to streamline operations, leading to downsizing and job losses.

(iv) **Policy Decisions** Government policies that prioritise capital intensive sectors or fail to promote labour intensive industries can exacerbate jobless growth.

(v) **Economic Conditions** Economic downturns or stagnation can result in businesses being cautious about hiring, contributing to unemployment despite overall GDP growth.

Importance of jobless growth is as follows

(i) **Economic Growth** Jobless growth still signifies overall economic expansion, which is crucial for improving living standards and infrastructure.

(ii) **Efficiency** Capital intensive techniques often lead to increased productivity and efficiency, which are vital for sustained economic development.

(iii) **Investment Opportunities** Higher profits from capital intensive sectors may translate into increased investment in other areas, fostering innovation and growth.

(iv) **Structural Transformation** Jobless growth can be a part of the broader structural transformation of the economy, as it shifts from agriculture to industry and services.

(v) **Policy Focus** Recognising jobless growth highlights the need for targeted policies to address unemployment, such as investments in education, training and job creation programmes.

5. Self-employment is least in urban areas as in urban areas, investment requirements are high to start with self-employment, also, it deals with risk so, generally people tries for regular salaried employment as it reduces risk and investment requirements. Moreover, people in urban areas are generally qualified and skill oriented to go for regular employment.

In rural areas, agriculture is the main occupation and generally all members of the family become the part of the agriculture which is self-employment. So, workforce in self-employment increases.

6. The period between 1990 to 2012 had been a significant one. Introduction of economic reforms in India has changed everything in India.

Variables shown in the given graph show that GDP growth rate has taken an upwards tread over the years whereas the situation of employment growth rate has seen major fluctuations while going down in overall trend.

GDP growth rate has increased from a meager 3.4% in 1991 to 7.8% in 2012. However the employment growth rate has shown declining trends from 1.5% in 1991 to 1.12% in 2012. Between the period 1999-2005 the employment generation rate was at peak since independence i.e. 2.28% p.a. with the corresponding GDP growth rate standing at a decent 6.1% p.a.

The gap between the two variables is maximum between the period 2005-10 when the employment growth rate hit the lowest in history of Independent India i.e. 0.28%. In the same period the GDP growth rate had hit the highest level since independence to the tune of 8.7% p.a. Indian economy has witnessed the peculiar phenomena of 'jobless growth' over all these years.

Learning from the situation government had put in serious efforts on employment front and brought it to a level of 1.12% p.a. between the period 2010-12. In all the period between 1990-2012 has been a real roller coaster ride for the India economy on the two front of GDP and employment growth rate.

7. The type of unemployment indicated in the above statement is disguised unemployment. It refers to a situation in which an extra input of labour generates no additional output. It is when marginal physical productivity of labour is zero or sometimes it becomes negative.

The paradox associated with disguised unemployment in rural areas of India is that while there are more members of a family are engaged in work, yet the gross income of the family is generally low.

This is because the surplus labour force does not contribute to any additional output or productivity, which means that the family's income is not proportional to the number of labourers. In fact, the extra labourers often add to the cost of production, as they need to be provided with food and other sources and this leads to lower net income.

8. (i) In the first part, disguised unemployment is being reflected. It refers to a situation in which an extra input of labour generates no additional output.

(ii) The causes of unemployment in India are given below

(a) **Slow Economic Growth** In Indian economy, the rate of economic growth is very slow.

This slow growth rate fails to provide enough employment opportunities to the rising population.

(b) **Rapid Growth of Population** Constant increase in population has been a grave problem of India. It is one of the main causes of unemployment.

(c) **Faulty Employment Planning** The five year plans in India have not been designed for employment generation.

(d) **Excessive use of Foreign Technology** There is lack of scientific and technical research in India due to its high cost. This has resulted in excessive use of foreign technology which has led to technical unemployment in our country.

CHAPTER -7

Environment and Sustainable Development

Types & Nos. of Questions

Multiple Choice Questions	-	28
Assertion-Reason Questions	-	8
Correct/Incorrect Statements	-	8
Case Based Questions	-	2 Cases, *each with four Questions*
Subjective Questions	-	10

Trend Analysis

On the basis of analysis of last 2 years' papers, it is found that on an average 2 Multiple Choice Questions, 1 Short Answer Type Question (Picture Based) and 1 Long Answer Type Question (Case Based) are asked from this chapter.

Focus Topics of the Chapter

- Meaning of Environment
- State of India's Environment
- Sustainable Development
- Strategies for Sustainable Development

Multiple Choice Questions

No. of Questions : **28** Suggested Time : **45 Minutes**

Direction Each of the question given below is Multiple Choice Question (MCQ) i.e. there are Four Options/ Choices for answer, out of which ONLY ONE is correct. You have to select the correct option. A response box is given with each option, mark (✓) in the box of the correct option. For each correct answer you will get 1 mark, while there is no penalty for incorrect answer or missed out questions.

1. .... capacity implies that the resource extraction is not above the rate of regeneration of the resource whereas .... means the ability of the environment to absorb degradation.

(A) Absorptive, carrying ☐
(B) Assimilating, absorptive ☐
(C) Carrying, absorptive ☐
(D) Ecological, carrying ☐

2. Identify, which of the following is not a correct function of environment?

(i) Exclusion of waste
(ii) Sustainance of life
(iii) Provide aesthetic services *[CBSE 2024]*

Codes

(A) Only (i) ☐ (B) Only (ii) ☐
(C) (ii) and (iii) ☐ (D) (i) and (ii) ☐

3. In an economy, when the rate of resource extraction is lower than the rate of regeneration of the resource, the environment may operate .... *[CBSE 2023]*

(A) within its carrying capacity ☐
(B) beyond its absorptive capacity ☐
(C) beyond its carrying capacity ☐
(D) beyond its aesthetic capacity ☐

4. Development to enhance our current living styles, without concern for posterity, will .... resources and .... environment at a pace that is bound to result in both environmental and economic crisis.

(A) enhance, preserve ☐
(B) deplete, degrade ☐
(C) restore, sustain ☐
(D) protect, improve ☐

5. "Only recently have we drifted away from the traditional systems and caused large scale damage to the environment and also our rural heritage." Now, it is time to go back.

In the context of the above statement, what role do traditional medical systems like Ayurveda, Unani, Tibetan and folk medicine play in healthcare?

(A) They are outdated and ineffective compared to modern medical practices ☐
(B) They provide complementary approaches to health and well-being, incorporating holistic and natural remedies ☐
(C) They are primarily used in rural areas due to lack of access to modern healthcare facilities ☐
(D) They are only relevant in certain cultural contexts and have limited applicability globally ☐

6. Identify the functions performed by the environment.

(i) It supplies resources
(ii) It assimilates waste
(iii) It sustains life
(iv) It provides inelegant services

Codes

(A) Only (i) ☐
(B) Both (i) and (ii) ☐
(C) Both (iii) and (iv) ☐
(D) (i), (ii), (iii) and (iv) ☐

7. What is the most accurate description of global warming?
(A) A rapid cooling of earth's atmosphere due to human activities ☐
(B) The process of reducing greenhouse gas emissions to stabilise earth's temperature ☐
(C) An increase in earth's average temperature primarily caused by human induced release of greenhouse gases ☐
(D) A natural cycle of temperature fluctuations unaffected by human influence ☐

8. Factors that contribute to global warming include
(i) burning of coal and petroleum products
(ii) afforestation
(iii) methane gas released in animal waste

Codes

(A) Only (i) ☐
(B) Both (i) and (ii) ☐
(C) Both (i) and (iii) ☐
(D) Both (ii) and (iii) ☐

9. "The 2023 ozone hole has been larger compared to 2022."
– European Environment Agency

What is the primary cause of ozone depletion in the stratosphere?
(A) High levels of carbon dioxide and methane compounds ☐
(B) High levels of chlorine and bromine compounds ☐
(C) High levels of sulfur dioxide and nitrogen oxides ☐
(D) High levels of oxygen and nitrogen compounds ☐

10. "This May was the warmest May ever. In fact, each of the last 12 months has set a new warming record for that particular month." – The Hindu

Which of the following is not an effect of global warming?
(A) Melting of polar ice resulting in increased sea levels ☐
(B) Increased volcanic activity ☐
(C) Disruption of drinking water supplies dependent on snow melts ☐
(D) More frequent tropical storms ☐

11. Identify the incorrect statement.
(A) Land degradation is solely caused by natural factors such as erosion and weathering ☐
(B) Land degradation leads to reduced agricultural productivity and loss of biodiversity ☐
(C) Overgrazing, deforestation and urbanisation are human activities that contribute to land degradation ☐
(D) Land degradation has no impact on water quality or availability ☐

12. Which of the following statements regarding land degradation is incorrect?
(A) Land degradation can result from unsustainable agricultural practices such as overgrazing and deforestation ☐
(B) Desertification is a form of land degradation characterised by the transformation of fertile land into desert-like conditions ☐
(C) Land degradation has no impact on biodiversity loss or ecosystem services ☐
(D) Soil erosion, salinisation and desertification are all examples of land degradation processes ☐

13. Mini-hydel plants are good for the environment because
(i) they generate electricity only for local areas
(ii) they do not change the land use pattern

(iii) they rely on the perennial streams [CBSE 2023]

Codes

(A) (i), (ii) and (iii) ☐
(B) (ii) and (iii) ☐
(C) Only (i) ☐
(D) (i) and (ii) ☐

14. Which environmental impact is commonly associated with both thermal and hydroelectric power plants?

(A) Air pollution due to emissions ofgreenhouse gases ☐
(B) Water pollution caused by discharge of heated water ☐
(C) Soil erosion and habitat destruction ☐
(D) Noise pollution from operational activities ☐

15. Which of the following relates to the function of CPCB?

(A) They investigate, collect and disseminate information relating to water, air and land pollution ☐
(B) They lay down standards for sewage/trade effluent and emissions ☐
(C) These boards provide technical assistance to governments in promoting cleanliness of streams and wells by prevention, control and abatement of water pollution ☐
(D) All of the above ☐

16. Which statement accurately describes the Central Pollution Control Board's (CPCB) identification of significantly polluting industries?

(A) CPCB categorises industries based solely on their size and revenue generation ☐
(B) CPCB categorises industries based on their potential environmental impact and pollution levels ☐
(C) CPCB categorises industries based on their geographical location and proximity to urban areas ☐
(D) CPCB categorises industries based on their compliance with environmental regulations ☐

17. In context of the following picture, choose the correct option.

The .... Movement aimed at protecting forests in the Himalayas. On 8th September, 1983, when the felling of trees was started in Salkani forest in Sirsi district, 160 men, women and children .... and forced the woodcutters to leave.

(A) Chipko, hugged the trees ☐
(B) Appiko, planted saplings ☐
(C) Van Mahotsav, protested ☐
(D) Green Revolution, demonstrated ☐

18. What fundamental aspect is integral to the definition of sustainable development according to UNCED?

(A) Maintaining economic growth at all costs ☐
(B) Striking a balance between meeting present needs, without compromising the ability of the future generation to meet their own needs ☐
(C) Focusing solely on environmental conservation without regard for social or economic factors ☐
(D) Exploiting natural resources without considering long-term consequences ☐

19. For the gobar gas plant to function, ... is fed to the plant and gas is produced which is used as fuel while the .... which is left over is a very good organic fertiliser and soil conditioner.

(A) cattle dung, chemical fertiliser ☐
(B) pesticides, slurry ☐
(C) agriculture run-off, organic compost ☐
(D) cattle dung, slurry ☐

20. In what way does the widespread adoption of Compressed Natural Gas (CNG) as a fuel in public transport systems benefit urban environments?

(A) By increasing greenhouse gas emissions due to the combustion of CNG ☐
(B) By reducing air pollution and improving air quality in urban areas ☐
(C) By contributing to soil pollution through CNG leakage from vehicles ☐
(D) By exacerbating noise pollution in densely populated areas ☐

21. In which of the following activities are earthworms commonly used to enrich soil?

(A) Aquaculture ☐
(B) Biocomposting ☐
(C) Biopest ☐ (D) Hydroponics ☐

22. The following image highlights .... source of energy.

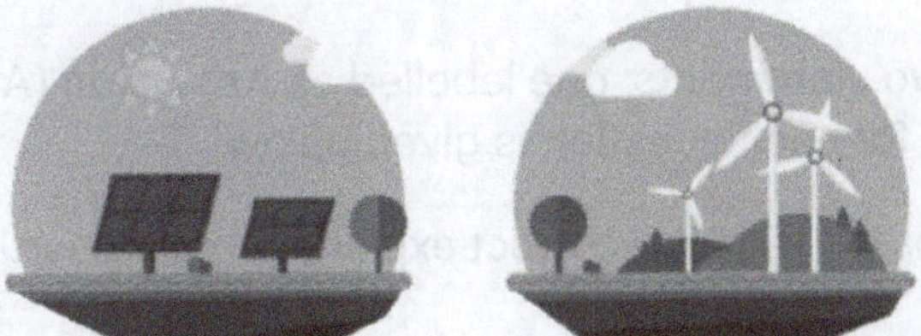

(A) renewable ☐
(B) non-renewable ☐
(C) conventional ☐
(D) non-conventional ☐

23. There are so many strategies being followed in the economy to achieve sustainable development. Which strategy is indicated in the following picture?

(A) Bio compost ☐
(B) Bio pest ☐
(C) Traditional knowledge and practices ☐
(D) None of the above ☐

24. Which of the following best describes a key difference between renewable and non-renewable resources?

(A) Renewable resources are finite and depletable, while non-renewable resources can be replenished over time ☐
(B) Renewable resources have lower environmental impact compared to non-renewable resources ☐
(C) Renewable resources are typically more expensive to extract and utilise than non-renewable resources ☐
(D) Renewable resources are derived from natural processes that can be sustained indefinitely, while non-renewable resources are finite and cannot be replenished ☐

25. The .... and .... extraction of both renewable and non-renewable resources has exhausted some of the vital resources and huge amount on technology and research is spent to explore new resources.

(A) inside, outside ☐
(B) intensive, extensive ☐
(C) inclusive, exclusive ☐
(D) adequate, inadequate ☐

26. Match the following

Column I		Column II
A. Global warming	(i)	Protection of forests
B. Montreal protocol	(ii)	Assess air quality
C. Appiko movement	(iii)	Ozone depletion
D. CPCB	(iv)	Environmental issue

Codes

	A	B	C	D	
(A)	(iv)	(iii)	(ii)	(i)	☐
(B)	(iv)	(i)	(iii)	(ii)	☐
(C)	(iii)	(iv)	(i)	(ii)	☐
(D)	(iv)	(iii)	(i)	(ii)	☐

27. Match the following

Column I		Column II
A. CNG	(i)	Neem trees
B. Photovoltaic cells	(ii)	Cattle dung
C. Biocomposting	(iii)	Lowered air pollution
D. Bio pest	(iv)	Solar energy into electricity

Codes

	A	B	C	D	
(A)	(iv)	(iii)	(i)	(ii)	☐
(B)	(ii)	(i)	(iii)	(iv)	☐
(C)	(iii)	(iv)	(ii)	(i)	☐
(D)	(iv)	(i)	(iii)	(ii)	☐

28. Match Column I with Column II.

Column I		Column II
A. LPG	(i)	Small turbines moved through streams
B. Gobar gas	(ii)	Liquefied petroleum gas
C. Wind power	(iii)	Dung cake and biomass
D. Mini-hydel plants	(iv)	Wind mills

Codes

	A	B	C	D	
(A)	(iv)	(i)	(ii)	(iii)	☐
(B)	(ii)	(iii)	(iv)	(i)	☐
(C)	(iii)	(iv)	(i)	(ii)	☐
(D)	(i)	(ii)	(iii)	(iv)	☐

Assertion-Reason Questions

No. of Questions : 8 Suggested Time : **15 Minutes**

Direction Each of the question given below consist of the two statements; one labelled as **Assertion** (A) and other as **Reason** (R). List of common options applicable for each question is given below

(A) Both Assertion (A) and Reason (R) are true and Reason (R) is the correct explanation of Assertion (A)

(B) Both Assertion (A) and Reason (R) are true, but Reason (R) is not the correct explanation of Assertion (A)

(C) Assertion (A) is true, but Reason (R) is false

(D) Assertion (A) is false, but Reason (R) is true

You have to select the codes as *A, B, C* or *D* as your answer to the question by marking (✓) in the response box given against each option.

1. **Assertion (A)** The rising population of developing countries and the affluent consumption and production standards of the developed world have placed a huge stress on the environment.

   Reason (R) Many resources have become extinct and the waste generated is beyond the absorptive capacity of the environment.

   (A) ☐ (B) ☐ (C) ☐ (D) ☐

2. **Assertion (A)** The threat to India's environment poses a dichotomy.

   Reason (R) The developmental activities in India have not adversely impacted its finite natural resources.

   (A) ☐ (B) ☐ (C) ☐ (D) ☐

3. **Assertion (A)** The high density of population and livestock and the competing uses of land for forestry, agriculture, pastures, human settlements and industries exert an enormous pressure on the country's finite land resources.

   Reason (R) India supports approximately 17 per cent of the world's human and 20 per cent of livestock population on a mere 2.5 per cent of the world's geographical area.

   (A) ☐ (B) ☐
   (C) ☐ (D) ☐

4. **Assertion (A)** Environment and economy are independent from each other.

   Reason (R) Development that ignores its repercussions on the environment will destroy the environment that sustains life forms.

   (A) ☐ (B) ☐
   (C) ☐ (D) ☐

5. **Assertion (A)** The major sources of air pollution are the pollutants from vehicles and industries.

   Reason (R) Categories of industries have been identified by CPCB which contributes to air pollution.

   (A) ☐ (B) ☐ (C) ☐ (D) ☐

6. **Assertion (A)** The long-term results of global warming are melting of polar ice with a resulting rise in sea level and coastal flooding, disruption of drinking water supplies dependent on snow melts, etc.

   Reason (R) Global warming is a gradual increase in the average temperature of the earth's lower atmosphere as a result of the increase in greenhouse gases since the industrial revolution.

   (A) ☐ (B) ☐ (C) ☐ (D) ☐

7. **Assertion (A)** In India, water pollution is widespread in urban areas where vehicles are the major contributors and in a few other areas which have a high concentration of industries and thermal power plants.

   Reason (R) Vehicular emissions are of particular concern since these are ground level sources and thus, have the maximum impact on the general population.

   (A) ☐ (B) ☐
   (C) ☐ (D) ☐

8. **Assertion (A)** India is naturally endowed with a large quantity of solar energy in the form of sunlight.

   Reason (R) With the help of photovoltaic cells, solar energy can be converted into electricity.

   (A) ☐ (B) ☐
   (C) ☐ (D) ☐

Correct/Incorrect Statements

No. of Questions : **8** Suggested Time : **15 Minutes**

Direction Each of the question given below consist of the two statements. List of common options applicable for each question is given below

(A) Both statements are correct
(B) Both statements are incorrect
(C) Statement I is correct and Statement II is incorrect
(D) Statement I is incorrect and Statement II is correct

You have to select the codes as *A, B, C* or *D* as your answer to the question by marking (✓) in the response box given against each option.

1. **Statement I** Environment is defined as the total planetary inheritance and the totality of all resources.

   Statement II A study of the environment calls for a study of the inter-relationship between these biotic and abiotic components of the environment.

   (A) ☐ (B) ☐ (C) ☐ (D) ☐

2. **Statement I** Absorptive capacity implies that the resource extraction is not above the rate of regeneration of the resource and the wastes generated are within the assimilating capacity of the environment.

   Statement II Carrying capacity means the ability of the environment to absorb degradation.

   (A) ☐ (B) ☐ (C) ☐ (D) ☐

3. **Statement I** Population growth and industrialisation have led to environmental challenges.

   Statement II Excessive resource consumption has outpaced the environment's ability to replenish, affecting supply-demand dynamics for environmental quality.

   (A) ☐ (B) ☐
   (C) ☐ (D) ☐

4. **Statement I** A UN Conference on Climate Change, held in Kyoto, Japan in 1997, resulted in an international agreement to fight ozone depletion.

   Statement II This agreement called for reductions in emissions of greenhouse gases by industrialised nations.

   (A) ☐ (B) ☐ (C) ☐ (D) ☐

5. **Statement I** India has abundant natural resources in terms of rich quality of soil, hundreds of rivers and tributaries, lush green forests, plenty of mineral deposits beneath the land surface, vast stretch of the Indian ocean, ranges of mountains, etc.

   Statement II The developmental activities in India have not resulted in pressure on its finite resources.

   (A) ☐ (B) ☐ (C) ☐ (D) ☐

6. **Statement I** In order to address two major environmental concerns in India, *viz.* water and air pollution, the government set-up the Central Pollution Control Board (CPCB) in 1984.

   Statement II State boards, through their district level officials, periodically inspect every industry under their jurisdiction to assess the adequacy of treatment measures provided to treat the effluent and gaseous emissions.

(A) ☐ (B) ☐ (C) ☐ (D) ☐

7. **Statement I** India is one of the ten most industrialised nations of the world.

Statement II This status has brought with it unwanted and unanticipated consequences such as unplanned urbanisation, pollution and the risk of accidents.

(A) ☐ (B) ☐ (C) ☐ (D) ☐

8. **Statement I** In areas where speed of wind is usually high, wind mills can provide electricity but it has adverse impact on the environment.

Statement II The initial cost of wind mills is high, but the benefits are quite low.

(A) ☐ (B) ☐ (C) ☐ (D) ☐

Case Based Questions

No. of Questions : 2 Suggested Time : **10 Minutes**

Direction This section contains 2 cases each having 4 questions of 1 mark each. You have to write the answer of each question based on the context of the related case.

Case 1 Economic development, which aimed to increasing the production of goods and services to meet the needs of a rising population, puts greater pressure on the environment. In the initial stages of development, the demand for environmental resources was less than that of supply. Now the world is faced with an increased demand for environmental resources, but their supply is limited due to overuse and misuse. Sustainable development aims at promoting the kind of development that minimises environmental problems and meets the needs of the present generation without compromising the ability of the future generation to meet their own needs.

Questions

(i) What effect does economic development have on the environment?

(A) Economic development alleviates pressure on the environment by reducing demand for resources ☐

(B) Economic development leads to increased demand for environmental resources, putting greater pressure on the environment ☐

(C) Economic development has no significant impact on environmental resources ☐

(D) Economic development enhances environmental conservation efforts by promoting sustainable practices ☐

(ii) Economic development .... demand for environmental resources, ... pressure on the environment.

(iii) What is the current situation regarding environmental resources, as described in the passage?

(A) Demand for environmental resources is decreasing due to conservation efforts. ☐

(B) Supply of environmental resources is increasing as technology advances. ☐

(C) Demand for environmental resources is increasing while their supply is diminishing due to overuse and misuse. ☐

(D) Both demand and supply of environmental resources are stable. ☐

(iv) Sustainable development promotes the kind of ...... that minimises environmental problems and meets the needs of the .... generation without compromising the ability of the future generation to meet their own needs.

Case 2 Sustainable development is the synonymous in the minds of many with the colour green and for good reasons. Twenty years ago, at the First Earth Summit at Rio de Janerio, in Brazil, world leaders set out what today is conventional wisdom: SOCIAL AND ECONOMIC HUMAN PROGRESS – cannot be divorced from environmental protection unless both are advanced together, both will flounder together.

Sustainable development is as much about health, education and jobs, as it is about the ecosystems. It is about ever widening inclusion and movement away from decisions that erode democratic space and do not address social inequality, intolerance and violence. Sustainable development is about changes that transform impoverished people, communities and countries into informed, educated healthy and productive societies.

It is about wealth creation that generates equality and opportunity. Sustainable development is about consumption and production patterns that respect planetary boundaries; it is also about increasing tolerance and respect for human rights at all levels. Building on human development legacy that oriented with economists like Amartya Sen and Mahbub ul Haq and was captured by the first Human Development Report in 1990.

United Nations Development Programme (UNDP) has long promoted alternative approaches to measure human progress, along with the Human Development Index (HDI). Today, we are building on this legacy by exploring how to adjust the index to reflect environmental sustainability, so that governments and citizens might better track real progress towards truly sustainable development. This must be our collective objective. *[CBSE QB]*

Questions

(i) Which of the following is not one of the ways to attain the goal of sustainable development?

(A) Use of cleaner fuels ☐

(B) Use of traditional knowledge and practices ☐

(C) Spreading awareness ☐

(D) Sticking to methods to promote inequalities ☐

(ii) State whether the given statement is true or false.

As per the UNDP Report education and health are the broader issues of human development.

(iii) Sustainable development and economic growth are .... (directly/indirectly) related.

(iv) **Assertion** (A) Sustainable development is about changes that transform impoverished people, communities and countries into informed, educated, healthy and productive societies.

Reason (R) Sustainable development advocates about wealth creation that generates socio-economic equality and opportunity.

Alternatives

(A) Both Assertion (A) and Reason (R) are true ☐

(B) Both Assertion (A) and Reason (R) are false ☐

Subjective Questions

Free Response Questions, Open-ended Questions etc.

No. of Questions : **10** Suggested Time : **65 Minutes**

1. "Recently Indians have drifted away from the traditional knowledge and practices and caused large-scale damage to environment." Explain how, adopting the traditional practices can be helpful in achieving the objective of sustainable development?

2. "The opportunity costs of negative environmental impacts are high." Defend or refute.

3. The environmental issues are increasing day-by-day and we have seen that the quality of the environment is deteriorated from last 20 years. What major changes you observe which leads to this deterioration?

4. "Sustainable development has become a catch phrase today. It is 'indeed' a paradigm shift in development thinking." Justify the statement. Also, explain any three strategies to achieve this.

5. "If the rate of resource extraction exceeds the rate of regeneration, it leads to reduction in carrying capacity of the environment." Discuss the rationale of the given statement with valid reasons.

6. Interpret the situation of earth as depicted in the given picture, with reference to current environmental challenges. *[CBSE 2023]*

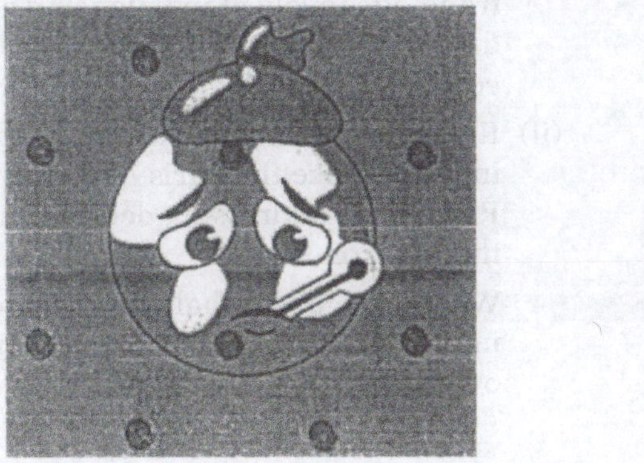

7. Highlight any two serious adverse environmental consequences of development in India. India's environmental problems pose a dichotomy- they are poverty induced and at the same time arise due to affluence in living standards. Is this true?

8. Analyse the impact of the following source highlighted in the image for conserving environment.

9. Read the following text carefully and answer the given questions on the basis of the same and common understanding

India has aimed to reduce the country's carbon intensity by approximately 45% by 2030. To achieve this 'green finance' plays a vital role. At the initial stages, green finance needs a big push from the government. The Indian government has identified projects worth ₹ 25,000 crore that will be financed by proceeds from Sovereign Green Bonds.

According to the framework approved by finance ministry, the sovereign green bonds will focus on financing public projects including renewable energy, climate change, clean transportation, sustainable water and waste management and pollution control.

Businesses that take green finance can get benefit in various ways. It can help them follow different environmental norms and regulations and thus avoid possible fines. Adopting sustainable developmental practices enhances brand value of businesses.

Customers tend to prefer brands that adopt clear sustainable development practices.

The energy-efficient and other sustainable development practices promoted by green finance also often help in saving cost, boosting profitability of businesses, etc.

Source *The Economic Times, 22nd April, 2023 (Modified)*

(i) Define sustainable development.

(ii) State the public project areas, where Sovereign Green Bond are focused.

(iii) How can businesses get benefit from green finance? *[CBSE 2024]*

10. "Deforestation in the Amazon Rainforest: Impact on Biodiversity and Climate"

The Amazon rainforest often referred to as the 'lungs of the Earth,' is the largest tropical rainforest in the world and home to unparalleled biodiversity. However, rampant deforestation driven by agricultural expansion, logging and infrastructure development poses a grave threat to its ecological integrity and global climate stability.

In recent decades, large swathes of the Amazon rainforest have been cleared to make way for cattle ranching, soybean cultivation and other forms of agribusiness. Illegal logging and mining activities further contribute to forest degradation, leading to loss of habitat for countless plant and animal species.

The destruction of the Amazon rainforest has far-reaching consequences for biodiversity conservation and climate regulation. Endangered species such as jaguars, giant river otters and harpy eagles face heightened risk of extinction as their habitats shrink. Moreover, the loss of tree cover disrupts the region's hydrological cycle, exacerbating droughts, floods and other extreme weather events.

Beyond its local and regional impacts, deforestation in the Amazon rainforest has profound implications for the global climate system.

The vast forest acts as a carbon sink, absorbing carbon dioxide from the atmosphere and helping to mitigate climate change.

However, when trees are cut down and burned, carbon stored in biomass is released into the atmosphere, contributing to greenhouse gas emissions and exacerbating global warming.

While governments of Amazonian countries have implemented conservation policies and established protected areas, enforcement remains a major challenge due to corruption, inadequate funding and conflicting interests. International efforts, such as the Paris Agreement and REDD+ (Reducing Emissions from Deforestation and Forest Degradation), aim to incentivise forest conservation and sustainable land management practices.

Local indigenous communities, who depend on the rainforest for their livelihoods and cultural identity, play a crucial role in conservation efforts.

Indigenous-led initiatives focused on sustainable resource management, eco-tourism and land tenure rights are essential for preserving the Amazon's ecological and cultural heritage.

(i) Assess the socio-economic drivers of deforestation in the Amazon region and the trade-offs involved in balancing economic development with environmental conservation.

(ii) Evaluate the effectiveness of international initiatives like the Paris Agreement and REDD+ in addressing deforestation in the Amazon region.
What are the key challenges hindering their implementation and how can they be overcome?

Answers

If your answer matches with the answer given here then put (✓) in the box otherwise put (✗). In case you did not attempt the question leave the box blank.

Multiple Choice Questions

1. C ☐	2. A ☐
3. A ☐	4. B ☐
5. B ☐	6. D ☐
7. C ☐	8. C ☐
9. B ☐	10. B ☐
11. D ☐	12. C ☐
13. A ☐	14. B ☐
15. D ☐	16. B ☐
17. A ☐	18. B ☐
19. D ☐	20. B ☐
21. B ☐	22. A ☐
23. B ☐	24. D ☐
25. B ☐	26. D ☐
27. C ☐	28. B ☐

Your Score__________ *(No. of Correct Answers)*

Assertion-Reason Questions

1. A ☐	2. C ☐
3. B ☐	4. D ☐
5. B ☐	6. B ☐
7. D ☐	8. A ☐

Your Score__________ *(No. of Correct Answers)*

Correct/Incorrect Statements

1. A ☐	2. B ☐
3. A ☐	4. D ☐
5. C ☐	6. D ☐
7. A ☐	8. B ☐

Your Score__________ *(No. of Correct Answers)*

Case Based Questions

1. (i) B ☐	(iii) C ☐
2. (i) D ☐	(iv) A ☐

Your Score__________ *(No. of Correct Answers)*

Explanations

Multiple Choice Questions

1. (C) Carrying, absorptive

2. (A) The environment does sustain life and provides aesthetic services. However, the exclusion of waste is not a correct function of the environment; instead, it involves managing and absorbing waste to maintain ecological balance.

3. (A) within its carrying capacity

4. (B) deplete, degrade

5. (B) They provide complementary approaches to health and well-being, incorporating holistic and natural remedies

6. (D) (i), (ii), (iii) and (iv)

7. (C) An increase in earth's average temperature primarily caused by human induced release of greenhouse gases

8. (C) Burning of coal and petroleum products releases carbon dioxide, a major greenhouse gas. Methane gas released in animal waste is another potent greenhouse gas. Afforestation, on the other hand, help to reduce global warming.

9. (B) High levels of chlorine and bromine compounds

10. (B) Increased volcanic activity

11. (D) Land degradation can significantly impact water quality and availability.

12. (C) Land degradation directly affects biodiversity loss and ecosystem services.

13. (A) (i), (ii) and (iii)

14. (B) Water pollution caused by discharge of heated water

15. (D) All of the above

16. (B) CPCB categorises industries based on their potential environmental impact and pollution levels

17. (A) Chipko, hugged the trees

18. (B) Striking a balance between meeting present needs, without compromising the ability of the future generation to meet their own needs.

19. (D) cattle dung, slurry

20. (B) By reducing air pollution and improving air quality in urban areas

21. (B) Earthworms are commonly used in biocomposting activities to enrich soil. They help break down organic matter and accelerate the decomposition process, resulting in nutrient-rich compost that enhances soil fertility and promotes plant growth.

22. (A) renewable

23. (B) Bio pest

24. (D) Renewable resources are derived from natural processes that can be sustained indefinitely, while non-renewable resources are finite and cannot be replenished

25. (B) intensive, extensive

26. (D) (iv) (iii) (i) (ii)

27. (C) (iii) (iv) (ii) (i)

28. (B) (ii) (iii) (iv) (i)

Assertion-Reason Questions

1. (A) Both Assertion (A) and Reason (R) are true and Reason (R) is the correct explanation of Assertion (A)

2. (C) Assertion (A) is true, but Reason (R) is false

3. (B) Both Assertion (A) and Reason (R) are true, but Reason (R) is not the correct explanation of Assertion (A)

4. (D) Assertion (A) is false, but Reason (R) is true

5. (B) Both Assertion (A) and Reason (R) are true, but Reason (R) is not the correct explanation of Assertion (A)

6. (B) Both Assertion (A) and Reason (R) are true, but Reason (R) is not the correct explanation of Assertion (A)

7. (D) Assertion (A) is false, but Reason (R) is true

8. (A) Both Assertion (A) and Reason (R) are true and Reason (R) is the correct explanation of Assertion (A)

Correct/Incorrect Statements

1. (A) Both statements are correct

2. (B) Absorptive capacity is the ability of the environment to absorb degradation.

Carrying capacity implies that rate of extraction of resources is not above the rate of their regeneration and wastes generated are within the assimilating capacity of the environment.

3. (A) Both statements are correct

4. (D) Statement I is incorrect and Statement II is correct

5. (C) Statement I is correct and Statement II is incorrect

6. (D) Statement I is incorrect and Statement II is correct

7. (A) Both statements are correct

8. (B) Windmills typically do not have adverse impacts on the environment in areas with high wind speeds and the operational benefits of wind energy usually outweigh the initial set-up costs.

Case Based Questions

1. (i) (B) Economic development leads to increased demand for environmental resources, putting greater pressure on the environment

(ii) increases, putting

(iii) (C) Demand for environmental resources is increasing while their supply is diminishing due to overuse and misuse.

(iv) development, present

2. (i) (D) Sticking to methods to promote inequalities

(ii) True

(iii) directly

(iv) (A) Both Assertion (A) and Reason (R) are true

Subjective Questions

1. The given statement is quite appropriate. Indian traditional practices were environment friendly and worked as complementary to the system and not its controller. The traditional agriculture system, healthcare system, housing, transport, etc. were intrinsically environment friendly.

The traditional practices used natural products and processes which are more or less free from side effects. For example by adopting medicinal plants/products we can conserve the resources and achieve the objective of sustainable development.

2. The statement is true. Negative environmental impacts incur significant opportunity costs on various fronts.

Firstly, the extensive exploitation of both renewable and non-renewable resources has depleted these valuable assets, necessitating substantial investments in technology and research to explore new resources.

Moreover, the health costs associated with degraded environmental quality, such as the decline in air and water quality, result in increased incidence of respiratory and water-borne diseases, leading to rising healthcare expenditures.

Additionally, global environmental issues like global warming and ozone depletion further strain government finances, contributing to higher opportunity costs. Therefore, the statement accurately reflects the substantial costs incurred due to negative environmental impacts.

3. Major changes that have been observed are

(i) **Rapid Industrialisation** The expansion of industrial activities, particularly in sectors such as manufacturing, mining and construction, has led to increased pollution of air, water and soil.

(ii) **Urbanisation and Infrastructure Development** Rapid urbanisation and infrastructure development, including the construction of roads, highways, buildings, and urban settlements, have led to habitat loss, deforestation and encroachment on natural ecosystems. Urban areas are often characterised by high levels of air and water pollution.

(iii) **Population Growth and Consumption Patterns** The growing population and changing consumption patterns have increased the demand for natural resources such as water, energy, land and raw materials.

Unsustainable consumption practices, including excessive use of fossil fuels, deforestation, overexploitation of natural resources and generation of waste, have put pressure on the environment and ecosystems, leading to depletion and degradation.

Overall, the deterioration of the environment over the past 20 years can be attributed to a combination of factors, including rapid industrialisation, urbanisation, population growth, unsustainable consumption patterns, agricultural practices and global environmental challenges such as climate change.

Addressing these issues requires concerted efforts at the local, national and global levels, including policy interventions, technological innovations, public awareness campaigns and sustainable development strategies aimed at balancing economic growth with environmental conservation and social equity.

4. The given statement suggests that sustainable development has gained widespread attention and popularity in contemporary discourse. It acknowledges that sustainable development represents a fundamental change or shift in how development is conceptualised and pursued.

There are many strategies to achieve sustainable development. Some of them are

(i) **LPG, Gobar Gas in Rural Areas** Households in rural areas generally use wood, dung cake or other biomass as fuel. This practice has several adverse implications like deforestation, reduction in green cover, wastage of cattle dung and air pollution.

To rectify the situation, subsidised LPG is being provided. In addition, gobar gas plants are being provided through easy loans and subsidy.

(ii) **Wind Power** In areas where speed of wind is usually high, wind mills can provide electricity without any adverse impact on the environment. Wind turbines move with the wind and electricity is generated. No doubt, the initial cost is high. But the benefits are such that the high cost gets easily absorbed.

(iii) **Solar Power through Photovoltaic Cells** India is naturally endowed with a large quantity of solar energy in the form of sunlight. Plants use solar energy to perform photosynthesis. Now, with the help of photovoltaic cells, solar energy can be converted into electricity. Plants use solar energy to perform photosynthesis. Now, with the help of photovoltaic cells, solar energy can be converted into electricity.

5. The environment is able to perform its functions uninterruptedly so long as the demand for these functions is within the carrying capacity of the environment. This means that the resources are not extracted beyond the rate of their regeneration.

If there is a disequilibrium (demand being more than supply), the environment fails to replenish itself and it will lead to environmental crisis.

Thus, to maintain a healthy environment, the carrying capacity of the environment must be valued and respected.

6. With reference to current environmental challenges, the situation of earth as depicted in the given picture is global warming.

The gradual increase in the average temperature of earth's lower atmosphere is called global warming. It occurs due to greenhouse gases (carbon dioxide, methane and other gases which have the capacity to absorb heat).

Different effects of global warming are described below
- (i) During the past century, the atmospheric temperature has risen by 1.1° F (0.6° C).
- (ii) Melting of polar ice resulted in increase in sea level.
- (iii) Disruption of drinking water supplies dependent on snow melts.
- (iv) Extinction of species.
- (v) More frequent tropical storms.
- (vi) Increased incidence of tropical diseases.

7. Two serious adverse environmental consequences of development in India are as follows
- (i) **Land degradation** Land in India has suffered degradation stemming mainly from unstable use and inappropriate management practices during the development process.
- (ii) **Air pollution** In India, air pollution is widespread in urban areas where vehicles are the major contributors and in a few other areas which have a high concentration of industries and thermal power plants.

  In 2016, personal transport vehicles (two-wheeled vehicles and cars only) constituted about 85% of the total number of registered vehicles. Thus, contributing significantly to total air pollution load.

This is true that India's environmental problems pose a dichotomy – they are poverty induced and, at the same time arise due to affluence in living standards.

On one hand, population explosion and widespread poverty has led to deforestation in India as the poor people in the rural areas are compelled to fell trees for earning their livelihood and for use as fuel, on the other hand, the growing demand for natural resources due to affluence in living standards in the urban areas is also equally responsible for the present environmental degradation.

8. Solar and wind energy play a vital role in conserving the environment and achieving sustainable development for several reasons
- (i) **Renewable and Clean** Solar and wind energy are renewable sources of energy that produce electricity without emitting greenhouse gases or other pollutants.

  By reducing reliance on fossil fuels, they help mitigate climate change and air pollution, contributing to improved environmental quality and public health.
- (ii) **Resource Conservation** Solar and wind energy harness naturally occurring resources i.e. sunlight and wind, that are abundant and widely available. By tapping into these resources, we can reduce the extraction and consumption of finite fossil fuel reserves, conserving natural resources for future generations.
- (iii) **Rural Electrification and Energy Access** Solar and wind energy can be deployed in remote and off-grid areas to provide electricity access to underserved communities.

  By bringing clean and affordable energy to rural regions, renewable energy technologies improve living standards, support education and healthcare services and empower communities to pursue sustainable development goals.
- (iv) **Environmental Conservation** Solar and wind energy help conserve natural habitats and ecosystems by reducing the need for land conversion and minimising habitat destruction associated with fossil fuel extraction and infrastructure development.

  By preserving biodiversity and ecosystem services, renewable energy supports healthy ecosystems and resilient communities.

Hence, solar and wind energy are essential pillars of sustainable development, offering clean, renewable and accessible energy solutions that promote environmental conservation, economic growth, social equity and energy security.

By harnessing the power of the sun and wind, we can build a more sustainable and resilient future for present and future generations.

9. (i) Sustainable development can be defined as an approach to the economic development of a country without compromising the quality of the environment for future generations.

(ii) The Sovereign Green Bonds will finance public projects including renewable energy, climate change, clean transportation, sustainable water and waste management and pollution control.

(iii) Businesses that take green finance can benefit in many ways

(a) It can help them follow different environmental norms and regulations and thus avoid possible fines.

(b) Adopting sustainable development practices enhances brand value of businesses.

(c) The energy-efficient and other sustainable development practices promoted by green finance helps in saving cost of production, boosting profitability of business.

10. (i) The socio-economic drivers of deforestation in the Amazon region are multi-faceted, including the expansion of agricultural frontiers, land speculation and infrastructure projects.

While these activities may provide short-term economic gains, they often come at the expense of long-term environmental degradation and loss of ecosystem services.

Balancing economic development with environmental conservation requires careful consideration of trade-offs, such as the importance of preserving biodiversity, mitigating climate change and safeguarding indigenous rights.

(ii) International initiatives such as the Paris Agreement and REDD+ represent important steps towards addressing deforestation in the Amazon region by providing frameworks for cooperation and financial incentives for forest conservation.

However, their effectiveness is limited by challenges such as lack of political will, insufficient funding and difficulties in measuring and monitoring forest carbon stocks.

Overcoming these challenges requires greater political commitment, increased financial support and improved governance mechanisms to ensure transparency, accountability and participation of local stakeholders in decision-making processes.

CHAPTER -8

Comparative Development Experiences of India and its Neighbours

Types & Nos. of Questions

Multiple Choice Questions	– 25
Assertion-Reason Questions	– 8
Correct/Incorrect Statements	– 8
Case Based Questions	– 2 Cases, *each with four Questions*
Subjective Questions	– 8

Trend Analysis

On the basis of analysis of last 2 years' papers, it is found that on an average 3 Multiple Choice Questions and 1 Short Answer Type Question are asked from this chapter. No case based question is asked but may be asked in coming exams.

Focus Topics of the Chapter

- Development Path of India, China and Pakistan
- Comparative Study of India, China and Pakistan
- An Appraisal of Development Strategies

Multiple Choice Questions

No. of Questions : **25** Suggested Time : **40 Minutes**

Direction Each of the question given below is Multiple Choice Question (MCQ) i.e. there are Four Options/ Choices for answer, out of which ONLY ONE is correct. You have to select the correct option. A response box is given with each option, mark (✓) in the box of the correct option. For each correct answer you will get 1 mark, while there is no penalty for incorrect answer or missed out questions.

1. Understanding the developmental processes pursued by the neighbouring nations allows nations to better comprehend their own .... and .... through their neighbours.

(A) threats, opportunities ☐
(B) economic, social stability ☐
(C) cultural, social ☐
(D) strengths, weaknesses ☐

2. Which of the following statements is incorrect?

(A) India initiated economic reforms in 1995 ☐
(B) The economic reforms initiated globalisation, liberalisation and privatisation ☐
(C) The economic reforms aimed at economic development ☐
(D) The economic reforms of India established a sound trade system ☐

3. Which of the following statements highlight the economic policy adopted by the People's Republic of China after its establishment?

(A) The government encouraged private ownership and entrepreneurship in all sectors ☐
(B) Critical sectors of the economy, enterprises and lands remained under individual ownership ☐
(C) The government brought all critical sectors of the economy, enterprises and lands under its control ☐
(D) The government decentralised control and allowed regional authorities to manage economic affairs independently ☐

4. "The Great Leap Forward (GLF) campaign, initiated in 1958, aimed at industrialising the country on a massive scale." The statement which focus on its impact is

(A) the campaign successfully achieved its goal of rapid industrialisation and economic growth ☐
(B) the encouragement of backyard industries led to sustainable economic development and prosperity ☐
(C) the commune system promoted collective farming and ensured efficient agricultural production ☐
(D) the campaign resulted in widespread famine and economic setbacks due to unrealistic targets and policies ☐

5. China's dual pricing system implemented during its economic reforms was characterised by

(A) fixed prices for all goods and services ☐
(B) market driven prices for all inputs and outputs ☐
(C) government setting prices for certain quantities, alongside market prices for the rest ☐
(D) privatisation of all state-owned enterprises ☐

6. Arrange the following events of China in chronological order and choose the correct alternative.

(i) Great proletarian cultural revolution
(ii) Great leap forward campaign
(iii) Introduction of economic reforms
(iv) First five year plan

Codes

(A) (ii), (iv), (iii), (i) ☐
(B) (iv), (ii), (i), (iii) ☐
(C) (ii), (iv), (i), (iii) ☐
(D) (iv), (i), (ii), (iii) ☐

7. "China did not have any compulsion to introduce reforms as dictated by the World Bank and International Monetary Fund to India and Pakistan", then, what drove China to implement economic reforms, diverging from its previous economic model?

(A) Political pressure from neighbouring countries ☐
(B) Recognition of inefficiencies in its centrally planned economy ☐
(C) Desire to assert dominance in the global market ☐
(D) Influence from international trade agreements ☐

8. It was found in China that establishment of infrastructure in the areas of education and health, land reforms, long existence of decentralised planning and existence of small enterprises had helped positively in the .... and .... indicators in the post reform period.

(A) social, political ☐
(B) social, income ☐
(C) political, income ☐
(D) technological, political ☐

9. How has China utilised the market mechanism to address social and economic needs, particularly in rural areas?

(A) By privatising land ownership and encouraging large-scale farming operations ☐
(B) By maintaining collective ownership of land while allowing individuals to cultivate it ☐
(C) By implementing strict land ownership regulations to prevent speculation ☐
(D) By outsourcing agricultural production to foreign investors for increased efficiency ☐

10. "The last time China's population saw a decline was in 1961, in the midst of a devastating four years famine following Mao's failed 'Great Leap Forward' campaign." – The Hindu

Which of the following best describes the primary aim of the Great Leap Forward (GLF) campaign initiated in 1958 in China?

(A) Encouraging rural communities to collectively cultivate land under the commune system ☐
(B) Setting-up industries in backyard locations to promote industrialisation ☐
(C) Establishing a system of government controlled industries to drive economic growth ☐
(D) Implementing policies to improve agricultural productivity and reduce famine ☐

11. .... and .... are the reasons for the slowdown of the Pakistan economy since independence.

I. Political instability
II. Over-dependence on remittances from abroad
III. Stable performance of agriculture sector
IV. Growth of service sector

Codes

(A) I and II ☐ (B) II and III ☐
(C) III and IV ☐ (D) I and IV ☐

12. What sequence of events contributed to the rise in foodgrain production following the introduction of the green revolution in Pakistan?

(A) Increase in mechanisation, increase in public investment ☐
(B) Decrease in mechanisation, increase in public investment ☐
(C) Increase in mechanisation, decrease in public investment ☐
(D) Decrease in mechanisation, decrease in public investment ☐

13. "Foreign exchange is an essential component for any country and it is important to know how it can be earned."
In context of this, which of the following was not a source of earning the foreign exchange for Pakistan?
(A) Remittances from Pakistan workers in the middle East ☐
(B) Exports of highly volatile agricultural products ☐
(C) Growing dependence on foreign loans ☐
(D) Sustainable export of manufactured goods ☐

14. According to scholars, which combination of factors is believed to contribute to the slowdown of the Pakistan economy?
(A) Political stability, over-dependence on remittances and foreign aid ☐
(B) Political instability, over-dependence on remittances and volatile agricultural performance ☐
(C) Economic diversification, over-dependence on foreign loans and political instability ☐
(D) Foreign investment, over-dependence on exports and volatile agricultural performance ☐

15. Identify the incorrect statement from the following.
(A) Pakistan has achieved self-sufficiency in the production of food ☐
(B) Pakistan has succeeded in developing its service and industry sectors at a fast rate ☐
(C) The use of modern technology is improving in Pakistan ☐
(D) The growth rate of GDP and its sectoral constituents have fallen in the 1990s ☐

16. "China has performed exceedingly well in various health and economic indicators."
Identify which of the following is not a health indicator?
(A) Infant mortality rate (per 1,000 live births) ☐
(B) Life expectancy at birth (years) ☐
(C) Percentage of people below poverty line (National) ☐
(D) Maternal mortality rate (per 1 lakh births) ☐

17. Which of the following best describes the type of economic system followed by India, China and Pakistan?
(A) India: Market economy, China: Traditional economy, Pakistan: Mixed economy ☐
(B) India: Mixed economy, China: Command economy, Pakistan: Mixed economy ☐
(C) India: Traditional economy, China: Mixed economy, Pakistan: Command economy ☐
(D) India: Command economy, China: Market economy, Pakistan: Traditional economy ☐

18. Which of the following statements accurately compares fertility rates and urbanisation levels in China, India and Pakistan?
(A) Fertility rates are high in China and low in both India and Pakistan, while urbanisation is high in India ☐
(B) Fertility rates are low in China and high in both India and Pakistan, while urbanisation is high in China ☐
(C) Fertility rates are low in China and high in India, while urbanisation is high in both China and India ☐
(D) Fertility rates are high in China and low in India, while urbanisation is high in Pakistan ☐

19. How the shift of employment and output from agriculture to industry and services is different in China, India and Pakistan?
(A) China has experienced a direct shift from agriculture to the service sector, while India and Pakistan have transitioned from agriculture to industry before moving to services ☐
(B) All three countries have experienced a direct shift from agriculture to the service sector ☐

(C) India and Pakistan have experienced a direct shift from agriculture to the service sector, while China has transitioned from agriculture to industry before moving to services ☐

(D) China and India have transitioned from agriculture to industry before moving to services, while Pakistan has experienced a direct shift from agriculture to the service sector ☐

20. Which additional set of indicators is crucial for evaluating a nation's progress and construction of human development index besides poverty reduction and sanitation improvement?

(A) Economic growth indicators ☐

(B) Education attainment metrics ☐

(C) Liberty indicators ☐

(D) Environmental sustainability measures ☐

21. On the basis of the data given below, identify the incorrect statement in terms of annual growth of GDP (%). *[CBSE 2023]*

Annual Growth of Gross Domestic Product (%) 1980-2017

Country	1980-90	2015-2017
India	5.7	7.3
China	10.3	6.8
Pakistan	6.3	5.3

Source *Key Indicators for Asia and Pacific 2016. Asian Development Bank Philippines : World Development Indicators 2018.*

(A) China was able to maintain near double-digit growth during the 1980s ☐

(B) Pakistan was ahead of India during 1980-2017 ☐

(C) India experienced a rapid rise in gross domestic product during 2015-17 ☐

(D) Both China and Pakistan experienced a decline in growth rate during 2015-17 ☐

22. **Trends in Output Growth in Different Sectors, 1980-2015**

Country	1980-90			2014-18		
	Agriculture	Industry	Service	Agriculture	Industry	Service
India	3.1	7.4	6.9	3.1	6.9	7.6
China	5.9	10.8	13.5	3.1	5.3	7.1
Pakistan	4	7.7	6.8	1.7	4.8	5.0

Which country has shown deceleration in all the three sectors?

(A) India ☐ (B) China ☐

(C) Pakistan ☐ (D) None of these ☐

23. Match the following

Column I	Column II
A. First five year plan of India	(i) 1953
B. First five year plan of China	(ii) Massive industrialisation
C. Great leap forward	(iii) Students and professionals were sent to work and learn
D. Great proletarian cultural revolution	(iv) 1951

Codes

	A	B	C	D	
(A)	(iv)	(i)	(iii)	(ii)	☐
(B)	(iv)	(i)	(ii)	(iii)	☐
(C)	(i)	(iv)	(ii)	(iii)	☐
(D)	(iv)	(ii)	(i)	(iii)	☐

24. Match the following

Column I	Column II
A. Special economic zones	(i) Pakistan
B. One child policy	(ii) Extent of democratic participation
C. Liberty indicators	(iii) Foreign investors
D. Very high fertility rate	(iv) China

Codes

	A	B	C	D	
(A)	(iii)	(i)	(iv)	(ii)	☐
(B)	(ii)	(iv)	(iii)	(i)	☐
(C)	(iii)	(iv)	(ii)	(i)	☐
(D)	(iv)	(ii)	(i)	(iii)	☐

25. Match the following

Column I	Column II
A. Economic reforms of China	(i) 2017
B. Economic reforms of Pakistan	(ii) 1949
C. People's republic of China	(iii) 1988
D. Last five year plan of India	(iv) 1978

Codes

	A	B	C	D	
(A)	(iii)	(ii)	(iv)	(i)	☐
(B)	(ii)	(iv)	(iii)	(i)	☐
(C)	(iv)	(iii)	(i)	(ii)	☐
(D)	(iv)	(iii)	(ii)	(i)	☐

Assertion-Reason Questions

No. of Questions : **8** Suggested Time : **15 Minutes**

Direction Each of the question given below consist of the two statements; one labelled as **Assertion** (A) and other as **Reason** (R). List of common options applicable for each question is given below

(A) Both Assertion (A) and Reason (R) are true and Reason (R) is the correct explanation of Assertion (A)

(B) Both Assertion (A) and Reason (R) are true, but Reason (R) is not the correct explanation of Assertion (A)

(C) Assertion, (A) is true, but Reason (R) is false

(D) Assertion, (A) is false, but Reason (R) is true

You have to select the codes as *A, B, C* or *D* as your answer to the question by marking (✓) in the response box given against each option.

1. Assertion (A) The Great Leap Forward (GLF) campaign faced numerous challenges.

Reason (R) Severe drought in China and conflicts with Russia disrupted industrialisation efforts and led to the introduction of the Great Proletarian Cultural Revolution.

(A) ☐ (B) ☐ (C) ☐ (D) ☐

2. Assertion (A) China's limited cultivable land area has led to a high dependence on farming for livelihoods, with over 80% of the population relying on agriculture until the 1980s.

Reason (R) China's suitable cultivation area is more as compared to India's cultivable land area.

(A) ☐ (B) ☐

(C) ☐ (D) ☐

3. Assertion (A) The developmental experiences of India and Pakistan have a lot of similarities.

Reason (R) Both India and Pakistan laid emphasis on creating a large private sector.

[CBSE 2024]

(A) ☐ (B) ☐

(C) ☐ (D) ☐

4. **Assertion (A)** The new leadership in China during the late 1970s was dissatisfied with the slow pace of economic growth and lack of modernisation under Maoist rule.

Reason (R) The Maoist vision of economic development, which emphasised decentralisation, self-sufficiency and avoidance of foreign technology and capital, was perceived as unsuccessful by the new leadership.

(A) ☐ (B) ☐ (C) ☐ (D) ☐

5. **Assertion (A)** Pakistan experienced economic growth during 1980's.

Reason (R) Financial support from Western nations and remittances from emigrants to the Middle East contributed to stimulating economic growth.

(A) ☐ (B) ☐ (C) ☐ (D) ☐

6. **Assertion (A)** Some scholars attribute that Pakistan's growth rate improved after the reform processes introduced in the country.

Reason (R) Political instability over a prolonged period was a contributing factor to Pakistan's declining growth rate.

(A) ☐ (B) ☐ (C) ☐ (D) ☐

7. **Assertion (A)** Scholars attribute the slowdown of growth and re-emergence of poverty in Pakistan's economy to the reliance on good harvests rather than institutionalised processes of technical change for agricultural growth and food supply.

Reason (R) The economy's performance in Pakistan fluctuated based on the success of harvests, with positive indicators during good harvests and stagnation or negative trends during poor harvests.

(A) ☐

(B) ☐

(C) ☐

(D) ☐

8. **Assertion (A)** During 1980's, economic growth rate of Pakistan was more than that of India.

Reason (R) Pakistan followed the path of mixed economic structure with equal participation of the public and the private sector. *[CBSE 2023]*

(A) ☐ (B) ☐

(C) ☐ (D) ☐

Correct/Incorrect Statements

No. of Questions : **8** Suggested Time : **15 Minutes**

Direction Each of the question given below consist of the two statements. List of common options applicable for each question is given below

(A) Both statements are correct
(B) Both statements are incorrect
(C) Statement I is correct and Statement II is incorrect
(D) Statement I is incorrect and Statement II is correct

You have to select the codes as *A, B, C* or *D* as your answer to the question by marking (✓) in the response box given against each option.

1. **Statement I** Until the 1980s, over 60% of the population in China depended on farming as their primary source of livelihood.

   Statement II The Chinese government took no efforts for diversification of livelihoods by encouraging people to engage in activities such as handicrafts, commerce and transport.

   (A) ☐ (B) ☐ (C) ☐ (D) ☐

2. **Statement I** Special Economic Zones (SEZs) policy has led to huge Foreign Direct Investment (FDI) flow to China.

   Statement II China's rapid industrial growth was the result of its economic reform in 1981. *[CBSE 2023]*

   (A) ☐ (B) ☐ (C) ☐ (D) ☐

3. **Statement I** The economic transformation occurring globally over the last two decades, partly due to globalisation, has implications for countries, including India.

   Statement II Nations are forming regional and global economic groupings such as SAARC, European Union, ASEAN, G-8, G-20, BRICS, etc, to strengthen their domestic economies.

   (A) ☐ (B) ☐ (C) ☐ (D) ☐

4. **Statement I** Nationalisation of consumer goods industries occurred in Pakistan during the 1970s.

   Statement II In the late 1970s and 1980s, Pakistan shifted its policy orientation towards denationalisation and the encouragement of the private sector.

   (A) ☐ (B) ☐ (C) ☐ (D) ☐

5. **Statement I** The Pakistan government provided incentives to the private sector, fostering a conducive climate for new investments.

   Statement II As China is the largest nation and geographically occupies the largest area among the three nations, its density is also highest.

   (A) ☐ (B) ☐ (C) ☐ (D) ☐

6. **Statement I** China has used the market mechanism to create additional social and economic opportunities for its citizens.

   Statement II In China, social infrastructure created by the government brought positive results in human development indicators. *[CBSE 2024]*

   (A) ☐ (B) ☐ (C) ☐ (D) ☐

7. **Statement I** Amongst India, China and Pakistan, China is the largest nation and has the highest population density.

   Statement II One-child policy introduced in the late 1970s in China led to a considerable decline in the population growth rate. *[CBSE 2023]*

   (A) ☐ (B) ☐
   (C) ☐ (D) ☐

8. **Statement I** Lack of political freedom and its implications for human rights are major concerns in Pakistan.

   Statement II In the last four decades, China utilised the market system without compromising its political commitment, leading to increased economic growth and poverty alleviation.

   (A) ☐ (B) ☐ (C) ☐ (D) ☐

Case Based Questions

No. of Questions : **2** Suggested Time : **10 Minutes**

Direction This section contain 2 cases each having 4 questions of 1 mark each. You have to write the answer of each question based on the context of the related case.

Case 1 India, China and Pakistan are three populous countries in South Asia with distinct historical, cultural and economic backgrounds. Despite facing similar challenges such as poverty, rapid urbanisation and environmental degradation, each country has pursued unique paths towards economic development.

India, the world's largest democracy, embarked on a path of economic liberalisation and reforms in the early 1990s. India's economy has diversified over the years, with significant contributions from sectors such as information technology, pharmaceuticals and services. However, India continues to rappel with challenges such as income inequality, bureaucratic inefficiency and inadequate infrastructure.

China, under the leadership of the Communist Party, underwent remarkable economic transformation since the late 20th century. Reforms in the late 1970s introduced market oriented policies while maintaining authoritarian political control. This approach led to rapid industrialisation, infrastructure development and poverty reduction. China's economy has become the world's second largest, driven by manufacturing, exports and foreign investment.

Pakistan faces challenges stemming from political instability, security concerns and governance issues. Despite possessing abundant natural resources, Pakistan's economy has struggled to achieve sustained growth. Efforts to stimulate economic growth through privatisation and deregulation have been hindered by corruption and inefficiency. Pakistan also faces socio-economic challenges.

India, China and Pakistan have pursued different models of economic development, reflecting their unique political, social and cultural contexts. While India opted for a democratic, market-oriented approach, China embraced market reforms within an authoritarian political framework. Pakistan, on the other hand, has grappled with political instability and governance issues, hindering its economic progress.

Questions

(i) .... has experienced rapid industrialisation and infrastructure development under an authoritarian political framework in South Asia.

(ii) What challenges have hindered economic growth in one of the countries, leading to periods of stagnation?

(A) Technological advancements ☐

(B) Political instability ☐

(C) Environmental sustainability ☐

(D) Infrastructural development ☐

(iii) .... sectors have made significant contributions to India's diversified economy.

(iv) Which of the following factors has hindered Pakistan's efforts to stimulate economic growth?

(A) Abundant natural resources ☐

(B) Privatisation and de-regulation ☐

(C) Corruption and inefficiency ☐

(D) Socio-economic challenges such as poverty and illiteracy ☐

Case 2 India and its neighbours – Pakistan and China, have very similar development strategies as an economy as a whole. All these three countries began towards their economic development at the same time. In addition, India and Pakistan attained independence in the year 1947. However, China was an independent economy in the year 1949.

India and Pakistan began with similar strategies for creating larger public sector units. And soon began working on raising public expenditure on social development.

All the countries began planning their development strategies in a very similar fashion. India made an announcement of its first five year plan in the year 1951. However, Pakistan made its five year plan announcement in the year 1956. China on the other hand, had made this announcement in the year 1953.

Questions

(i) When did China become an independent economy?

(A) 1945 ☐ (B) 1947 ☐
(C) 1949 ☐ (D) 1952 ☐

(ii) ……….. and ……….. are the neighbour countries of India.

(iii) When did India launch its first Five Year Plan (FYP)?

(A) 1947 ☐ (B) 1949 ☐
(C) 1951 ☐ (D) 1956 ☐

(iv) Pakistan announced its first five year plan in the year ……… .

Subjective Questions

Free Response Questions, Open-ended Questions etc.

No. of Questions : **8** Suggested Time : **55 Minutes**

1. How do regional and economic groupings foster economic growth, enhance competitiveness and address shared challenges and what factors determine the effectiveness and sustainability of participation in such groupings for member economies, explain with context of India?

2. When all the three countries, India, China and Pakistan started their developmental journey almost at the same time, then which policies of all the three countries make them standing apart?

3. Although the policies initiated by China before reforms were focused on infrastructural development to support rapid industrialisation and transformation of the economy, what according to you, made China to bring economic reforms so early than India and Pakistan?

4. "Scholars find son preference as a common phenomenon in India, Pakistan and China." Justify the given statement in the light of skewed sex ratio. *[CBSE 2024]*

5. How do human development indicators, such as life expectancy and education levels, compare and interact with income indicators, like GDP per capita, in assessing the overall well-being and quality of life within a society?

6. Compare and analyse the following information related to Annual Growth of Gross Domestic Product (GDP) of India and China. *[CBSE 2023]*

Annual Growth of Gross Domestic Product

Country	1980-91	2015-17
India	5.7	7.3
China	10.3	6.8

Source *Asian Development Bank Philippines, World Development Indicator-2018.*

7. Analyse the data given in the following table

Sectoral Share of Employment and GVA (%) in 2018-19

Sector	Contribution to GVA			Distribution of Workforce		
	India	China	Pakistan	India	China	Pakistan
Agriculture	16	7	24	43	26	41
Industry	30	41	19	25	28	24
Services	54	52	57	32	46	35
Total	100	100	100	100	100	100

8. **SINO:-PAK FRIENDSHIP CORRIDOR**

The China-Pakistan Economic Corridor (CPEC) has deepened the decades-long strategic relationship between the two nations. But, it has also sparked criticism for burdening Pakistan with mountains of debt and allowing China to use its debt-trap diplomacy to gain access to strategic assets of Pakistan.

The foundations of CPEC, part of China's Belt and Road Initiative, were laid in May 2013. At the time, Pakistan was reding under weak economic growth. China committed to play an integral role in supporting Pakistan's economy.

Pakistan and China have a strategic relationship that goes back decades. Pakistan turned to China at a time when it needed a rapid increase in external financing to meet critical investments in hard infrastructure, particularly power plants and highways. CPEC's early harvest projects met this need, leading to a dramatic increase in Pakistan's power generation capacity, bringing an end to supply side constraints that had made rolling blackouts a regular occurrence across the country. Pakistan leaned into CPEC, leveraging Chinese financing and technical assistance in an attempt to end power shortages that had paralysed its country's economy. Years later, China's influence in Pakistan has increased at an unimaginable pace.

China As Pakistan's Largest Bilateral Creditor

China's ability to exert influence on Pakistan' economy has grown substantially in recent years, mainly due to the fact that Beijing is now Islamabad's largest creditor.

According to documents released by Pakistan's finance ministry, Pakistan's total public and publicly guaranteed external debt stood at $ 44.35 billion in June 2013, just 9.3 percent of which was owed to China.

By April 2021, this external debt had ballooned to $ 90.12 billion. With Pakistan owing 27.4 percent – $ 24.7 billion of its total external debt to China, according to the International Monetary Fund (IMF).

Additionally, China provided financial and technical expertise to help Pakistan build its road infrastructure, expanding North-South connectivity to improve the efficiency of moving goods from Karachi all the way to Gilgit-Baltistan (PoK).

These investment were critical in better integrating the country's ports, especially Karachi, with urban centers in Punjab and Khyber-Pakhtunkhwa provinces.

Despite power asymmetries between China and Pakistan, the latter still has tremendous agency in determining its own policies, even if such policies come at the expense of the long-term socio-economic welfare of Pakistani citizens.

Source *https://www.usip.org/publications/2021/05/pakistans-growing-problem-its-china-economic-corridor-modified*

(i) Outline and discuss any two economic advantages of China Pakistan Economic Corridor (CPEC) accruing to the economy of Pakistan.

(ii) Analyse the implication of a bilateral 'debt-trap' situation of Pakistan *vis-a-vis* the Chinese economy.

Answers

If your answer matches with the answer given here then put (✓) in the box otherwise put (✗). In case you did not attempt the question leave the box blank.

Multiple Choice Questions

1. D ☐	2. A ☐
3. C ☐	4. D ☐
5. C ☐	6. B ☐
7. B ☐	8. B ☐
9. B ☐	10. B ☐
11. A ☐	12. A ☐
13. D ☐	14. B ☐
15. B ☐	16. C ☐
17. B ☐	18. B ☐
19. C ☐	20. C ☐
21. B ☐	22. C ☐
23. B ☐	24. C ☐
25. D ☐	

Your Score__________ *(No. of Correct Answers)*

Assertion-Reason Questions

1. B ☐	2. C ☐	3. C ☐
4. A ☐	5. A ☐	6. D ☐
7. A ☐	8. B ☐	

Your Score__________ *(No. of Correct Answers)*

Correct/Incorrect Statements

1. B ☐	2. C ☐	3. A ☐
4. D ☐	5. C ☐	6. A ☐
7. D ☐	8. D ☐	

Your Score__________ *(No. of Correct Answers)*

Case Based Questions

1. (ii) B ☐	(iv) C ☐
2. (i) C ☐	(iii) C ☐

Your Score__________ *(No. of Correct Answers)*

Explanations

Multiple Choice Questions

1. (D) strengths, weaknesses

2. (A) India initiated economic reforms earlier, in 1991, not in 1995. These reforms aimed to liberalise the economy, encourage globalisation, privatise state-owned enterprises and stimulate economic development.

3. (C) The government brought all critical sectors of the economy, enterprises and lands under its control

4. (D) the campaign resulted in widespread famine and economic setbacks due to unrealistic targets and policies

5. (C) government setting prices for certain quantities, alongside market prices for the rest

6. (B) (iv), (ii), (i), (iii)

7. (B) Recognition of inefficiencies in its centrally planned economy prompted China to reform its economic system towards a more market oriented approach.

8. (B) social, income

9. (B) By maintaining collective ownership of land while allowing individuals to cultivate it combines the benefits of collective ownership, ensuring stability and equitable distribution of resources, with individual cultivation rights, promoting agricultural productivity and rural development.

10. (B) The Great Leap Forward (GLF) campaign aimed to rapidly industrialise China by encouraging people to set-up small-scale industries in their backyard locations.

11. (A) I and II

12. (A) Increase in mechanisation, increase in public investment

13. (D) Sustainable export of manufactured goods

14. (B) Political instability can disrupt economic activities and deter investment, while over-dependence on remittances and volatile agricultural performance can introduce uncertainties and hinder sustainable economic growth.

15. (B) While Pakistan has made progress in various sectors, including services and industry, describing the development as 'at a fast rate' may not accurately reflect the pace of growth in these sectors.

16. (C) The percentage of people below the poverty line is an economic indicator, reflecting the income or wealth distribution within a population.

17. (B) India: Mixed economy, China: Command economy, Pakistan: Mixed economy

18. (B) Fertility rates are low in China and high in both India and Pakistan, while urbanisation is high in China

19. (C) India and Pakistan have experienced a direct shift from agriculture to the service sector, while China has transitioned from agriculture to industry before moving to services

20. (C) Liberty indicators reflect the extent of political freedoms, civil liberties and human rights within a country, which are important aspects of human development.

21. (B) Pakistan was ahead of India during 1980-2017

22. (C) Pakistan has shown deceleration in all three sectors. This indicates a slowdown in economic growth across various sectors such as agriculture, industry and services.

23. (B) (iv) (i) (ii) (iii) 24. (C) (iii) (iv) (ii) (i)

25. (D) (iv) (iii) (ii) (i)

Assertion-Reason Questions

1. (B) Both Assertion (A) and Reason (R) are true, but Reason (R) is not the correct explanation of Assertion (A)
2. (C) Assertion (A) is true, but Reason (R) is false
3. (C) Assertion (A) is true, but Reason (R) is false
4. (A) Both Assertion (A) and Reason (R) are true and Reason (R) is the correct explanation of Assertion (A)
5. (A) Both Assertion (A) and Reason (R) are true and Reason (R) is the correct explanation of Assertion (A)
6. (D) Assertion (A) is false, but Reason (R) is true
7. (A) Both Assertion (A) and Reason (R) are true and Reason (R) is the correct explanation of Assertion (A)
8. (B) Both Assertion (A) and Reason (R) are true, but Reason (R) is not the correct explanation of Assertion (A)

Correct/Incorrect Statements

1. (B) Both statements are incorrect
2. (C) Statement I is correct and Statement II is incorrect
3. (A) Both statements are correct
4. (D) Statement I is incorrect and Statement II is correct
5. (C) Statement I is correct and Statement II is incorrect
6. (A) Both statements are correct
7. (D) Statement I is incorrect and Statement II is correct
8. (D) Statement I is incorrect and Statement II is correct

Case Based Questions

1. (i) China
   (ii) (B) Political instability
   (iii) Information technology, pharmaceuticals and services
   (iv) (C) Corruption and inefficiency
2. (i) (C) 1949
   (ii) China, Pakistan
   (iii) (C) 1951
   (iv) 1956

Subjective Questions

1. Participation in regional and economic groupings presents opportunities and challenges for India's growth trajectory. By engaging in such groupings, India can access larger markets, promote exports and attract foreign investment, thereby stimulating economic growth.

   Furthermore, collaboration within regional frameworks can facilitate the sharing of best practices, technology transfer and infrastructure development, which are crucial for addressing India's developmental challenges.

   There is also an increasing eagerness on the parts of various nations to try and understand the developmental processes pursued by their neighbouring nations as it allows them to better comprehend their own strengths and weaknesses *vis-a-vis* their neighbours.

   In the unfolding process of globalisation, this is particularly considered essential by developing countries like India as they face competition not only from developed nations but also amongst themselves in the relatively limited economic space enjoyed by the developing world.

2. India's emphasis on democratic governance, mixed economy with a focus on state-led industrialisation through five year plans and policies promoting education and technological advancement contributed to its unique trajectory.

   China's adoption of centralised planning under a single party system, coupled with market reforms and export oriented industrialisation, propelled its rapid economic growth.

   Pakistan facing political instability and frequent changes in governance, struggled to maintain consistent economic policies, hindering its developmental progress compared to its neighbours.

   Therefore, while all three countries began their developmental journeys' around the same time, their differing policy approaches and governance structures have led them to stand apart in terms of economic development outcomes.

3. The policies initiated by China were focused towards industrial development through massive industrialisation and transformation of the economy, but still reforms were brought in 1978 without any compulsion as the new leadership at that time in China was not happy with the slow pace of growth and lack of modernisation in the Chinese economy under the Maoist rule.

   They felt that Maoist vision of economic development based on decentralisation, self-sufficiency and shunning of foreign technology, goods and capital had failed. Despite extensive land reforms, collectivisation, the Great Leap Forward and other initiatives, the per capita grain output in 1978 was the same as it was in the mid-1950s.

4. Both rural and urban populations have economic and traditional incentives to prefer sons over daughters. Sons are preferred as they provide the primary financial support to the parents.

   A woman changes her surname to her husband's surname after marriage. For some families, one's daughter-in-law's name instead of a daughter's name would be added in the book of family tree.

   Therefore, if a family had no son, the fortune and name of the family would have no legal heirs. The choice of small families also affects the people's views on the sex of their child.

5. The relationship between human development indicators and income indicators is complex and multi-faceted. While income indicators like GDP per capita provide a measure of a country's economic output, human development indicators such as life expectancy, literacy rates, and access to education offer insights into the quality of life and well-being of a population.

   However, it's crucial to recognise that high income doesn't always guarantee high human development, as factors like income inequality, access to healthcare, education and social services play significant roles.

   Conversely, countries with lower income levels can still achieve high levels of human development through effective social policies and investments in education and healthcare.

   Therefore, a holistic approach that considers both income and human development indicators is necessary for a comprehensive understanding of societal progress and well-being.

6. From the given information, we can analyse the Annual Growth of GDP of India and China in the following ways

(i) In the initial years (during 1980-90), China's GDP growth rate was higher than that of India. China was able to maintain near double-digit growth during the 1980s.

(ii) India experienced a rapid rise in GDP during 2015-17. India's GDP growth rate increased from 5.7% to 7.3% which indicates that the Indian economy was able to sustain growth overtime.

(iii) China experienced a decline in growth rate during 2015-17 that indicates a possible slowdown in the economy.

7. In 2018-19, with 26 per cent of its workforce engaged in agriculture, its contribution to the GVA in China is 7 per cent. In both India and Pakistan, the contribution of agriculture to GVA were 16 and 24 per cent, respectively, but the proportion of workforce that works in this sector is more in India.

In Pakistan, about 41 per cent of people work in agriculture, whereas, in India, it is 43 per cent. 24 per cent of Pakistan workforce is engaged in industry but it produces 19 per cent of GVA.

In India, industry workforce account for 25 per cent but produces goods worth 30 per cent of GVA.

In China, industries contribute to GVA at 41 and employ 28 per cent of workforce. In all the three countries, service sector contributes highest share of GVA.

In the normal course of development, countries first shift their employment and output from agriculture to industry and then to services. This is what is happening in China as can be seen from table, but in India and Pakistan, the shift is taking place directly to the service sector.

Thus, in all the three countries the service sector is emerging as a major player of development. In the 1980s, India, China and Pakistan employed 17, 12 and 27 per cent of its workforce in the service sector respectively. In 2019, it has reached the level of 32, 46 and 35 per cent, respectively.

8. (i) China has become famous for its 'debt-trap diplomacy' in recent times. Under this China provides financial and technical expertise/ assistance to help various nations to bring them under its direct or indirect influence.

The first and the foremost implication of the diplomacy is that Beijing has now become Islamabad's largest creditor. According to documents released by Pakistan's finance ministry, its total public external debt stood at $ 44.35 billion in June 2013, just 9.3 percent of which was owed to China.

By April 2021, this external debt had ballooned to $ 90.12 billion, with Pakistan owing 27.4 percent – $ 24.7 billion– of its total external debt to China, according to the IMF.

(ii) Non-monetary exchange transactions are not included in the estimation of gross domestic product on account of practical difficulties like non-availability of reliable data. Although these activities enhance public welfare which may lead to underestimation of GDP.

e.g. Kitchen gardening, services of homemaker, etc.